MODERN COLONIZATION
BY MEDICAL INTERVENTION

D1453170

Studies in Critical Social Sciences Book Series

Haymarket Books is proud to be working with Brill Academic Publishers (www.brill.nl) to republish the *Studies in Critical Social Sciences* book series in paperback editions. This peer-reviewed book series offers insights into our current reality by exploring the content and consequences of power relationships under capitalism, and by considering the spaces of opposition and resistance to these changes that have been defining our new age. Our full catalog of *SCSS* volumes can be viewed at www.haymarketbooks.org/category/scss-series.

Modern Colonization by Medical Intervention

U.S. Medicine in Puerto Rico

Nicole Trujillo-Pagán

Haymarket
Books
Chicago, IL

First published in 2013 by Brill Academic Publishers, The Netherlands.
© 2013 Koninklijke Brill NV, Leiden, The Netherlands

Published in paperback in 2014 by
Haymarket Books
P.O. Box 180165
Chicago, IL 60618
773-583-7884
www.haymarketbooks.org

ISBN: 978-1-60846-419-7

Trade distribution:
In the U.S. through Consortium Book Sales, www.cbsd.com
In the UK, Turnaround Publisher Services, www.turnaround-psl.com
In all other countries by Publishers Group Worldwide, www.pgw.com

Cover design by Ragina Johnson.

This book was published with the generous support of Lannan Foundation
and the Wallace Action Fund.

Printed in Canada by union labor.

10 9 8 7 6 5 4 3 2 1

Library of Congress Cataloging-in-Publication Data is available.

MIX
Paper from
responsible sources
FSC® C103567

Para Liani

CONTENTS

LIST OF TABLES AND FIGURES

Tables

Figures

CHAPTER ONE

A MATTER OF LIFE AND DEATH

Most people probably associate colonization with fatal phenomena, such as the smallpox epidemic that accompanied westward expansion and decimated Native American populations. Others reflect on more coercive forms of conquest, such as the expanding Spanish empire that forced indigenous groups to choose between religious conversion or death. Understanding colonialism as a matter of life and death is common in the ways we think about older forms of colonization, but rare in how we think about the modern period. Life and death nonetheless take on new symbolic meanings through modern forms of warfare and colonization. As Rudyard Kipling suggested, to take up the "white man's burden" meant involving white American men in "the savage wars of peace...[to] bid the sickness cease" (1899: 4). Following the bloody Civil War, most Americans were reassured that the relatively small number of soldiers who died in conflict during the Spanish-American War of 1898 was a cost of war. Many soldiers died from sickness in the latter struggle, but medical officers produced extraordinary results healing injured soldiers and improved medicine's status. Americans hoped the war would support modernization at home and abroad, which included better control over contagious diseases they believed were imported into the United States (Espinosa, 2009). The war appealed to their nationalistic pride and bolstered a self-serving sense of engaging in a humanitarian cause. As part of their promise to "give...the advantages and blessings of enlightened civilization," U.S. colonial administrators claimed they would end oppression and promote progress in Puerto Rico (Miles in Herrmann, 1907: 33). Through its repeated references to mortality rates, the U.S. colonial administration used life and death to measure its success in the old-new colony.

Because of its own history as a British colony, some Americans supported the decolonization of Spanish colonies at the end of "the splendid little war," but the United States pursued a new course of political administration that challenged its trajectory of territorial annexation (Hay in Thayer, 1916: 337). The United States became a colonizing power at the end of a global wave of modern colonization in the 1890s, which challenged the political ideals of democracy. U.S. political leaders entered into a complex negotiation with their national identity. To resolve the contradictions of democracy and colonization before national and international

audiences, U.S. political authorities built upon the sense they had a civilizing mission to spread freedom and modernization. A new U.S. colonial
administration crafted a discourse on tutelage and Americanization that
relied on claims to represent the public interest, which implicated both
medicine and the administration of public health.

The Spanish-American War was the first significant conflict following
wide acceptance of germ theory, which implied a new role for medicine
and public health within the colonial administration. U.S. colonial administration took on the "white man's burden" on an island where the death
rate was double that of the United States and entered a second war against
death (Hoff, 1900: 796). They promoted colonial interventions as a form of
benevolent humanitarianism and used public health to justify their imperial desires (Tyrrell, 2010). In their reports, U.S. military officers revealed
an alternate narrative about public health in Puerto Rico. They were
particularly concerned about contagious diseases among their soldiers.
U.S. military officers ordered that sanitation efforts be conducted as emergency measures. They established new sanitation regulations modeled on
the United States and asserted control over the island's treasury, which
they used to carry out a compulsory smallpox vaccination campaign.

The smallpox campaign was not only a medical intervention, but also a
form of social and political espionage that aided the development of the
colonial administration. It "became a means to gather vital data on the local
topography, political institutions, and indigenous peoples-making those
exotic tropical places legible to their new rulers" (Willrich, 2011: 124). This
data served the military administration's interest in expanding its surveillance over remote and inaccessible areas, for instance enabling the arrest of
the "White Eagle," José Maldonado (Picó, 2004: 92). The smallpox campaign
also modeled how medical interventions could concede and justify "almost
unlimited legal authority" to police a new subject population (Willrich, 2011:
124). Foreshadowing the role of medicine in consolidating the U.S. colonial
administration's legitimacy, the smallpox campaign was considered the U.S.
Army's first co-operative civil public health program (Wintermute, 2011).
U.S. military officers promoted the illusion their efforts were cooperative,
but they ultimately privileged their own leadership. For instance, the smallpox campaign's architect, Dr. Azel Ames, explained it was "always in name,
a civil undertaking," but ordered under military supervision and authority
and "organized and directed wholly by medical officers of the Army" (1903:
302). Under military direction, the smallpox campaign compelled broad
compliance from municipal mayors, local physicians and the island's residents under threat of fines and imprisonment (Rigau-Pérez, 1985). General
John Van Rensselaer Hoff justified these forms of coercion when he asserted,

"the real reason why we are in the Antilles today is because our people had determined to abate a nuisance constantly threatening their health, lives, and prosperity. Of course there were other factors...but all of these only helped to emphasize the fact that Spain was maintaining a pesthole at our front door...[Puerto Rico] stretched a threatening hand toward our shore" (Hoff, 1900: 796). By asserting government's right to protect its people from invasion, military and medical metaphors were merged and the U.S. colonial administration that ensued engaged in a different kind of battle after the war that used public health to colonize Puerto Rican society.

During the military administration that lasted from 1898 to 1900, military officers positioned the United States in relation to Puerto Rican interests using two dominant narratives that were eminently ideological. Their narrative about public health associated a general humanitarian interest in the island's progress with the rejection of the island's uncivilized and primitive past. It emphasized the U.S. military's leadership over public health interventions officers' associated with an order and a kind of modernization that purportedly served the public interest. The narrative rejected the Spanish colonial legacy by describing it as a slow and degenerative decay that led Puerto Ricans to consider premature deaths as normal. U.S. colonial administrators used death as a metaphor to promote their own legitimacy in conquering the tropics.

The narrative associating death with a colonial past was reproduced by American soldiers and travelers who visited the island and other new colonial possessions. In Puerto Rico, these observers informed an imperial gaze that was impressed by funeral processions and alarmed by what they saw as overcrowded cemeteries where human remains were exposed (Allen, 1901; Bryan, 1899; Herrmann, 1907; King, 1929). Cemeteries were both a symbol and a target for displacing the Spanish colonial legacy and consolidating U.S. colonial authority (Urrego, 2002). For instance, in *Our Islands and Their People,* a photographer places himself in a dominant relationship to the colonial legacy through the colonizing frame of a photograph and in reference to both the "X" he marked on the photo to indicate where Columbus "first landed" and to contrast the "Spanish gentleman" sitting at the edge of a grave site (see Figure 1; Bryan, 1899: 337). The photographer contrasts his active gaze with the static posture of onlookers in the center of the photo and, in the lower-right corner, the casual demeanor of a cigarette-smoking grounds keeper who appears to be smiling. The caption contrasts the owners of the cemeteries with the temporary rental of graves, which implied the former's callous attitude toward the symbol of death when it explains bones were "thrown promiscuously into the common pit" (Bryan, 1899: 337). This implication

Figure 1. "Conquering Death." Cemetery and Boneyard at Aguadilla, Porto Rico (in Bryan, 1899: 337).

is reinforced by the image of the keeper who rests his feet on the human bones and holds up two skulls as both proof and spectacle for the consumption of multiple U.S. audiences who viewed the picture.

Other photographs exposed Puerto Ricans' otherness in terms that contrasted death and reproduction. Across approximately fifty books that were published between 1898 and 1914, images of Puerto Rico associated poverty with inefficient production as an aspect of the Spanish colonial legacy (Thompson, 2007). The narrative of naturalized death and inefficient production involved uncontrolled reproduction. For example, a U.S. volunteer in the war explained he had seen five funerals, which he believed meant that ten births had occurred because of the high birth rate (Herrmann, 1907). Pictures focused obsessively on naked children to underscore the shifting dynamic of paternal authority and control over both production and reproduction.[1] This authority implied a form of

---

[1] According to Thompson (2007), this "obsession" was, without exception, shared across all fifty books.

colonial control that espoused an ideology of tutelage over an island that was treated and represented as a child. Similarly, U.S. colonial authorities focused on children, schooling, families, sexuality and reproduction (Briggs, 2002; Lopez, 2008; Negron De Montilla, 1975). This ideology was negotiated in relation to native elite ideas about the nation and its honor, which were expressed through the conceptualization of a *gran familia puertorriqueña,* or a grand Puertorrican family. The ideas of Puerto Rico's native elites reflected a society profoundly structured by race, class and gender (Findlay, 1999; Rodríguez-Silva, 2012).[2]

The narrative of conquering death contributed to a discourse that portrayed the U.S. administration as an exceptional form of benevolent colonial rule. The project of benevolence and the mission of tutelage meant the U.S. colonial administration adapted to conditions existing in their colonies and they enrolled native elites in developing and reproducing this image (Go, 2007). In Puerto Rico, the U.S. colonial administration used the narrative of death to claim they shared a goal with the native elite: the island's progress. U.S. colonial authorities adapted a pre-existing discourse about how inefficient labor compromised the island's modernization and economic development and defined reproduction as a problem for a population that was overwhelmingly young and inefficient in its productive capacity. The narrative of conquering high death rates complemented the one on high birth rates, which implied fewer workers were able to fulfill the purportedly shared goal. Although both groups sought to modernize production, they had competing ideas about modernization and progress. U.S. colonial administrators and the island's elite also had different ideas about who should benefit from production. The narrative on death nonetheless centered the U.S. colonial administration and Puerto Rico's physicians on a shared objected and promoted consensus regarding interventions that targeted workers. In order to develop the island's productive capacity, U.S. colonial administrators reasoned they had to regenerate the labor of men (Middeldyk, 1903; Hoganson, 1998; Rigau-Pérez, 2010). They adapted an existing medical/hygienic discourse through public health interventions that involved men (physicians, laborers, administrators, elites) in the project of regenerating masculine labor.

A second dominant battle narrative was more closely tied to the colonial relationship and the public health administration. In this narrative,

---

[2] Throughout the text, "native" refers to a person born in Puerto Rico of any parentage.

U.S. colonial officers claimed native politicians were self-interested and expressed doubts about Puerto Ricans' ability to govern themselves. This narrative reflected other U.S. reformers' strategic attempts to expand their influence by creating what was essentially a false dichotomy between formal electoral politics and patronage on the one hand, and the public administration on the other (Rosenbloom, 2008). In the United States, the dichotomy fostered a sense that administration was "governed by principles that were analogous to 'laws of nature'" (Rosenbloom, 2008: 59). In Puerto Rico, U.S. colonial administrators used this dichotomy as a rhetorical strategy. They insisted political patronage was a legacy of Spanish colonization on the island and reproduced the illusion politics could be removed from the work of administration.

For U.S. colonial administrators, the administration became a critical point of intervention. They had been assigned a task that "had no parallel in the previous history of our country" and had little instruction from "the act of Congress [which] is very brief, and makes no direction of the manner in which the military was to be superseded by the civil government" (Allen, 1901: 14). With little direction from Congress, U.S. colonial administrators had to depend on native support to carry out the work of tutelage and to foster Americanization and implement "American customs and policy" on the island (Davis, 1900b: 10). Following the military strategies developed under the U.S. occupation of the island, they had to eliminate what they perceived was the negative legacy of the Spanish colonial regime on Puerto Rican affairs. On the one hand, U.S. colonial administrators wanted to distinguish themselves from this "unfamiliar" legacy that caused discontent and social and economic unrest (Davis, 1900b). In the transition to a civil government, for instance, military governor George W. Davis repeatedly differentiated his actions from those of authoritarian Spanish Governor Generals who carried out arbitrary administrative decisions that "systematically rejected, individual initiative of every sort" (1900b: 7). On the other hand, U.S. colonial administrators insisted Puerto Ricans had inherited the Spanish legacy in not only language, but also temperament, lifestyle, manners and political beliefs. U.S. colonial administrators blamed the Spanish influence for being unsympathetic with "the innovations of American laws, customs, and progress" and negatively influencing political affairs through the press (Hunt, 1904: 10). U.S. colonial administrators wanted to eliminate this influence because they saw it as an obstacle that impeded U.S. colonization and the penetration of U.S. capital. As a result, Governor Charles H. Allen considered himself "fortunate" he had unrestricted authority to set up the civil government (1901: 14).

U.S. colonial administrators adapted to local conditions and used their broad administrative powers to control the island's insular and municipal administrations. They engaged in a different kind of battle to undermine Puerto Ricans' claims of effective representation. As part of this second battle narrative, U.S. colonial administrators insisted the Spanish colonial legacy had compromised Puerto Ricans' ability to engage in fair politics and promote the public interest. For instance, Leo Stanton Rowe cast Puerto Ricans as political fanatics whose beliefs "became a kind of religion" (1904: 235). He alleged that the task of "education and example" was made more difficult not only because U.S. colonial administrators had to "secure the active support of the native population," but also because natives used "public service for personal ends" (1904: 224, 229). In order to intervene in what they claimed were patronage politics, the U.S. colonial administration targeted what they considered "primitive" municipal governments (Davis, 1900b; Go, 2008; National Civil Service Reform League, 1902; Rowe, 1904; Willoughby, 1909, 1910). This strategic decision worked to appease Puerto Ricans' anxieties about political autonomy. For instance, the island had gained political autonomy under Spain in 1897 and municipal governments had already enjoyed greater autonomy since 1872. By targeting municipal governments, U.S. colonial administrators believed they could work at the local level to promote tutelage, intervene in what they construed as patronage politics and undermine the political mobilization and influence of groups they perceived to be out of sympathy with the change in sovereignty. As a result, administrators like Governor Davis could assert the withdrawal of troops and extension of autonomy was dependent "solely on the people themselves" demonstrating they could serve the public interest through "towns well governed" (Davis, 1900b: 10–11).

For U.S. politicians on and off the island, municipal governments' relative autonomy was a profoundly political and rhetorical strategy aimed at promoting the legitimacy of U.S. colonial authority. For instance, after visiting the island in November 1906, President Theodore Roosevelt affirmed the symbolic limits of municipal government's autonomy when he claimed "the difficult matter of granting to the people of the island the largest measure of self-government that can with safety be given at the present time" was reflected in municipal governments who enjoyed "complete and absolute autonomy" (1906: 5). According to Roosevelt, this indicator of Puerto Ricans' capacity for self government was monitored by the insular government and the U.S. colonial governor only exercised his authority to remove municipal officials when they jeopardized "the interests of the people of the island; and under such circumstances it has been fearlessly used to the immense benefit of the people (Roosevelt, 1906: 5). Roosevelt emphasized the people and their interest in order to claim the United States was their effective representative. In an effort to obscure and legitimize U.S. political domination, Roosevelt suggested democratic representation came not from the people or even from above, but instead from the outside influence of the United States.

Roosevelt's repeated metaphor of the people was a consistent and strategic ploy used by a majority of U.S. colonial administrators to give symbolic weight and significance to their shared mission of tutelage. Administrators imbued the metaphor with meanings about race, modernity and civilization that made a critical distinction between the people and the Puerto Rican elite. For instance, Davis explained Puerto Ricans were used to subservience and "the Spanish race" had never been able to establish and maintain good government (1900a: 45). Davis belied his ambivalence about the legacy of colonial authority and its implications on racial difference and Puerto Ricans' capacity for self-government when he used the Census to establish that "the pure white are in a considerable majority," but distinguished "say 75 per cent of the males over 21 years of age...[who] are of the class usually called peons" (1900b: 16–17). His distinction between the Spanish race and peons was at least partly provoked by the rural violence accompanying the U.S. invasion, which indicated class interests between social groups on the island were as significant as relations between dominator and subaltern (García, 2000; Picó, 2004). For U.S. colonial administrators, however, the people and the public interest did not necessarily extend to a variety of social groups characterizing Puerto Rican society in the early-twentieth century, including a diverse political, intellectual and landed elite, local administrators, academically-trained professionals and a wide variety of medical practitioners on the island, urban workers and artisans, cattle farmers and a diverse group of small and medium planters that included tenant farmers and sharecroppers. Instead, U.S. colonial administrators defined the people as landless peasants.

For U.S. colonial administrators, the overwhelming majority of Puerto Ricans were peons who were degenerated by poverty, debt and old laws. As a consequence, Davis claimed there was no difference between "negro and the peon" whom he described as "pale, sallow, and often emaciated beings" that descended in a surprising contrast from the Spanish "conquistadores" (1900b: 18). For Davis, the relative meaning of Puerto Ricans' whiteness was indicated by the description he quoted from a text, *The*

English in the West Indies. His description did not indicate the reference came from the text's section on "negro morals" (Froude, 1888: 48–51). Davis' semantic imposition of implied and recognized European and African ancestry indicated his ambivalence about Puerto Ricans' whiteness and his ideas about racial degeneration in the tropics. He concluded the text's moral characterizations "apply with full force to these people" and his quote underscored the primitive nature of Puerto Rican peons who "sin, but they sin only as animals...They eat, drink, sleep, and smoke, and do the least in the way of work they can. They have no idea of duty, and therefore are not made uneasy by neglecting it" (Froude in Davis, 1900b: 18). Davis implied work was a measure of racial degeneration and attitudes about work were part of the Spanish colonial legacy in Puerto Rico.

Davis was not the only U.S. colonial administrator who used the peon to criticize the native elite and the administration of municipal government. Through repeated references to the peon that imbued the symbol with meaning, a variety of U.S. audiences reproduced the assertion the island was not ready for the responsibilities of a democratic government. By justifying its effort to displace the effects of "old laws" on the peon, for instance, the U.S. colonial administration legitimized and consolidated its authority. The repeated references also worked to generalize an immediate interest in developing the peon's productive capacity. Dr. Ames explained: "agriculture is basic...78.6 percent of the entire population is practically rural and essentially agricultural... a very small fraction of the percent named will represent those in the rural districts exempt from labor... 'labor problems' relate almost wholly to the agricultural toiler, his interests, condition, and needs" (1901: 380). The needs of the agricultural toiler, the peon, became the symbol of public interest, which U.S. colonial administrators like Davis and Ames used to displace blame for limiting territorial autonomy onto a small elite they marked through contrasting and belittling references like "a very small fraction of the percent... exempt from labor" (Ames, 1901: 380). These associations became important tropes for an array of groups who used them to navigate the colonial relationship.

The distinction between "the Spanish race" and peons was as critical to U.S. colonial administrators as it was to the native elite, because these so-called peons became an object in the fierce competition for representing the public and its interests. For Puerto Rican elites who were not Spanish, but instead were born on the island and made up a native elite, the bodies of rural peasants, the so-called *jíbaro,* were constructed as both

symbol and myth of Puerto Rico as a sick nation. In the nineteenth
century, liberal elites imagined the *jíbaro* as barefoot and isolated in a
rural tropical environment because of Spanish colonial repression. They
used this construct to project their own dissatisfaction with the lack of
modernizing reforms under the Spanish colonial regime. Elites also saw
the *jíbaro* as a white victim of Spanish colonialism and as a sick patient
that could be cared for, which had particular political salience because
"scientific theories...linked a nation's prospects for development to the
racial make-up of the population" (Loveman, 2007: 81; Cubano-Iguina,
2005; Rodríguez-Silva, 2012; Scarano, 1996, 1999; Trigo, 2000; Trujillo-Pagán,
2003). The ideal of caring for the *jíbaro* shifted under a new colonial
regime, but the *jíbaro* continued to play a crucial role as elites navigated
new racial distinctions and radical changes in the political economy of the
island. After 1898, the *jíbaro* remained white but became the symbol of a
national identity "threatened by North American economic and cultural
domination" (Scarano, 1996: 1404; Guerra, 1998). He was refashioned as not
only a sick patient who required care, but also one whose behavior
reflected Puerto Ricans' primitive nature and lack of capacity for self-government (Go, 2008). For both U.S. colonial administrators and Puerto
Rican physicians, medical intervention became a powerful new political
force within an otherwise ambiguous and ostensibly dangerous tropical
landscape.

U.S. colonial administrators' paternalistic association of broader political autonomy and self-government with reforms to the local administration implied a unique role for municipal governments and local physicians
in fostering American customs and policy on the island. Through their
repeated references to mortality, the significance of the peon and public
interest were amplified and became indicators of Puerto Ricans' capacity
for self-governance. U.S. colonial administrators also expanded the metaphor of patients' pallor to enlist physicians in sharing their claim to represent the public interest. Ultimately, U.S. colonial administrators hoped
physicians would regenerate not only the peon's pallor, but also municipal governments and the native elite who competed to represent his interests. At the local level, physicians went into another battle waged in the
name of public health, through sanitation surveillance and policing,
and in relation to a variety of distinct and competing social groups. The
form in which Puerto Rico was colonized by the United States implicated
a profound and enduring competition between U.S. colonial administrators and the native elite in establishing the meanings of duty, authority
and work.

Economy and Social Conditions: Labor and Hunger

The island's transition from a military to a civil government did not occur without tragedy. Hurricane San Ciriaco hit the island in 1899 and devastated lives by increasing morbidity and mortality. In Utuado, the death rate was 81% (Hoff, 1900: 797). Mortality also increased in municipalities far from the storm's path from the southeastern to the northwestern corners of the island. For instance, in Ponce and Yauco mortality jumped by about 10% from what it had been in 1890 (Hoff, 1900: 797). A wave of reports from sanitation inspectors on the resulting conditions of hunger and public protest resurrected the specter of death and ruined U.S. military administrators' narrative of conquest. For instance, Dr. George G. Groff of the Superior Board of Health (SBOH) explained the cyclone and poverty in municipalities were responsible for the "unsightly... [and] unhygienic" conditions existing in cemeteries, which included, in Utuado, bodies "left to the dogs – one body already having been consumed by these animals... human remains are seen scattered on the ground. Numberless clothes of the deceased, coffins, etc., are also visible" and in Hatillo, "the walks are white with human bones" (in Hoff, 1901: 610).

A natural hazard turned into a disaster through the pre-existing conditions of hunger and the political decisions that were made after the hurricane's impact. U.S. military authorities introduced a series of policies that were continued by the civil government and that recreated the sense of a faltering recovery. For instance, the change in sovereignty had reduced agricultural production on an island that had already become reliant on imported food. Most Puerto Ricans could not afford iron-rich meat and this commodity had already become a particularly powerful symbol of colonial dependence by the end of the nineteenth century (Coll y Toste, 1892; Rodríguez-Silva, 2004). This concern had even been shared by municipal councils loyal to the Spanish colonial administration (San Juan Ayuntamiento, 1888). The hurricane compounded the lack of food, but the Charity Board required Puerto Ricans to work in order to access food relief (Hoff, 1900; Schwartz, 1992). The social problems relating to food and the administration's demand to intensify labor production were compounded the following year by the Foraker Act, which structured the civil government. Under U.S. colonial authority, Puerto Ricans' political subordination compromised employment levels and industrial recovery. As workers' wages fell to half what they had been under Spanish authority, Puerto Ricans intensified their demands for greater political autonomy.

The disastrous political conditions critically affected coffee production. The hurricane's path devastated coffee-producing municipalities and compromised the island's major export crop. Colonial policies compounded the calamity in a variety of ways, which included the exclusion of coffee from tariff protections and denying a loan for the industry's recovery. A complete revolution in the industry also implied a dramatic reduction in the availability of domestically-produced food that was grown interspersed with coffee bushes. Agricultural production on the island had already encouraged increased reliance on imported foodstuffs in the late-nineteenth century, but when the Foraker Act devalued the Spanish peso, the relative price of food increased. As a member of the Planters, Bankers, and Merchants' Association of Puerto Rico explained, "our people are starving...and the island is in a worse condition under the rule of Gov. Allen than it ever was before, even when Spain held sway" (*New York Times,* 25 April 1901).

The social conditions following the hurricane benefitted the importation of U.S. products into the island at the expense of the Puerto Ricans and their economy. For instance, in Figure 2, the political cartoon implies the unequal relationship between the United States and Puerto Rico using symbols of unequal trade. Several commodities are emphasized in the cartoon, including Puerto Rican coffee that did not enjoy favorable market conditions in the United States. The peasant holding the coffee seems engaged in a negotiation with a much taller and powerful Uncle Sam, whose height compares to the ships that carry imports and exports from the island. This representation of Uncle Sam is suggestive of how the United States controlled trade and the importation of commodities. Although manufactured clothing, machinery and yarn are included on the margins of the image, what is emphasized in the center of the cartoon and in the negotiation between the peasant and Uncle Sam, involves basic foods like meat, condensed milk and lard. On the right side of the image, Uncle Sam casually consumes luxury goods with one hand in his pocket while smoking a pipe. In contrast, the barefoot peasant negotiates with the "the only purveyor" who keeps a pair of shoes beyond his reach and behind the store's glass.

Following the 1899 hurricane, workers who didn't or couldn't migrate to urban areas to find work, faced a decline in employment and wages. Many agricultural workers could barely meet their basic needs through seasonal labor and their work became increasingly irregular as coffee planters scaled back production. Several reports on labor conditions varied in their estimates of daily wage rates, typically between .30 to .60 cents

Figure 2. "U.S. Porto Rico's Only Purveyor", Drawing by Mario Brau de Zuzuárregui, in Colección de Dibujos de Mario Brau (1904-1915). Reproduced with permission from Colección Puertorriqueña del Sistemas de Bibliotecas, Universidad de Puerto Rico, Recinto de Río Piedras.

a day, but the data collected in a 1904 informal survey among 22 workers on a coffee plantation indicated pickers (who were paid based on volume picked) averaged about 12 to 16 cents per day (Weyl, 1905). The 1905 report on labor conditions also found a dozen eggs that were probably produced locally cost about 24 cents (Weyl, 1905). Meanwhile, U.S. colonial administrators insisted the low wages exceeded the cost of living and explained "if they [country laborer] receive the money they will not work" (Post, 1907: 23).

Like other forms of disaster, famines are produced through political and economic decisions. Samuel Gompers visited the island as part of the American Federation of Labor's investigation of complaints and claimed he had never seen such hunger or misery. He emphasized his disappointment through contrasting references to the "healthful and invigorating" climate that made the island productive (Gompers, 1904: 4). Hoff also mentioned a "famine" had followed the hurricane and "many thousands during the past year...have starved outright," but he was quickly drowned out by other colonial administrators (1900: 799; 2006: 121). For instance, the Secretary of the Superior Board of Health rejected the claims of the American press as "calamity howlers" (Smith, 1900). In a letter to the Editor of *The Great Round World,* Dr. William Fawcett Smith (1901) also warned food relief would be a "calamity" that discouraged labor supply and encouraged a harmful "pauperizing tendency." U.S. colonial adminis-trators concurred in a ubiquitously repeated narrative that workers were responsible for their impoverished condition. They referred, for instance, to drinking or gambling habits that should be controlled through govern-ment regulation (Weyl, 1905).

Medicine: Hookworms

The disaster that followed the 1899 hurricane seemed to reach its peak in 1904. Many coffee farmers hoped for the best after waiting the five years it took for their bushes to produce fruit. In the meantime, they had weath-ered a loss of credit and markets, a lack of tariff protections in U.S. markets, increased competition from Brazilian exports, lowered world market prices for coffee, and the loss of a labor force that had migrated to the coast for work in sugar production. Coffee planters' dissatisfaction with the U.S. colonial administration drove many to join the new Unionist Party. They joined a broad political coalition of various sectors of Puerto Rican society.

The Unionist Party delivered a landslide electoral victory in 1904, dra-matically undermining the influence of the Republican Party that was favored by U.S. colonial authorities. Governor William H. Hunt openly recognized that Puerto Ricans "want more, not less, self-government" and they felt "bitterly toward the United States and its policies in Puerto Rico" (1904: 10). He nonetheless restated his position from the previous year that "the present form of government ought not to be changed now" (1904: 12). Instead, he proposed a bill that acted on the 1899 discovery of hookworm on the island. Hunt redirected politicians' attention to a parasite that is more frequently known as a roundworm. He lobbied for the island's funds to be directed toward providing resources to create the Commission for the Study and Treatment of Anemia in Puerto Rico.

The Commission was part of a broader campaign whose demonstra-tions grew out of a scientific discovery and a subsequent survey, both of which had recognized the importance of diet. The survey also consid-ered hookworm a problem that was generalized across a variety of social groups in Puerto Rico. By late 1904, however, the Commission emphasized the origins of hookworm in coffee-producing regions and asserted the parasite undermined rural workers' productivity and their lives. Although the hookworm is a factor in iron-deficiency, the hookworm campaign's directors frequently asserted a broader claim that they could cure tropical anemia. They began promoting a message of salvation that was alternately framed in religious, economic and military terms. Appealing to both physicians and planters, the directors promised once they cured anemia, Puerto Rico "will enter upon an era of prosperity which to-day [sic] our most extravagant dreams can not [sic] foreshadow" (Ashford and Gutiérrez Igaravidez, 1911: 22). They began their efforts at the Bayamon Municipal Hospital where both physicians and politicians could "observe the practical work and the results of treatment" (Commission for the Study and Treatment of Anemia, 1904: 9). Armed with medical men as soldiers and medicine as their weapon, the hookworm campaign moved into battle to demonstrate "the cause of the anemia of our *jíbaros* [rural peasants]. It's a worm! Not climate, nor food, nor bad hygiene, nor malaria, nor anything of that sort, but a worm-an intestinal worm!" (Ashford, 1934: 5) According to the U.S. colonial officers that directed the campaign's earliest developments, starvation couldn't explain anemia in Puerto Rico because the peon had food in abundance and "many nations eat bananas as their staple article of food, and maintain good physical development" (1903: 392). Two months later, the campaign advanced its operations into Utuado, "the most hungry of all of the Porto Rican municipalities" (Ashford and Gutierrez Igaravídez, 1911: 29).

The discovery of hookworm on the island had not been initially significant to the U.S. colonial administration. In a field hospital the U.S. Army set up as part of the relief effort, one of its medics found hookworm ova in patients' feces. Dr. Bailey K. Ashford's findings were referenced in Hoff's 1900 report on "the white man's burden" in Puerto Rico, but they weren't used to explain the island's mortality rate. The young medic went back to the United States and returned to the island two years later. His enduring interest in the hookworm still hadn't received the U.S. administration's financial or logistical support. Instead, he began a survey of hookworm infection through the support of Walter W. King, an assistant surgeon of the U.S. Public Health and Marine Hospital Service and Dr. Luis Aguerrevere, a Puerto Rican physician and director of the Tricoche Hospital who provided critical space and resources.

Despite these humble origins, the hookworm campaign that ensued gained support among the island's physicians and its political and labor leaders. Its popularity among these groups shaped public health and medical efforts on the island. The campaign also influenced hookworm control interventions in the United States and internationally through the Rockefeller Foundation. Through the hookworm campaign, Puerto Rican physicians participated in the international development of modern tropical medicine. This participation drew them into a specialty that had significant implications beyond the medical community. On the one hand, tropical medicine's development was rooted in bacteriology (germ theory) and focused on parasites in tropical climates (Caponi, 2002). Tropical medicine provided institutional support for new research and scientific development in and beyond the colony. On the other hand, medical schools institutionalized tropical medicine as a specialty through the colonial administrations in European colonies (Peard, 1999). This implicated Puerto Rican physicians in a politic that went beyond their geographic and national boundaries.

Tropical medicine implies difference, which has traditionally involved competing narratives about race. In other contexts, tropical medicine became a way for whites to colonize the "other." For Puerto Rican physicians, it became a way to negotiate the meaning of embattled national identity and whiteness in relation to both U.S.-Anglo-Saxon institutions and the "Spanish race." The unique role of tropical medicine in shaping the meanings of race meant that Puerto Rican physicians' participation in the hookworm campaign built on a pre-existing cultural repertoire that had labored to reconcile the implications of racial mixture on national identity. At the end of the nineteenth century, liberal physicians who sought political autonomy under Spanish colonial authority were critical to the national project of regenerating blood they associated with the "Spanish race" (Cubano-Iguina, 2005; Rodríguez-Silva, 2012). At the beginning of the twentieth century, the same elite struggled to reconcile the Spanish legacy under U.S. colonial authority. Even if racial mixing implied Puerto Ricans weren't white by Anglo-Saxon standards, elite physicians argued the majority of the islands' residents should be considered white because of their European ancestry.

For a select group of medical practitioners in Puerto Rico, tropical medicine became a profound endeavour that shaped their relationship to the U.S. colonial state, the idea of Puerto Rico as a nation and the sick patient. The doctor-patient relationship was embedded in a colonial-national struggle for elites' authority over modern progress. Through their patients who were viewed as clinical material, Puerto Rican physicians not only developed tropical medicine on island, but also fostered their relationships with both U.S. and Latin American medicine and engaged in international debates for scientific and professional recognition. Through a campaign that began with national debates on the hookworm, Puerto Rican physicians recreated their leadership in a radically-altered social hierarchy. They worked toward shaping this hierarchy to their advantage in not only professional, but also national terms that implicated political elites, labor and race.

As inheritors of the Spanish race and its legacy on the island, Puerto Rican physicians played a singular role in simultaneously navigating the colonial and the municipal administrations and promoting the public interest vis-à-vis the so-called peon. They were profoundly implicated in a colonial struggle to transform the island's native elite. On the one hand, many liberal elite physicians led the island's political changes at the end of the nineteenth century. Some were central to the mobilization and developments of the Autonomist Party on the island, while others were involved in separatist activities on and off the island. Physicians like Julio J. Henna had actively pursued Puerto Rico's independence from New York through a segment of the Cuban Revolutionary Party. Others, like Dr. Ramón Emeterio Betances, worried about U.S. intentions to annex Puerto Rico (in Scarano, 1998). On the island, physicians were also the first to mount protests against the military occupation and U.S. colonial government (Henna and Zeno Gandia, 1899). On the other hand, the physicians involved in the hookworm campaign also competed among a diverse elite in their claim to represent the rural laborer who became a symbol of the public interest.

The campaign associated the hookworm with the legacy of servitude under Spanish colonization because it caused a "pallor of years, of centuries" (Ashford, 1934: 3). According to Ashford and many other U.S. audiences concerned with some version of liberty and "the physical emancipation of Porto [sic] Rico," the hookworm also distinguished "the poor man [from] the well-informed and better class of Porto [sic] Ricans, who were well fed and well shod, and therefore protected from infection, being skeptical and having centuries of prejudice behind them" (Grinnell, 1914: 719, 721). Through many published documents and photos and ideas that were publicized among a variety of Puerto Rican and U.S. audiences, the campaign's medical men claimed to represent the poor man, the peon and the *jíbaro*, which referred to the same category of rural agricultural working men. They shared U.S. colonial administrators' conflation of this man with the public interest, which they claimed to promote by distinguishing themselves from the so-called "better class" (Grinnell, 1914: 721). For physicians who participated in the campaign, their interests were not simply about negotiating colonial authority or the change in political sovereignty. Instead, many municipal physicians participated in the campaign in order to realize a goal of greater professional autonomy from municipal governments' influence and authority. Other campaign physicians hoped to use the campaign to improve a social position that had been compromised by U.S. colonial authority, which included increased difficulties obtaining compensation and competition for markets of patients. The campaign's new medical men distinguished themselves from a variety of social groups because, as the campaign's directors insisted by referring to both established elites and competing practitioners, "this lack of mental contact, of a common ground of interest between the jibaro and the better class of Porto Ricans drives the former to charlatans for his medical advice" (Ashford and Gutierrez Igaravidez, 1911: 15).

Method

In this book I use a variety of data to understand the context of public health and tropical medicine in Puerto Rico at the turn of the century. Local, insular and U.S. government reports elucidated the political context in which these institutions developed.[3] Evidence in the form of unpublished reports, correspondence and local regulations were obtained from archival sources in the United States and in Puerto Rico. The book also refers to a variety of medical, biographical and medico-literary texts that were authored in the period from 1850 to 1950. Dr. Manuel Quevedo Báez, the founder of Puerto Rico's medical association, reflected that biographies were as difficult to construct as oil paintings. The task of developing physicians' biographical data was facilitated by supplementing the data sources outlined above with Census data, government appointment rosters, and physician directories that were published in early-to mid-twentieth century. These sources were also supplemented with an unsystematic review of newspapers published during the period to identify themes in how medicine was advertised and popularized.

I use these texts to elucidate changes in medical discourse about the profession and its relationship to national development. I identified themes to understand how narratives about medicine and health were developed. The major themes in these narratives involved labor and national progress. My analysis assumes narratives are like stories that are used to develop and negotiate ideas. These narratives shape multiple and competing meanings that inform a broader discourse institutionalizing shared definitions of reality (Berger and Luckmann, 1966; Foucault, 1980).

---

[3] In this text, "local" refers to the municipal administration. "Insular" refers to the centralized government administration of the island. U.S. government reports were federal documents published by the U.S. Government Printing Office.

My analysis assumes narratives were developed not only through written language because multiple texts also used photographs and drawings to tell stories. I pay attention to these images in my analysis of how narratives overlap, compete and/or complement one another.

The Scholarship on Public Health, Tropical Medicine and Hookworm in Puerto Rico

Historians who study Puerto Rico share a popular belief that public health institutions developed at the beginning of the twentieth century began to solve the crisis of Puerto Rico's high mortality rate. This shared perspective centers on the hookworm campaign, which they assume cured rural peasants of parasitic infection. Many Puerto Ricans also applaud the early U.S. colonial administration for developing a campaign they believe cured islanders of the broader disease diagnosed as anemia. Even commentators who are most critical of colonialism share the view that the campaign was one of the U.S. colonial administration's positive legacies. For instance, the national newspaper credits the campaign's perceived success for many contemporary Puerto Rican medical institutions.

This narrative is somewhat confirmed by the campaign's documents and the historical record on medicine's development in Puerto Rico. The narrative tying the campaign to institutional development was much clearer. The campaign developed a professional elite and laid the institutional framework for the development of medical authority and science on the island. This professional elite included many of the campaign's medical men who developed their research and administrative influence to form the island's first medical school. Although U.S. colonial administrators took credit for these developments, it was Puerto Rican physicians who had to negotiate the terms of colonization beyond the administration and in relation to the U.S. medical profession in order to develop medicine on the island. The terms of colonization reflected Puerto Rican physicians' ambivalent position: they sought to expand their associations with U.S. medicine, but many shared significant concerns about U.S. colonization (Lo, 2002).

The narrative that credits the hookworm campaign with curing anemia and reducing the island's mortality rate is less clear. The campaign provided medical attention to many patients and attempted to cure them of uncinariasis, a disease caused by significant and persistent hookworm infection. Despite the campaign's claims to cure an island-wide epidemic, however, its records document important distinctions between the number of patients who were treated and a much smaller proportion who were cured of infection. The campaign could not control reinfection in rural areas and did not intervene in significant ways within coastal and urban areas where hookworm was not a significant source of disease. Several bodies of scholarship suggest the campaign's claims about the peon as patient, and the resulting narrative of the campaign's success, should be reconsidered.

Medical historians find physicians were largely unable to reduce mortality prior to the mid-20th century (Colgrove, 2002). At the beginning of the twentieth century, when the hookworm campaign began in Puerto Rico, colonial medicine could not win major victories in conquering death. "Doctors could deal with trauma, perform some surgical marvels, prescribe quinine for malaria, vaccinate for smallpox, and not much else" (Patterson, 1989: 511). Similarly, as early as 1903, physicians doubted hookworm infection was lethal. Charles Wardell Stiles, a U.S. physician who claimed scientific recognition for discovering the *necator americanus* species of the hookworm, suggested "uncinariasis *per se* is not quite so fatal... I am not disinclined to the belief that...deaths attributed to uncinariasis in man are in reality due to a second disease which the patient was not able to withstand because of the preexisting hookworm infection (1903: 53). Ashford's claim that hookworm infection could be fatal had important implications, but may have reflected the co-existence of other diseases among patients, including tropical sprue that implicated some measure of nutritional deficiency (Lim, 2001).[4] Despite his initial claims, Ashford eventually conceded hookworm was not fatal in other parts of the world, including the U.S. South (Ashford, 1928; Crosby, 1987). These assertions suggest the dominant narrative crediting the campaign for a dramatic reduction of the death on the island is part of a political discourse on the legacy of U.S. colonization and part of the history of science "that has centered, classically, in the formal stories...to exalt the heroism...or the valor of great men of science" (Caponi, 2003: 136).

The narrative of the anemia campaign's successes should also be contextualized in relation to Puerto Rican society in the early twentieth century. Scholars consistently find the colonial context mattered (Espinosa, 2009). They challenge unqualified claims of medicine's triumph over

---

[4] Blood analysis cannot distinguish between pernicious anemia and tropical sprue (Maldonado, 2010). Although "diet alone is not an effective therapy," tropical sprue reflects a nutrient imbalance (Preston, 2001: 226; Lim, 2001).

death and disease (Ileto, 1988). They are also more cautious in defining success and note claims are historically variable and more narrowly defined in terms of controlling specific diseases (Birn, 2009). Medical historians have determined that the dramatic reductions in death rates observed during the twentieth century were largely due to advances in diet, sanitation and improved standard of living (Colgrove, 2002; Rigau-Pérez, 2000b; Szreter, 1988). The relationship between diet and disease, at least in the in the late-nineteenth century United States, was part of a debate between germ theorists who wanted to develop "the sophisticated tools of bacteriology" and reformers who wanted to improve social conditions" (Colgrove, 2002: 729). In Puerto Rico, however, U.S. colonial administrators had singular authority in shaping this debate through a medical intervention whose broad claim to reducing mortality was more narrowly designed to control hookworm disease. The Puerto Rican hookworm campaign was initiated through U.S. colonial administrators' authority and two military officers in particular, Ashford and King, controlled the campaign's early leadership and mission. Puerto Rican physicians who inherited this structure were compelled by the campaign's mission to privilege medical treatment over sanitation. Ashford did not believe sanitation campaigns could eradicate hookworm and he was particularly concerned regulations could compromise the campaign's ability to cultivate favorable public opinion (Ashford in Farley, 1991; Ashford, 1909, 1913a). Dr. Pedro Gutiérrez Igaravídez, the Puerto Rican director of the campaign, conceded some role for patient education, but ultimately concurred with Ashford's overall assessment (Ashford and Gutierrez Igaravidez, 1911). As a result of its directors' pessimistic ideas, and despite many campaign physicians' interest in improving sanitation, the campaign's efforts to educate patients about hookworm infection or promote sanitation measures were inconsistent. The campaign's medical men prioritized treatment; research was a secondary priority that sacrificed other efforts, including interactions with individual patients. Despite other alternate ideas about the cause of anemia and appropriate interventions within and beyond the campaign, the directors' political and professional interests shaped the campaign and delimited more systematic efforts at developing rural sanitation. These interests meant more systematic and coordinated efforts to improve sanitation occurred only after public health and medical research had developed as distinct endeavors on the island.

Another body of scholarship that delimits the narrative on the hookworm campaign's success centers more specifically on anemia and professional authority. In terms of the campaign's administration, we now recognize that reinfection makes medical interventions centered on treatment and controlling hookworm infection unsustainable (Diemert, Bethony and Hotez, 2008). In terms of the campaign's broad claims for authority and prestige, we now know that anemia is not a single disease, but rather a condition caused by a variety of diseases. Historians have explored the changing meanings of anemia over time and in relation to professional identity. They find that as the prestige of the medical profession developed in the early twentieth century, "a handful of physicians" labored to establish the legitimacy of "the anemias," which were distinct from:

> [other] dramatic diseases with which patients rapidly identified. Neither did they evoke widespread fear. To most patients, the anemias were unknown and unappreciated until specialists identified and explained them [...] According to the blood specialists, anemia was an insidious presence, crippling workers, women, black people, and other people in the prime of life [...] The anemias inculpated the moral character of particular patients as well as the state of society, and these diseases suggested the need for a specialist to examine the relationship of medical knowledge to social policy (Wailoo, 1999: 5).

As Keith Wailoo makes clear, the "production of knowledge about the blood" was tied to professional identity (1999: 3). His examples indicate cultural and economic changes shaped medical specialists' and professionals' ideas about blood and disease. This insight was no less true for the political changes that followed the abolition of slavery and liberalization in Puerto Rican politics in the late-nineteenth century. Of course ideas about blood and purity were critical to the way Spanish colonization had established itself in the Americas and they defined race and maintained social hierarchies around caste. By the late-nineteenth century, although bacteriology had been widely accepted among many prominent Puerto Rican physicians and they had begun to consider the role of parasites in disease, blood continued to inform loyalties and differences. Ideas about blood indicated elite anxieties about the consequence of miscegenation on their authority and ability to wage claims for political equality as a Spanish province (Trigo, 2000; Goode, 2009). Ideas about blood implicated the nation's identity. Although the idea of shared blood tied Puerto Ricans to a Spanish legacy, liberal elite physicians crafted a medical/hygienic discourse that constructed the nation as sickened by the colonial regime. The meanings of shared blood changed under the U.S. Empire and the Spanish legacy was challenged by an ostensibly different Anglo-Saxon future (Cubano Iguina, 2005).

Under U.S. colonial authority, new medical knowledge about the blood transformed narratives of political loyalties and racial difference. Despite U.S. colonial authorities' efforts to distinguish their modern governance from the Spanish colonial legacy, they promoted forms of medical knowledge that complemented governance and blood and government remained intimately connected (Kramer, 2006; Kauanui, 2008; Quijano and Wallerstein, 1992). Ashford, a representative of U.S. Empire and a colonial administrator, frequently blamed enslaved persons from Africa for introducing the hookworm in Puerto Rico. This claim contradicted his explanation that the hookworm was unable to survive in hot and dry conditions on the coast where slaves had historically been concentrated. Ashford reproduced these contradictions by distinguishing worm carriers from patients who were worm sick and claiming blacks were less likely to suffer uncinariasis. In essence, Ashford defined racial difference through disease immunity: race determined immunity as much as immunity defined race (Feliú, 2001: 161). This distinction about racial immunity enabled Ashford to appeal to another pre-existing idea among Puerto Rico's native elite about the limited influence of miscegenation on the nation's racial identity. Puerto Rican elites had attempted to resolve their post-abolition anxieties about mixed blood by associating the island's isolated, rural and mountainous interior regions with whiteness and racial purity. The hookworm campaign that built its work from these ideas concluded the blood of a peon, a rural peasant alternately referred to as a *jíbaro,* was especially vulnerable to infection. Like white anxieties about tropical climates and tropical difference, the *jíbaros'* whiteness was compromised by a disease that reduced his hemoglobin levels, changed his blood and made him weak.

After 1904 in Puerto Rico, hookworms took on ferocious power. Through frequent published reports and visits from prominent politicians and local residents, the campaign's medical men explained that hookworm caused anemia by feeding on their host's blood. The species Ashford had identified, the *necator americanus,* is distinguished because it is toothless. Instead, the hookworm burrows into the host's intestinal walls and causes chronic blood loss, which can lead to protein deficiencies (malnutrition) and iron-deficiency anemia.[5] The hookworms also

---

5   Iron deficiency can delay mental function (normal thinking and processing skills) and cause fatigue that impairs the ability to do physical labor. According to the Centers for Disease Control (CDS), there are two main causes of iron deficiencies. First, people may not absorb adequate amounts of iron from food. The causes of poor iron absorption include both diet and parasitic infection. Second, iron deficiencies are also caused when people lose blood. One way of losing blood includes hookworm infection, which causes blood loss in relation to the number of worms an infected person carries. Hookworm

produce eggs that are evacuated by the individual (the host) through her/his feces, which in late-nineteenth and early-twentieth century were typically deposited in open areas on the soil. When workers walked with their bare feet on this soil, the hookworm larvae penetrated the skin, reinfected the same or another individual, and travelled through the blood to the intestines, thus reproducing the hookworm's lifecycle (see also Anderson, 2006; Coelho and McGuire, 2006). In Puerto Rico, the hookworm was particularly well adapted for reproduction in the humid and shady environment of rural coffee-producing regions.

The campaign associated the hookworm with the legacy of servitude, slavery and Spanish colonization. It purported to use modern U.S. medical science to restore the negative consequence of the Spanish colonial legacy. By regenerating the *jíbaro's* blood, Puerto Rican physicians believed they could restore life to labor, coffee production and the medical profession. The campaign's reports of hemoglobin levels and bodily practices (defecation and hygiene, residence and farm and family structure, visits to the clinic, compliance with medical treatment instructions, etc.) not only underscored patients' lack of modern hygiene, but they also served to surveille patients' practices and refract Puerto Ricans' capacity for self-governance. To the extent medical scientists could restore their patients' blood, they could regenerate the progress of the nation. Puerto Rican physicians working with the campaign repeatedly measured patients' hemoglobin levels and kept meticulous records of their research. They labored to restore a proud legacy of conquering not only death from hookworm's infection, but also from the legacy of Spanish colonial rule. For Puerto Rican physicians entering into the new and developing specialty of tropical medicine, blood represented a critical measure of whiteness, vigor and the potential for promoting development in the tropics. By restoring hemoglobin levels, Puerto Rican physicians also worked to mediate the implications of U.S. colonial tutelage on their status and, as Ashford implied, take advantage of their "chance to become famous" by supporting the campaign's work (1934: 71).

Indeed, many Puerto Ricans did become well known as medical scientists on and off the island when their efforts influenced hookworm

---

infection can cause and/or exacerbate iron-deficiency anemia. Both explanations are related. For instance, improved diet and iron supplements can compensate for the effects of hookworm infection (Stoltzfus et al., 1997). Despite our understanding of the relationship between diet and iron-deficiency anemia, however, interventions that intend to control hookworm infection are generally not designed to reduce iron deficiency (Stoltzfus et al., 1997).

campaigns in Latin America (Ashford, 1934; García and Quevedo, 1998). On the island, their work was taken up by the Rockefeller Foundation through the International Health Board (IHB) in 1920. The Rockefeller Foundation was arguably the world's most important agency of public health work before the World Health Organization was founded in 1948. Scholars who have studied the IHB's efforts outside of Puerto Rico have consistently found its efforts were tied to U.S. Empire and neo-colonial intervention. More specifically, their scholarship finds public health interventions ignored labor conditions that promoted hookworm infection. Instead, the IHB's programs reshaped both public health and politics in less-developed countries (Birn, 1996; Birn and Solórzano, 1999; Farley, 2003; Palmer, 2009). In essence, the IHB used hookworm campaigns to promote U.S. capital and increase laborers' capacity for hard work. The IHB's projects incorporated and built upon the work of pre-existing programs. In Puerto Rico, the work of making the island safe for U.S. capital and the IHB's programs had been well developed. As in the other colonies, however, these earlier programs struggled to reconcile nationalist impulses with the ideal of modernization, the colonial state, the "civilizing process...[and] the medical mobilization of civic potential" (Anderson, 2006: 4; Scarano, 1999).

This historical scholarship on medicine and anemia is a starting point for re-imagining the Puerto Rican hookworm campaign in terms of these complex professional and political battles and providing a context for understanding parasitic infection, disease and medical intervention. The number of worms infecting a person, also known as worm burden, distinguished worm-carriers from the worm-sick. Although many Puerto Ricans would be re-infected by the hookworm, the campaign reduced worm burden among their patients, improved their quality of life and reduced their experience of dis-ease. The concept of reducing worm burden was perhaps most significant in illustrating how the Puerto Rican hookworm campaign's success was tied to a medical and administrative intervention. This distinction was significant. In terms of medicine, the hookworm campaign was an intervention centered on the island's physicians, which included both elite and rank-and-file practitioners. It fostered a collective identity among the island's academically-trained physicians, many of which were not among the elite, based on a new medical specialty: tropical medicine. By appealing to rank-and-file practitioners, the campaign fostered a new cadre of professionals whose research was tied to similar regional developments in Latin America and internationally through the Rockefeller Foundation and the IHB.

In terms of its administrative intervention, the IHB eventually focused on reducing worm burden and removing "the largest possible number of worms from the largest possible number of persons" (1922: xxv). The hookworm campaign's earlier emphasis on individuals reflected the ways it competed to represent and use the public interest in order to influence the native elite and municipal governments. Ashford eventually recognized problems with the campaign's early interventions because individual treatment that focused on "expelling all hookworms" was expensive and the repeated administration of these vermifuges increased unpleasant side effects (1928: 15). Some campaign physicians wondered whether the thymol they dispensed caused some patients' deaths.[6] The dispensary method also compromised treatment because several campaign physicians recognized patients did not take the medication once they got home. Other campaign physicians observed many patients didn't return to the clinic and discontinued treatment altogether. Some of the campaign's medical men preferred betanaphthol and the Rockefeller Foundation eventually found oil of chenopodium, which was being used in 1900 in Indonesia, was "more powerful than thymol, while at the same time it was cheaper, easier to administer, and, in the minds of the patients, less unpleasant to take" (1922: xxiv). By focusing on the provision of medical treatment, however, the hookworm campaign also expanded its social and political influence among municipal governments, local elites, rank-and-file physicians and other rural populations.

The example of Dr. Azel Ames indicates how medicine could have such significant political effects. As noted above, he was credited as the architect of the compulsory smallpox campaign in Puerto Rico and reported on labor conditions to the Department of Labor. What appears an unusual position today is a product of how physicians developed their status, promoted their functional specificity and maintained their professional authority through the late-twentieth century. This facet of professional identity was a historical development that expanded physicians' authority by translating "cultural and professional dominance into moral and medical language" (Conrad, 2008: 197). The medical profession expanded its jurisdiction into social areas that were previously viewed as forms of crime or sin and that were beyond its proven technical competence, such as

---

[6] Subsequent research on the island and in the United States suggested the negative side effects of thymol were primarily limited to nausea, weakness, dizziness and stomach discomfort, but "given certain patient debilities, or if taken in the wrong way and not followed at the proper interval by a purge, could be fatal" (Palmer, 2010: 73; Stiles, 1913).

alcoholism, mental illness, or child abuse. They "medicalized" social problems to expand their authority. As physicians brought phenomena that
were seen as socially disruptive under their control, medicine came to
play an important role in creating a socially-accepted reality, defining
interventions and reproducing social structure (Engelhardt, 1996).
Medical judgments could and still can change cultural conceptions and
standards of what is normal, acceptable, or dangerous. By defining health
as the ability to work, for instance, physicians participate in social control
and in the reproduction of capitalism (Waitzkin, 1991).

Although these explanations delimit the hookworm's ferocious power,
they do little to explain the enduring narrative about the campaign that
began in 1904. The context of this narrative involves the histories of colonial medicine. Historians demonstrate that developments in modern
medicine made the idea of conquering the tropics possible and promoted
new and different forms of colonial expansion during the nineteenth and
early twentieth centuries (Farley, 1991; Worboys, 2000). European empires
saw medicine as a way to promote their own progress and expand into
what they had defined as undeveloped and inaccessible areas. In this analysis, medical discourse became an ideological expression of European
conquest and its need to create a colonial order by fabricating difference
(Arnold, 1993). In the United States, colonial medicine also informed the
"white man's burden." It became a way of gaining legitimacy and authority
that complemented the colonial administrations' civilizing mission. As
the President of the Rockefeller Foundation explained, the tropics had to
be conquered in order to control disease transmission from "other lands"
and to protect the importation of valuable products. It was "one war the
world needs" (Vincent, 1923). He also explained that "conquering the tropics" involved not only "the germs, parasites and infective insects that
thrive in hot and humid countries [but also] The primitive social organization among tropical peoples" (Vincent, 1923: 52).

Historians of colonial medicine have more recently turned to U.S. colonization, but their studies have not been comparative. This raises the
question of what distinguishes U.S. medicine or U.S. colonization from its
European counterpart. Mariola Espinosa's research on Cuba suggests U.S.
colonial medicine was not unlike its European counterparts. U.S. medicine and public health complemented colonial and neo-colonial discipline and Cuban physicians became critical to maintaining Cuban
independence. In *Epidemic Invasions* (2009), Espinosa argues the U.S. fear
that yellow fever epidemics were introduced from Cuba, motivated U.S.
colonization of the island. She recognizes a Cuban physician, Carlos

J. Finlay, who deserved credit for identifying the mosquito that carried yellow fever. She also places Cubans at the center of efforts to promote sanitation and prevent a yellow fever epidemic from recurring. In this analysis of an independent country, Cubans occupied center stage in preventing recolonization by controlling epidemics. Cubans denied their public health efforts were inferior to the United States, but the colonial relationship influenced the terms of independence and compelled them to pursue unpopular and expensive sanitation measures that the United States did not effect in its own southern cities (Espinosa, 2009).

In his analysis of medicine and public health in the Philippines, Warwick Anderson suggests U.S. colonization was distinguished by liberal American ideals of self-government. He focuses on how U.S. medicine was embedded in the project of Americanizing Filipino adults, which involved managing resistance and forming new identities. In *Colonial Pathologies* (2006), Anderson describes the development of public health through sanitation as part of the U.S. colonial administration's "benevolent assimilation" of Filipinos. Anderson also pays close attention to race and tropical medicine as a product of white concerns about soldiers' health in the tropics and a way of asserting racial superiority and masculinity. Anderson understands tropical medicine as part of a "progressive occupation" that informed the U.S. colonial administration's "'civilizing project'-a 'nation-building' program" (2006: 47). In his analysis, tropical medicine was not only a way of reproducing racial difference, but also a method to promote the surveillance and discipline of a subject population.

The analysis of how U.S. medicine complemented U.S. colonization has not resolved the question of what, if anything, distinguished either from their European counterparts. In his analysis of how ideas of hygiene influenced the possibility of political self-government, however, Anderson indicates U.S. military officers worked to make tropical medicine in the Philippine Islands "the lingua franca of modern tropical medicine" (2006: 73). The implication was that U.S. colonial administrators pursued an interest in distinguishing U.S. Empire and its administrators complemented this effort in relation to an international scientific community. A dominant method for pursuing this interest involved not only advancing tropical medicine, but also reforming public administration on the island. As in the Philippines, U.S. colonial administrators in Puerto Rico drew on reform movements in the Unites States to shape their ideas about promoting self-government through tutelage.

Many scholars who study colonialism consider the United States exceptional and assert its liberal government shifted colonial forms of expansion from imperialism to liberal internationalism (Kaufmann, 2001). This scholarship argues that, while U.S. colonization was informed by the ideals of white supremacy, U.S. expansion was driven more by a desire for land and resources and less by the need to dominate others. In their analyses, U.S. government authorities mobilized their economic and cultural resources to pursue economic and missionary opportunities and establish a new international order that is known as Americanization.

More recently, however, Julian Go (2008) argued that U.S. and European empires were not so distinct. Instead, colonialism adapted to different conditions it encountered and in relation to native elites. Go rejects the all-or-nothing proposition espoused by many scholars that argue U.S. colonialism's emphasis on tutelage was effectively imposed or simply rejected. Instead, he considers tutelage a "cultural project" and found Americanization was negotiated by the native elite in different contexts and over time (2008: 27). In his analysis, negotiation took place not only through culture, but also in relation to the administration that was critical to the civilizing mission and tutelage. Influenced by reform movements in the United States, U.S. colonial authorities saw public administration as the lynchpin for transforming politics, gaining legitimacy in the colonies and promoting tutelage. For instance, the investigative commissions in Puerto Rico informed U.S. authorities of Puerto Ricans' expectations and interests, which became critical to colonial governance. As a result, elites gained significant political participation in the political administration even as power was concentrated among a few U.S. colonial authorities.

Go resolves the apparent contradiction between self-government and tutelage by explaining that, for U.S. colonial authorities, democratic self-government involved limiting the power of elites to promote "government by the people" and "the mass of the population" (2008: 40). More specifically, self-government "referred to collective and individual self-government" and paralleled "the government of the individual self by the self...self-repression...[and] organized self-control" (2008: 43–44). In essence, Puerto Ricans were integrated in the administration in symbolic gestures that made "the colonial state into a 'school of politics'" (Go, 2008: 49). Puerto Ricans were reappointed to municipal posts and "inundated...with signs" that included speeches, proclamations and written texts, but U.S. colonial administrators "kept the highest posts of government for themselves... [and] had ultimate veto power over all legislation. They further constructed a system of surveillance...[and] retained the power to remove officials at will and intervene into municipal affairs as needed" (Go, 2008: 51–52). In this way, the administration became an "object lesson" in good government where Puerto Ricans could "learn through example" (Go, 2008: 52). Go's explication can be used to understand how the hookworm campaign's "object lessons" in sanitation implicated not only individual patients, but also the administration of public health at insular and local levels and elite and municipal physicians. The campaign was not only a medical intervention on the profession and individual patient's lives, but it also participated in transforming Puerto Rican society and politics.

Perspectives on U.S. medicine and U.S. colonization have generally considered the native elite as a group that alternately accommodated or resisted domination. Although Go challenges this presumed dichotomy, he reproduces the presumption that the native elite was a homogenous group. For instance, he presumes "nearly all sectors of Puerto Rican society warmly welcomed the American forces" and asserts "the elite even accepted the idea of tutelary rule" (Go, 2008: 55). Historians of Puerto Rico have also noted the ways elites welcomed the invading U.S. forces, but scholars like Fernando Picó find a puzzling discrepancy that challenge the idea of a homogenous native elite. He uses two examples of events within Utuado and Fajardo that demonstrate how the elite bubbled "over with patriotic prose in defense of the Spanish territory in June and then, with the same fervor, proclaims in August its allegiance to the Stars and Stripes" (Picó, 2004: 39). Picó resolves the discrepancy by recognizing the elite was divided between conservatives who supported Spanish colonial authority and "anti-Spanish youths from prominent *criollo* families" (41).

Although Picó recognizes the *criollo* elite "mobilized the masses to acclaim the Americans and reorganized the municipal administration to set up its own political program," he does not develop his analysis of the two interrelated phenomena indicated by his examples. First, physicians were critical in defining distinctions within the elite. Even within the prominent *criollo* elite, liberals were divided between a majority who favored an autonomous government under the Spanish republic and a small, disorganized minority that promoted separatist movements. Physicians were critical to the development of the Autonomist Party, but they were also well represented in the latter group by the end of the nineteenth century. Their regional associations and families were also fractured by economic interests in either coffee or sugar, which promoted the latter's support for autonomy under Spain or potential annexation and incorporation in U.S. markets.

Second, ethnic and economic indicators were limited in their ability to predict physicians' politics. Many physicians were not only liberals, but also professionals. They were likely part of what Francisco Scarano has referred to as a modernizing, intermediate elite between workers and large landowners who "abhorred the institutions and practices that gave such groups their power and prestige...[and were] tormented by the contradictions of colonial life" (1998: 598). If some liberal elites had a pact with Spanish colonial authority, physicians like Jose Celso Barbosa y Alcalá, Jose Gomez Brioso and Felix Tio y Malaret were important leaders of a radical faction that rejected this pact. They were most likely to cultivate cross-class alliances and promote their leadership in organized efforts to regain *criollos'* control of the island's economic fortunes (Negron Portillo, 1990; Meléndez, 1993). Under the U.S. colonial administration, physicians also helped reshape and redefine the meanings of the colonial condition, or coloniality, on the island (Quijano, 2008).

Physicians were not only distinguished by politics, but also by social status based on academic training in Europe and the United States. The small number of academically-trained physicians on the island insulated them somewhat from being heavily subordinated to political patronage and several cases demonstrated political conflicts between municipal physicians and mayors. Physicians' training also gave them a unique ability to navigate political influence within municipal governments. Through medicine and the doctor-patient relationship, physicians were uniquely positioned in intimate relation with patients. Physicians employed by municipal governments found their work overlapped with that of other private practice physicians, including liberal elite physicians who were among the island's political and intellectual elite. Many municipal physicians maintained their own independent practice. Municipal appointments also distinguished many rank-and-file practitioners from more influential physicians. As a result, like the peons who were targeted by the hookworm campaign's medical interventions, municipal physicians also became an object of fierce professional and political competition between the native elite and U.S. colonial administrators. Liberal elite physicians had been leaders in the struggle to reform Spanish colonial influence during the late-nineteenth century, but the meanings of the professional as political shifted after the change in sovereignty. Through the hookworm campaign, U.S. colonial authorities worked to cultivate a new professional elite among physicians and undermine claims for greater political autonomy in the early twentieth century.

This book is an attempt to navigate these political and professional battles. The change of sovereignty implied a radical shift in the structure of the colonial relationship, which was reflected in the meanings of anemia and the public interest. The U.S. colonial administration included native elites in the administration, but also cultivated municipal physicians to facilitate local interventions on municipal governments and residents. In this book I explore the ways the changing administration of public health promoted not only new "object lessons" under U.S. colonial authority, but also competition between political groups in relation to the metaphor of public interest. This competition involved a diverse elite in negotiating the terms of U.S. colonial authority and shaped the colonial relationship. Their outcome implicated not only medicine and the public health administration, but also Puerto Rico as a nation and Puerto Ricans as colonial subjects.

I focus on the development of sanitation, public health and tropical medicine in Puerto Rico where the professional was undoubtedly political. Sanitation involved regulations and new forms of policing urban and rural populations under the U.S. colonial administration. Many Puerto Ricans understood the new forms of promoting sanitation, particularly where they involved food inspection, as a colonial imposition and a reflection of their lack of "territorial" autonomy. In contrast, tropical medicine developed through the hookworm campaign demonstrated Puerto Rican physicians' professional expertise. It reflected an alternate form of colonial authority that was directed not only at patients, but also political elites and coffee planters. Although the campaign improved physicians' status, the development of tropical medicine was part and parcel of the development of colonialism and capitalism on the island. With the support of the U.S. colonial administration, physicians developed a new social location as intermediaries between labor, politicians and employers.

Chapter Outline

Chapter 1 provides a context for understanding traditional narratives about colonialism, and specifically U.S. colonization, and anemia. The chapter focuses on the meaning of insular and local autonomy and the fortunes of the coffee industry. Under Spanish colonial authority, the coffee industry became a dominant export in the late-nineteenth century and influenced its limited claims for autonomy rather than independence. *Criollo* elites and professionals fostered their desire for autonomy through municipal governments where they established tenuous forms of local control. During the military occupation, municipal governments retained much of their former authority. It established the premise that Puerto Ricans should prove themselves capable of self-governance to U.S. colonial authorities. In developing the civil government in 1900, however, even these limited promises were undermined when the U.S. President-appointed Executive Council and Governor redefined municipal governments and fostered the division between Puerto Rico's dominant political parties. U.S. colonial authority also effectively undermined municipal government's authority when they were restructured in 1902. At the insular level, colonial policies created the conditions for the decay of the coffee industry and the immiseration of its workers. I locate the political meanings of anemia within this political context and the underlying narrative of disaster, which involved not only the 1899 hurricane, but also a variety of transformations related to U.S. colonial rule. For U.S. colonial administrators, anemia remained tied to the island's political and economic fortunes even as they shifted the meanings of local autonomy. The increasing centralization of public health under U.S. colonial authority implied new political significance for some elites at the expense of local control.

Chapter 2 focuses on the development of public health in Puerto Rico under the U.S. colonial administration. The administration of public health was part of how the United States sought to compete with other empires in colonizing populations. Although poverty and hunger were important themes in early U.S. colonial administration's narratives about Puerto Ricans, the colonial administration's interventions in public health were ultimately guided by American ideals of individualism, work, and local government. In this chapter I discuss quarantines and the compulsory smallpox vaccination campaigns as two examples of how the U.S. colonial administration worked through civil governments and native physicians. Ultimately, sanitation became the dominant, albeit unpopular form of public health organized through the insular government. The hookworm campaign also emerged as a public health effort at the municipal level. Public health fostered native physicians' direct and indirect relationships with the U.S. colonial government and physicians working indirectly with the administration, through the campaign, ultimately fostered the separation of preventative and curative medicine in Puerto Rico.

Chapter 3 explains the process through which Puerto Rican medicine struggled to develop a professional identity and the ways physicians' work was transformed under the colonial administration. Physicians were particularly notable among social reformers on the island due to their status, based on their physical and social care of the nation. The U.S. colonial administrators cast physicians' social and political involvements as a corruptive influence on scientific medicine, and compelled them to abandon their previous involvement in politics and the social development of the rural and urban poor. Facing the increased inability to organize medical practitioners on the island, physicians opted to incorporate their medical association, the *Asociación Médica de Puerto Rico* (AMPR), within the American Medical Association.

Chapter 4 discusses anemia as a discourse that implicated questions of national identity. In late-nineteenth century Puerto Rico, elite physicians used a medical/hygienic discourse to imagine rural peasants as *jíbaros* in ways that promoted the physicians' own authority. These discursive constructions were not only professional, but also tied to the relationship between labor, production, and the colonial relationship. In the early twentieth century, physicians adapted this discourse to a radically altered social and economic context. The emerging medical discourse emphasized death in a way that implicated the regeneration of labor and production in relation to a modern colonial administration. The resulting medical discourse surrounding anemia shifted from an ailment caused by a poor diet, an explanation that indirectly challenged Spanish colonialism, to one that emphasized infection by a "tropical" parasite. The resulting attention to hookworm and individual behavior over the social context in which infection occurred shifted attention away from economic and class oppression and implicitly blamed the patient for his/her suffering.

Chapter 5 provides a summary of the main points and arguments of the manuscript. Here I summarize my discussion of how the U.S. colonial administration used tropical medicine to gain legitimacy. I also review the social transformation of the island, which displaced many native elites, but provided new opportunities for developing professional status among physicians. I consider the implications of this relationship in terms of the development of public health and medicine in Puerto Rico, particularly in relation to public health work and medical education. This discussion suggests class prejudice influenced the ways native physicians ultimately reproduced the idea that Puerto Ricans could not govern themselves.

CHAPTER TWO

ANEMIA AND AUTONOMY

The colonial relationship shaped by the U.S. military officers and subsequent colonial administrators reflected two dominant concerns. The first and most immediate concern surrounded the rural disorder and violence that accompanied the invasion. Although military officers relied on forceful metaphors, their soldiers were made up primarily of volunteers who soon shipped off to the United States. As a result, officers and colonial administrators tried to walk a fine line between their interest in distinguishing U.S. colonial from its Spanish predecessor and stabilizing a colonial order. They seemed to wobble in this balancing act when a devastating hurricane hit the island less than a year after the U.S. military government had been established on the island. Their authority was increasingly challenged by shifting political alliances and the increased worker mobilization. Recognizing that their authority was threatened at the local level, U.S. colonial administrators resorted to interventions on municipal governments in order to stabilize the U.S. colonial order. In order to implement these interventions, U.S. colonial authorities centralized key decision-making power, but worked with and selectively relied on native politicians, legislators, and administrators.

When U.S. officers established the military government, they treated the island's sanitation conditions with emergency measures. More emergencies followed a year later, when the 1899 San Ciriaco hurricane wreaked havoc, resulting in extensive loss of life and property. The occupying military force implemented relief measures, including a provisional tent hospital, to deal with the wounded and the dramatic increase in disease. The emergency work of establishing colonial order was aided by the U.S. Army medic who headed this hospital, Dr. Bailey K. Ashford. He claimed he discovered the true scientific cause of "the Puerto Rican epidemic" and the source of Puerto Rico's economic problems. For Ashford, the epidemic was the rural peasants' anemia that made them weak, lazy and inefficient workers. The ensuing campaign to eradicate this epidemic, and the hookworm to which it was attributed, became the early colonial administration's greatest success, winning approval among Puerto Rican medical professionals, colonial administrators, U.S. presidents and contemporary Puerto Rican historians.

The hookworm campaign became a symbol for a variety of transformations related to U.S. colonial rule. The parasite's appearance under the
microscope ushered in the earliest large-scale medical intervention into
the lives of what had previously been considered a largely inaccessible
rural peasantry. The campaign's directors argued hookworm infection was
particularly marked among the white peasants of the island's rural interior
region where it seemed to suck not only the blood of its host, but also the
fortunes of a region known for coffee production. The hookworm's appearance coincided with the disaster that compromised coffee production
and accompanied U.S. colonial policies that undermined the industry's
recovery. Similarly, the hookworm's hosts were made increasingly visible
as patients in the field hospitals and dispensaries that structured the
campaign. The microscope moved the worm from the coffee fields into
the laboratory and represented an ideal of modern progress and efficient
production. As the campaign's discourse on anemia developed across the
island, it transformed the public health administration at the municipal
level and undermined local claims for greater political autonomy.

In the late-nineteenth century, the strength of the coffee industry had
tied Puerto Rico and its elites to Spanish export markets and delimited
political claims for reform. This economic relationship distinguished the
island's markets from its Cuban counterparts whose exports were built on
sugar and depended on U.S. consumption. Unlike Cubans, Puerto Ricans'
struggle for independence had been largely disorganized. Meanwhile, as
the coffee industry expanded, land was increasingly consolidated under
control of peninsular Spaniards. The 1868 *Grito de Lares,* an unsuccessful
separatist revolt in the heart of a coffee-producing region, reflected the
increasing discontent of small and medium-sized landowners who were
overwhelmingly native-born *criollos* and experienced the unequal benefits of the industry's growth. These landowners shared concerns about the
influence of peninsular Spaniards more broadly with other *criollo* elites
and educated professionals who chafed under Spanish domination. In the
wake of the revolt, organized political parties fought successfully to liberalize the island's politics and gain autonomy under Spanish rule.

In their struggle for autonomy, many liberal Puerto Rican elites treated
the nation as diseased and anemia as a political cause. Elite physicians like
Cayetano Coll y Toste blamed Spanish control for the peasants' poor diet.
Coll y Toste protested Spain's control over food imports and the municipal
tax structure, which he blamed for almost doubling the cost of meat.[1]

---

[1] Taxes were based on income and "even day laborers were called upon to contribute
with a third of their annual salaries" (Carrasquillo, 2006: 43).

He claimed food prices forced rural laborers, the *labriego*, to consume rotten codfish (1914: 178–1799). Other elites similarly blamed Spain's colonial repression for driving peasants into remote rural areas where they became ill and could not access medical attention. The liberal elite used anemia as an ideological tool to challenge "the local Spanish authorities indirectly, by presenting themselves as the caretakers of a victimized lower class" (Trigo, 2000: 82). They treated anemia as a metaphor for a curable condition of colonial abuse and its consequent effects on the "diseased state" of the Puerto Rican nation. Elites used this metaphor to promote demands for national self-determination and bolster their own authority, but it also served to displace attention from harsh working conditions (Trigo, 2000).

After 1898, the discourse on anemia shifted under U.S. colonial authority. A new scientific narrative on anemia remained tied to the island's political and economic fortunes, but shifted the meanings of local autonomy. Ashford later reflected, "coffee is the country gentleman's crop, the poor man's crop, the Puerto Rican's crop" (1913a: 360). His observation tied a nation to the coffee industry's farmers and peasants even as it obscured agricultural recapitalization following 1899 and the continued expansion of a rural proletariat. The social and economic transformations facing the coffee industry were also reflected in the transformation of the island's class structure and shifting political alliances. The different meanings of insular and municipal autonomy elucidated the competing politics of centralized authority and local control under the U.S. colonial administration. The meaning of anemia also changed and was reshaped in relation to a nationalist politics surrounding autonomy.

Puerto Rico began the nineteenth century as a relatively isolated and neglected Spanish colony, but ended the century as a conflict-ridden island that had witnessed the dramatic growth of population and agriculture. These developments were shaped by three significant immigrant waves. In the late-eighteenth century, a small wave of migration came from the Canary Islands, the Dominican Republic and South American countries that were fighting for independence, particularly Venezuela. This wave was complemented by immigration following the 1815 *Real Cédula de Gracias,* or "Decree of Grace," which gave white immigrants with capital, i.e., slaves, the ability to enter Puerto Rico (Gonzalez, 1980). By the mid-nineteenth century, other English, French, Dutch and Irish immigrants had joined Puerto Rico's Spanish and African populations and created *criollos,* a creole class of natives who developed the island's coffee industry. A third wave of immigrants came to Puerto Rico from the Spanish peninsula around the middle of the nineteenth century. Peninsular Spaniards, or *peninsulares,* had more capital than *criollos* and were favored by the Spanish government. Meanwhile, *criollos* were almost entirely excluded from participating in the island's administration (Picó, 1986).

Peninsulares played a central role in the development of capitalism on the island, particularly in relation to sugar production. By the mid-nineteenth century, the sugar industry experienced a crisis in competition with international markets and *peninsulares* sought commercial opportunities in Puerto Rico's mountainous interior where coffee production predominated. They moved into rural towns as merchants and their financial capital colonized Puerto Rico's mountainous interior. *Peninsulares* controlled debts and credit and used land titles became a form of economic exchange between themselves and farmers. They used their capital to concentrate landholdings, displacing many *criollo* landowners and rural peasants and promoting the formation of a rural proletariat (Bergad, 1983a). As merchants, *peninsulares* carried debts to control credit prices and profit from the higher market price they obtained for selling coffee (Dietz, 1986).

Despite their increased dispossession, *criollos* could grow subsistence crops among coffee bushes, which made it ideal for peasant and small-scale production. The emergence of a rural proletariat of landless workers, or *jornaleros,* represented the declining fortunes of a diverse "class in transition" after the mid-1880s, which had included *agregados* (service tenants), *arrendatarios* (renters), sharecroppers and semi-nomadic independent farmers on unowned or crown land, or farmers who lacked a title to their land. Although people could work temporarily for wages or access to land, but classification as *jornalero* was the most dreaded because it "implied the absolute domination by landowners" (Bergad, 1983a: 89). These groups made up the island's peasantry, which amidst debate over the distinction, may refer to a group uncommitted to the "production of commodities or profit" (Wolf in Dietz, 1986: 52). The problems with creating a labor market and ensuring labor supply for large-scale agricultural production were persistent and sometimes, "land was accumulated not to be put into production but precisely to gain control of the peasant labor living on it" (Dietz, 1986: 42).

Peninsulares' capital not only had an important influence on the economic shifts occurring within the coffee industry, but also produced commensurate shifts in the labor market. Both sugar and coffee plantations struggled for an adequate labor supply and sought to control the mobility of landless populations in rural areas. In 1849, the Spanish Governor had passed the *Ley General de Jornaleros,* or General Law of Rural Workers, which required all nonprofessional and nonpropertied men to find work on farms. The law also formalized relationships between *hacendados* and landless *jornaleros* because it required the latter to carry their passbooks, the *libreta,* at all times, or risk being imprisoned. In the *libreta,* employers recorded employment and made notes about workers' conduct. The *libreta* also allowed municipal authorities, particularly *comisarios de barrio* or what would be akin to a neighborhood police commissioner, to monitor *jornaleros'* work, behavior and movements. Workers were imprisoned for vagrancy if they were not carrying their *libreta,* lacked employment (squatters), or if they received negative comments from employers. Although many scholars note the various ways workers resisted the *libreta,* it nonetheless served to restrict workers' mobility, increase their dependence on employers and formalize tenancy agreements (Bergad, 1983a; Picó, 1993; Scarano, 1996).

After the *libreta* was abolished in 1873, it was replaced by new forms of labor control. One equally formal, if extralegal, institution involved accumulating debt in the *tienda de raya* (García Leduc, 2003; Bergad, 1983). In these cases, workers were paid in credit that could be used at what was essentially a company store or local stores that were affiliated in some way with farm owners. The system of paying workers in these alternate forms of credit and currency, known as *riles* (unofficial metal coins) or *vales* (vouchers), obligated workers to make their purchases in forms that reproduced their debt and subservience to farmers (García Leduc, 2003). Another way the *libreta* re-emerged was through a form of identification card, *cedulas de vecindad.* These forms of identification limited workers' mobility because travel and relocation had to be approved by mayors. *Cedulas* were checked by a rural militarized police force. Through these *cedulas,* municipal governments also benefitted from labor control because they could fine, imprison or force laborers to work on public projects, particularly in maintaining and constructing roads (Carrasquillo, 2006; Figueroa, 2005).

Although *criollos* were too weak to dominate municipal governments and their social mobility was blocked by the colonial administration, they formed part of an "economic base" that could influence how colonial policy was implemented and bend it to local purposes (Carrasquillo, 2006). In particular, professionals enjoyed "a relatively privileged and influential position" at the municipal level where they could "exercise some political leverage and share in political power and patronage" (Dietz, 1986: 58). Professionals were mainly *criollos* "educated abroad as lawyers, teachers, and doctors, and who often were the descendants of displaced creole hacendados." In this way, professional influence through municipal governments became a critical way of negotiating and challenging Spanish colonial authority (Cubano-Iguina, 1998). The significance of local, municipal autonomy persisted under U.S. colonization, particularly in relation to public health.

Peninsulares within the *hacendado* class were "basically uncultured, arrogant, and conservative" (Gonzalez, 1980: 13). They "despised and oppressed the native poor, and were, in turn, hated by them" (Gonzalez, 1980: 13). As a result, despite the ways in which *jornaleros* working in mountainous rural areas were structurally constrained by *hacendados* as a class, many projected the source of their domination in ethnic terms onto merchant *peninsulares* (Picó, 1986). *Peninsulares'* mercantile wealth and distance from farms contrasted with *jornaleros'* poverty and *hacendados'* debts. Enmity between Puerto Rico and Spain intensified when the Spanish government increased tariffs to subsidize its attempt to regain control of the Dominican Republic. As tensions escalated, Spain introduced a series of special laws during the 1860s, to restrict separatist activities in Puerto Rico. In response to the escalation of repressive legislation and the spread of indebtedness, *criollo* workers and farmers seized the rural municipal town of Lares for two days, in September 1868. Although the *Grito de Lares* revolt has been characterized alternately as a local revolt motivated by debt and restricted access to capital, and as a separatist, anti-colonial revolt, it led Spain to liberalize its policies toward Puerto Rico. Spain granted Puerto Rico greater municipal autonomy, allowed political parties to form and abolished slavery in 1873.

Puerto Rican society was divided along the lines of not only ethnicity, but also social class and political affiliation. The demand for autonomy intensified after the island experienced a financial crisis in 1886–1887 and liberals formed the Autonomist Party. Although the party may have been seen as representing *criollo* interests, in fact, this conflation may have been more propaganda than reality as native-born elites were also active in the royalist and conservative parties (Scarano, 1996). What is more certain is that these demands were met with a wave of increased repression in what became known as the *compontes* of 1887, or a wave of arrests, torture and threats against many native elites who were suspected of being involved in radical or separatist activities. Some fled into exile where they continued to struggle for separation from Spain through alliances, for instance, with the Cuban Revolutionary Party. Despite its demands for political liberalism, however, the Autonomist Party obscured conflicts with working and lower classes that sought a greater degree of reform

(Carrion, 1983; Figueroa, 2005; Picó, 1993). These tensions eventually drove autonomists apart in 1897: Luis Muñoz Rivera favored a fusionist pact with Spanish authority and José Celso Barbosa favored a greater degree of autonomy. Barbosa encouraged laborers to join his Orthodox Autonomist Party (*Partido Autonomista Ortodoxo*).

Criollo ideas on Puerto Rican autonomy were threatened by organized labor. While many urban workers affirmed the defense of a distinct national identity against dominant Spaniards, others saw the idea of a nation as meaningless and patriotism as an instrument of the dominant classes. For the developing labor movement, politics and patriotism distanced workers from their true demands. Organized labor sought to build an international socialist union because it believed "where there are bosses there are slaves, and where there are slaves, there cannot be a nation" (Quintero Rivera, 1981). The threat of the labor movement resulted not only from socialist ideas, but also workers' new political significance. Artisans organized guilds and associations that, while not explicitly political, had bettered their members' material conditions. In 1893, Barbosa led the development of a cooperative society, *El Ahorro Colectivo* and encouraged professional leadership, including that of physicians and pharmacists. While the collective may have had some socialist tendencies, only three years later the Spaniard, Santiago Iglesias, arrived on the island to promote a seemingly apolitical (not formally involved in electoral politics) and explicitly socialist movement (Negrón-Portillo, 1990). In 1897, literate workers and illiterate taxpayers gained increased political influence through the *Carta Autonomica* (a form of constitutional autonomy), which granted the island self government and extended universal suffrage to all men over 25 years of age.

By 1898, Puerto Rico was a deeply divided island. Separatists affiliated with the Cuban Independence Movement encouraged the United States to intervene on behalf of Puerto Rico and eradicate Spanish colonialism on the island. They shared an unlikely agenda with many *peninsulares* whose interests supported U.S. intervention in favor of modernizing sugar production and expanding export markets to the United States. The rapidly developing labor movement also sought to eradicate Spanish colonialism as an impediment to social and human solidarity. *Criollos,* however, faced larger contradictions in reconciling their liberal ideology. On the one hand, many *criollos* who had interests in sugar associated it with a broader international market and therefore critical to the island's material progress. They believed a U.S. invasion would push *peninsulares* out of municipal and insular posts and give them greater power (Picó,

1993). On the other hand, many *criollos* favored autonomy under Spanish protection in order to bring exploitative relations of production under their control (Quintero Rivera, 1981).

Many Puerto Ricans believed U.S. intervention would introduce a new phase of democracy and modern progress. As a result, they welcomed the U.S. invasion of 1898. On the eve of the change in sovereignty, particularly in rural, coffee-producing areas, workers believed their violent demands for reform would be protected by U.S. democracy and they became violent in their resistance to landowners' exploitation (Picó, 2004: 1993). They formed bands that attacked Spanish homes, businesses and processing plants, settled scores with owners of the haciendas and their foremen, set fire to their homes and warehouses, re-appropriated the stored goods and undermined other symbols of Spanish hegemony. While the U.S. military fought Spaniards in the Spanish-American War, Puerto Ricans violently resisted the control of large landowners.

A "New" Colonial Structure

The Treaty of Paris, signed on December 10, 1898, ceded Puerto Rico to the United States at the end of the Spanish-American War. The majority of Puerto Rico's elite initially welcomed what they believed to be a temporary military occupation by the United States who had supported their struggle against Spanish colonialism. The period during which the U.S. military would eradicate the "Spanish legacy" and train Puerto Ricans in the ways of democracy, however, had no date of expiration. Instead, an indefinite period of U.S. control and democratic tutelage followed military rule.

The United States claimed its involvement in Puerto Rico overthrew Spanish colonialism and promoted liberal democracy. In contrast to its policy of establishing settlements in acquired territories, the presence of U.S. military officials on the island was limited to "top levels of public administration, the federal judicial branch, the public education system, and few capitalists interested in investing in Puerto Rico" (Argüelles, 1989: 17). The military occupation itself lasted a year and a half. During the occupation, the U.S. military was responsible for administrating the island and "Executive Order No. 101" gave military governors absolute and supreme authority to replace municipal officials. The U.S. military administration was followed by a civil government in May of 1900, however, and neither made immediate changes to the local public health administration (*beneficencia*) vis a vis municipal governments.

The civil government structured by the Foraker Act introduced Charles H. Allen as the first U.S. civil governor for Puerto Rico. The new government also included a restructured judicial system, a legislative assembly consisting of a President-appointed Executive Council and a thirty-five member popularly-elected House of Delegates. The structure outlined by the Foraker Act formalized the political and colonial relationship between the United States and Puerto Rico. For instance, the civil governor was an American appointed by the U.S. President; this ensured colonial control over any legislative action from the House. The act also distinguished U.S. colonialization from the former Spanish colonial regime by including native representation, which extended to the U.S. Congress in the form of a non-voting Resident Commissioner. These appointments underscored Puerto Ricans' lack of formal political power at federal and insular levels. The act subordinated Puerto Rico to all federal laws in effect in the United States. Through the Executive Council, the U.S. federal government also reinforced its control over political decisions at the insular level. For instance, of the eleven members of the Executive Council, six seats were filled by U.S. citizens. The Executive Council ensured the U.S. citizens controlled its activities. The U.S. colonial governor also monopolized decision-making power on the island through his veto power and political influence. The Executive Council also named other U.S. citizens to key policy-making positions, thereby influencing the "direction of socioeconomic development and ideological training" (Dietz, 1986: 87).

U.S. colonial authorities claimed to establish democracy on the island, but controlled the insular administration and shaped significant socioeconomic changes on the island. This influence was reflected in the initial crisis and dramatic erosion of the coffee industry (see Table 1). The crisis began when Spain and Cuba imposed tariffs on Puerto Rico's coffee. U.S. markets failed to compensate for the loss and coffee production decreased dramatically. The erosion of coffee markets was compounded by natural disasters. The San Ciriaco hurricane hit the island on August 8, 1899 and intensified farmers' dispossession. Less than ten months after the U.S. military occupation began, the hurricane caused a significant crisis itself. It was among the worst in Puerto Rico's recorded history, killing approximately 3,400 people and leaving many others without shelter, food, or work.

Problems concerning markets and natural disasters were compounded by U.S. colonial policies. For instance, following the hurricane, military governor General Guy Henry temporarily suspended mortgage disputes and foreclosures in February 1899. Rather than alleviate dispossession,

Table 1. Value of Coffee Exports From Puerto Rico (in US Dollars).[1]

Calendar, 1892	5,671,759
Calendar, 1893	6,966,729
Calendar, 1894	7,147,821
Calendar, 1895	5,695,327
Calendar, 1896	8,318,543
Calendar, 1897	7,323,559
July 1898-June 1900	7,515,129
Fiscal, 1900–1901	1,678,765
Fiscal, 1901–1902	3,195,662
Fiscal, 1902–1903	3,970,574
Fiscal, 1903-June 22, 1904	3,839,373

[1] (Hunt, 1904: 22).

however, lenders stopped accepting land as collateral. Farmers who could have obtained credit were forced to sell larger parcels to obtain capital. The legislation also affected workers as the loss of credit most often resulted in a loss of wages (Dietz, 1986). Faced with worsening economic conditions, many subsistence farmers sold their land.

Colonial policies increased the island's dependence on U.S. markets. The hurricane ruined almost 80% of the coffee plantations on the island and made planters increasingly dependent on foreign capital, but there were no tariff protections for coffee in U.S. markets and it could not compete with less expensive South American imports (Dietz, 1986). In contrast, tariff protections gave the Puerto Rican sugar industry access to U.S. markets and integrated the island into the mainland's economy. The Foraker Act removed limits on the size of land that a single person could own, which promoted the ability of U.S. capitalists to acquire and expand their land holdings. As they consolidated land on the island, they also established their political and economic dominance and worked through colonial legislation to stimulate the growth of the sugar industry (Cabán, 1999). The sugar monoculture that emerged intensified the island's dependency on U.S. markets. Coffee not only represented a means of increasing Puerto Rico's economic independence from the United States and diversifying its export base, but was also the primary means of subsistence for those families that depended on its production.

The effects of the Foraker Act and the loss of work, home, food and property value following the hurricane were particularly devastating among coffee farmers. The hurricane had destroyed farmlands, especially in the mountains where coffee plantations were located. For many destroyed coffee farms, it would take another five years before new bushes could produce a crop. The ability to finance this recovery was compromised both by the loss of capital among coffee *hacendados* and the repeated defeat of a proposed agricultural loan in the Executive Council (Hunt, 1904: 18–21; Baralt, 1999). As the shifts in the Puerto Rican economy grew in magnitude, so did the numbers of coffee farmers who were negatively affected by them. Coffee farmers formed the core of political resistance from 1900 to 1929 and gave rise to a variety of social class and political conflicts that dominated the period. Despite subsequent changes to the colonial relationship in 1917 through the Jones Act that granted Puerto Ricans U.S. citizenship, the period between 1900 and 1929 demonstrated an "indisputable unity" in the conflicted relationship between coffee farmers, organized labor, the native elite and the U.S. colonial administration (Scarano, 1993: 624–625).

Bread and Butter Issues

The hurricane's impact on coffee farms also affected other subsistence crops, which were planted among coffee bushes to provide them shade and protection from the wind. Nonetheless, U.S. military officers felt the reports of hunger and half-starved workers following the hurricane were exaggerated. For instance, Major Van Hoff directed the Charity Board's relief efforts. Dominated by three Americans, the Board sought to restrict food relief to workers. Initially, the Board attempted "a new Yankee version of the libreta" that would require workers to obtain a signature for their work cards, from an employer, to obtain relief (Schwartz, 1992: 325). The Board soon abandoned the cumbersome scheme in favor of delegating responsibility for food distribution to planters. By making food relief conditional on work, the Board promoted labor supply. The Board's relief efforts "hoped to preserve the existing relations of production and ensure a supply of reliable and inexpensive labor" (Schwartz, 1992: 316).

Although the hurricane destroyed food crops on an island that was already importing food, Governor Davis similarly believed half-starved workers should be paid less in order to promote the competitiveness of Puerto Rican export prices. The problems of hunger and malnutrition intensified when the monetary exchange outlined in the Foraker Act devaluated the Spanish *peso* relative to the U.S. dollar, which effectively undermined the buying power of Puerto Ricans at the same time that the price of food increased. Still a year after the Act was passed, in a study of labor conditions on the island, Azel Ames blamed the climate for poverty because it encouraged "indolence" (1901: 379). He noted wages were only about 30 cents a day, but reasoned low wages were justified because rural populations had better access to food in a productive tropical environment. He ignored changing forms of land tenure and shared many other U.S. colonial administrators' judgment that rural workers went hungry because they lacked incentive. Ames (1901) estimated the cost of food for an individual for a day ranged between 3 to 20 cents, but insisted that workers should not face hunger. His figures also failed to account for the variability in agricultural wages, which were determined based on production. In contrast, Walter Weyl recorded more detailed data on wages and food prices. He found wages could vary significantly within a occupation even within the same municipality. For instance, his data showed coffee cultivators could make between 10 and 40 cents a day. Weyl also included data on food prices, which indicated that workers could not count on savings from seasonal agricultural labor to make it through a day, much less the year. As indicated in table 2, for instance, eggs could cost as much as .24 cents.

U.S. colonial administrators' association of hunger with labor indicated the ways they used food as a form of labor control. They were particularly concerned about preserving a labor force to support production and the development of public projects, including road construction. The chief

Table 2. Average Food Prices in Ponce Market, 1905.[1]

	Cost/lb.
Rice	0.04
Beans, red	0.06
Bread and biscuits	0.06
Eggs (market)	0.19
Eggs (store)	0.24
Codfish	0.08
Beef	0.10
Sugar	0.05
Plantain	0.02
Sweet Potatoes	0.01

[1] (Weyl, 1905: 779).

engineer of the irrigation service considered food a "way of holding men on the job" as food prices continued to increase exponentially, doubling over a 5-year period by 1919 (chief of the insular bureau of labor in Marcus, 1919: 16). In order to compensate for an unstable work force, the engineer took 25 cents out of the daily wage to pay for three meals. Although the *libreta* had proved too cumbersome for the Charity Board, colonial administrators nonetheless adapted other forms of labor control that were similar to the *vales* used by planters under the Spanish colonial administration. They participated in turning food into an instrument of labor control because they believed "the whole barefoot population...will not work except under the prospect of starvation" (Swift in Schwartz, 1992: 313).

The relationship between the worker and the island's fortunes was powerfully refracted in these bread and butter issues that were ultimately determined by relations of colonial dominance. The island depended on U.S. consumers for export markets and imported products, particularly for its food supply. This posed severe problems for the average resident's ability to buy food and encouraged both poverty and a scarcity of food that resulted in malnutrition and hunger for many. The development of this dependence is reflected in two values. Table 3 demonstrates the increasing value of imports between 1901 and 1914. Table 4 indicates the higher value products imported by Puerto Rico. Rice, rice, a staple in the Puerto Rican diet, was the highest value import.

Party Politics

The Puerto Rican Republican Party and the *Partido Federal Americano* (Federal Party), both established in 1898, became particularly disillusioned by the Foraker Act and U.S. colonial control. The parties were

Table 3. Value of Imports for Selected Years, 1901–1914.[1]

	United States	Other Countries	Total
1901	6,965,408	1,952,728	8,918,136
1905	13,974,070	2,562,189	16,536,259
1907	25,686,285	3,580,887	29,267,172
1911	34,671,958	4,115,039	38,786,997
1912	38,470,963	4,501,928	42,972,891
1914	32,568,368	3,838,419	36,406,787

[1] (Yager, 1914: 7).

Table 4. Higher-Value Imports from the United States, 1914.[1]

Product	United States	Other Countries	Total
Rice	5,306,364	11,247	5,317,611
Iron and steel, manufactures of	2,644,008	87,488	2,731,496
Cloth	2,324,584		2,324,584
Pork, pickled	1,653,155		1,653,155
Wheat Flour	1,608,504		1,608,504
Leather, and manufactures of	1,399,994	39,992	1,439,986
Fish: Dried, smoked, or cured	558,553	643,021	1,201,574

[1] (Yager, 1914: 7).

founded by José Celso Barbosa and Luis Muñoz Rivera, respectively, and originated in their resistance to Spanish colonialism. Their platforms initially supported Puerto Rico's annexation to the United States as a state, but for different reasons. The Republican Party was largely made up of professionals, including many lawyers, doctors, pharmacists and engineers, who professed pro-American sentiment because statehood represented a new Americanized social order of liberalism and modernity. Republicans enjoyed the official support of the colonial administration (Dietz, 1986: 96).[2] In contrast, the Federal Party represented large- and medium- sized propertied interests in sugar and coffee that sought to promote Puerto Rican agriculture. Although it initially welcomed the island's affiliation with the United States and favored free trade with the United States, the Federal Party demanded political rights, particularly self-government and wide autonomy for municipalities. The party leader, Muñoz Rivera, considered the Foraker Act undemocratic. The party was less favored by the U.S. colonial administration.[3]

---

[2] Labor was divided among support for the Republican Party and those who sought to remain independent of politics. Workers who favored the Republican Party included artisans organized as the *Federación Regional*. The Free Federation of Labor (*Federación Libre de los Trabajadores*) formed in October of 1898 and established the Worker Socialist Party. The latter party joined the Federal Party in 1902 (Carrion, 1983; Scarano, 1993).

[3] U.S. President Taft resented Muñoz Rivera's challenges to American authority and the Unionist Party's increased popularity, which affected Washington's reaction to conflict. The party's 1902 victory in the House encouraged new challenges to U.S. power, including

The issue of municipal autonomy was of particular consequence for the Federal Party (later the Unionist Party) and would influence municipal physicians' work in sanitation and public health. The Party sought to expand political authority and local autonomy through municipal governments. This strategy reflected the longer trajectory of using municipal governments to negotiate colonial authority and expand the native elites' influence. The spirit of local autonomy was embedded in the political gains *criollos* made under the Spanish colonial regime and in the Autonomic Charter. The Federal Party's two members in the Executive Council protested in vain against the appointment of a special committee by Secretary of the Executive Council, Hunt. They then sought to amend the special committee's proposal for redrawing municipal boundaries on the island, which was "a classic example of gerrymandering at its worst (some of the districts were not even contiguous, as ordered by the Foraker Act)" (Trías Monge, 1997: 53). Finally, the members unsuccessfully proposed the Federal Party's plan for redrawing municipal boundaries. They resigned and the Federal party withdrew from the popular election of the House because they believed the colonial government was not impartial (Picó, 1986). The laws passed in 1902 structuring municipal governments under the U.S. colonial administration centralized municipal governments under the U.S. governor's authority and dramatically undermined the influence of local mayors, particularly in relation to police and tax collection (Silvestrini and Luque de Sánchez, 1992). At the same time, municipal physicians remained under the authority of mayors and local councils.

The Republican Party shifted when a prominent member began a "regeneration" campaign in 1902. Through public presentations and a writing campaign, Rosendo Matienzo Cintrón built public support for the regeneration of an essential puertorrican personality that existed above political party differences. He argued this personality was threatened by U.S. colonial domination.[4] In opposition to "the offensive regime," this campaign influenced the Federal Party's reorganization as the Unionist Party in 1904.[5] The Unionist Party consolidated the Federal Party, factions

---

party support for projects to improve agriculture, extend the U.S. Constitution to Puerto Rico and petition Congress to modify its relationship to Puerto Rico (Silvestrini and Luque De Sanchez, 1992: 402).

[4] Unionists rejected the Executive Council as partial and unrepresentative (Scarano, 1993: 631).

[5] Their goal was undermined by the Unionists party's failure to unify the parties, which recast the Unionists as simply another political party. Conflict over the status and

of the Republican Party, the mountain peasantry, professionals and, at least temporarily, organized labor. It found particularly strong support among coffee plantation owners who protested governmental support of the sugar and tobacco industries dominated by U.S. interests.[6] The party's nationalism defended specific class interests and defined its goal as self-government, but the demand for political autonomy did not equate to independence. Instead, the party "accepted all possible solutions of the colonial problem: autonomy, complete annexation, or independence as a protectorate, as had been implanted in Cuba in 1902" (Scarano, 1993: 630).

As a result of both widespread support and the enfranchisement of all men over the age of twenty-one, the Unionist Party won the majority vote in 1904 and remained the dominant political party in Puerto Rico until 1928. The party's popularity intensified hostilities with the colonial administration. For instance, the Unionist Party-controlled House of Representatives attempted to pass laws in 1909 opposed by then-Governor H. Regis Post and the majority of the Executive Council.[7] In reaction, Post ordered the House to approve the next year's fiscal budget and set a deadline for approval. When the term expired and the House failed to approve a budget, the government found itself amidst a political crisis that was resolved by the Taft administration that sided with Post by passing the Olmstead amendment and allowing the prior year's fiscal budget to remain in force.[8] This political maneuver undermined the influence of the House and gave increased importance to the President-appointed Executive Council in supervising Puerto Rico's affairs. Following his controversial administration and the increasingly fragmented political context that ensued, Post resigned.

---

relationship of the party to the colonial administration also created immediate distance between the parties. For Republicans who remained within the Pro-American Republican Party, the "true" Puerto Rican remained to be developed through the process of Americanization. In contrast, the Unionist Party rejected the idea of receiving U.S. citizenship without governmental reform. As a result of the Republican Party's continued support for the colonial administration, and despite its lack of popular support, it continued to enjoy the sympathies of the U.S. colonial administration (Scarano, 1993).

[6] The Unionist Party "had deep roots among the coffee growers, the mountain peasantry, and the professional groups. Its influential *hacendados* were not exactly pro-labor nor did the labor leaders share the party's interest in the defense of Puerto Rico's personality and its sense of cultural regionalism" (Carrion, 1983).

[7] Amidst increasing tensions between the House and the Executive Council, the Unionist Party met in 1907 to strategize a formal opposition to the Foraker Act through a legislative boycott (Silvestrini and Luque De Sanchez, 1992: 406).

[8] President Taft considered the Unionists' challenge a reflection that the House had too much power and that Puerto Ricans had not yet learned the art of good government (Silvestrini and Luque De Sanchez, 1992: 407).

Despite the Unionist Party's popularity and dominance in insular politics, its attempt to reconcile divergent interests led to disillusionment. On the one hand, the goal of defending a unified "puertorrican personality," irrespective of class differences, was increasingly untenable. The party's "influential *hacendados* were not exactly pro-labor nor did the labor leaders share the party's interest in the defense of Puerto Rico's personality and its sense of cultural regionalism" (Scarano, 1993: 635). The party also worked against the interests of organized labor. As a result, the dominant labor party ran its own candidates in the 1906 elections. On the other hand, support for independence within the party also undermined broad support for a resolution in favor of autonomy under U.S. protection. Other factions of the Unionist party felt independence was an unachievable ideal. Associated with the American Federation of Labor, the labor party could not support independence. Finally, several prominent leaders left the Unionist Party and formed the Independence Party in 1912.[9]

In summary, U.S. colonial dominance was primarily concerned with the needs of U.S. markets and Puerto Rican interests were increasingly defined in relation to U.S. capital. Similarly, political rights were delimited by the United States in terms that imposed U.S. colonial authority without addressing long-standing demands for political reform. In these ways, the U.S. federal and colonial administrations defined the island's economic and political needs. Meanwhile, nationalist definitions of the Puerto Rican "personality" competed with colonial definitions, but they reflected political and class-based interests that were increasingly dependent on, and compromised by, U.S. politics and capital.

The island's social structure experienced significant changes under the U.S. colonial administration in the interests of U.S. capital. For instance, as the sugar monoculture developed, infrastructure developed (e.g., road building) in support of sugar cultivation. Education also expanded dramatically in support of the economy's development, which primarily benefited U.S. capitalists.[10] The social infrastructure developed not only in

---

[9] The supporters of an Independence party argued that no party could successfully support all possible options: autonomy, statehood, or independence. While general support within the Unionist Party for autonomy and independence grew, those factions of the party headed by Muñoz Rivera felt that independence was an unachievable ideal. The labor party's ties to the American Federation of Labor (AFL) compromised its ability and interest in pursuing independence for Puerto Rico. The founders of the Independence party were Matienzo Cintrón, Manuel Zeno Gandía, Luis Lloréns Torres, Eugenio Benítez Castaño and Pedro Franceschi (Scarano, 1993: 635).

[10] The increasing centralization of productive wealth in the hands of U.S. capitalists, and the few associated Puerto Ricans, was tied to an educational policy that met industrial needs, including needlework (Dietz, 1986: 118–119).

relation to U.S. capital, however, but was also mediated through the colonial administration's native representatives on the island.[11] Although Puerto Ricans' definitions of social progress were increasingly influenced by Americanization and U.S. reformers during the Progressive Era, the broader desire for modernizing the island was also shaped in relation to the Spanish colonial legacy. For instance, the meaning of local autonomy through municipal governments continued to represent an alternate political terrain for organizing politics and professional influence. Similarly, as the case of the Board of Charities' food relief demonstrated, U.S. colonial administrators adapted bureaucratic imperatives in relation to emerging forms of labor discipline.

Anemia, Autonomy and the Public Health Administration in Puerto Rico

The hookworm campaign and the emerging politics surrounding anemia were ultimately medical and administrative interventions that transformed the meanings of local autonomy, professional influence, and the relationship between work and access to food. Ashford rejected the dominant paradigm shared by both Puerto Rican physicians and the U.S. colonial administration to explain anemia. Rather than hunger, he argued a parasite explained peasants' diminished capacity for labor. This explanation blamed the hookworm for sucking nutrients from victims' blood and draining peasants' lives. In important ways, the Puerto Rican hookworm campaign paralleled a colonial interest in minimizing the significance of economic dislocation and hunger. For instance, in the civil government's first annual report, Governor Allen explained "the cry of 'destitution' was raised more for political effect than from any necessities based upon actual conditions" (1901: 22).

The campaign's trajectory closely followed a radical transformation of the island's coffee industry and *criollo* misfortunes. On the one hand, it targeted peasants in coffee-producing areas that had only recently threatened the presumably peaceful transfer of colonial authority. Military officers Ashford and Walter W. King, his collaborator, presented the campaign as a humanitarian and economic effort to improve the lives of peasants who found themselves increasingly dispossessed and hungry. On the other hand, it held out a promise of broader economic development

---

[11] Unlike the United States, the Puerto Rican educational system was highly centralized. Its development involved a cultural struggle over shifting values, including debates on the superiority of English (Carrion, 1983: 175).

through increased worker productivity. In particular, the campaign associated itself with the recapitalization of coffee production. Ashford insisted the coffee industry had not modernized its methods and the loss of land could not explain its changing fortunes (Ashford, 1913a). Instead, Ashford and the campaign's physicians consistently emphasized labor productivity. For instance, they argued coffee production was undermined by the sick worker whose productivity was compromised by hookworm disease (uncinariasis). The worker was also blamed for propagating the hookworm because he was undisciplined and defecated "anywhere it may be convenient for him to do so" (Commission for the Suppression of Anemia in Puerto Rico, 1905: 24).

The campaign also worked to reconcile competing interests. It responded to the U.S. colonial administration's concerns about filth. U.S. colonial administrators' interventions on the public health administration were influenced by germ theory and promoted public hygiene as a way of attracting foreign investments.[12] In contrast, native elites had focused on personal hygiene as a matter of behavioral norms that implied the island's modernization. The hookworm campaign reconciled both sets of values by associating "soil pollution" with economic decay. For instance, despite recognizing that shoes could mediate the effects of walking barefoot and being infected with the hookworm, the campaign did not promote this intervention. Instead, Ashford insisted that "to compel the poor jibaro to buy shoes would seem unjust" because of the inconvenience and expense it caused (1913b: 67). Ashford designed the campaign to attract rural laborers to clinics where physicians could treat what he defined as both a medical and economic problem.

The Puerto Rican hookworm campaign's interest in regenerating the rural peasant was a product of both nationalist and colonial desires. In the nineteenth century, Puerto Rican elites constructed the *jíbaro* as a victim of Spanish colonialism and considered his anemia normative (Trigo, 2000; Trujillo-Pagán, 2003). After 1898, elites began to see the *jíbaro* representing a national identity "threatened by North American economic and cultural domination" (Scarano, 1996: 1404; Guerra, 1998). In the hookworm campaign, however, Ashford repositioned himself (and by association the U.S. colonial administration) as a leader in a fight against the island's anemic economy. Ashford also represented the campaign in political terms that lambasted native elites as self-interested politicians. He insisted the

---

[12] "Public hygiene" referred to the inspection of food, public and private establishments and collecting and reporting vital statistics.

campaign should be above politics, but his claims about science were nonetheless political instruments.

For instance, as demonstrated by Figure 3, one political cartoonist clearly tied the hookworm campaign to a "cure" for independence. On the cover of the November 17, 1915 edition of *La Democracia,* edited by Luiz Muñoz Rivera, the drawing positions Ashford in relation to tropical medicine and in opposition to a box labeled *"fiebre de independencia,"* or fever of independence. Ashford holds a worm, which indicates his attempt to cure the parasite that is associated with this fever. His desk includes other images of modern science and politics, including a bottle labeled what appears to be *fiebre republicana,* which implies the Republican Party could also be used to cure the fever. Although not a part of the original image reproduced below, the newspaper caption of *"La Fiebre de Ahora,"* or the current fever, included a short poem that suggested disgrace and dishonor (*"negra honrilla"*) had betrayed science.[13]

Ashford married Maria Asunción López Nussa, a Puerto Rican woman clearly embedded in the intellectual and political elite of Mayaguez. This union gave him access to prominent physicians vis a vis Ashford's brother in law. Dr. Rafael Augusto Lopez Nussa followed in his brother-in-law's footsteps and similarly completed his medical degree at Georgetown University. Like Ashford, Lopez Nussa cultivated professional influence in Ponce where the latter spent most of his life. In his biography, Ashford (1934) also referred to his father in law's prominence to mediate adverse situations. Ashford's father-in-law, Ramón Belisario López, founded the prominent Puerto Rican daily newspaper, *La Correspondencia* (Brau, 1959). The newspaper was purchased by Dr. Rafael del Valle y Rodríguez of nearby Aguadilla in 1902, which suggested the close symbiotic relationship between liberal elite physicians and the intellectual elite (Brau, 1959). The purchase of the press was notarized by a prominent member of the local *criollo* elite, Santiago Palmer, who had been elected as Mayaguez's mayor during the U.S. military occupation of the city (Herrmann, 1907). Ashford's sister-in-law was married to Mariano Riera Palmer who was elected as Mayaguez's mayor in 1908. Riera Palmer (1907) was the only Unionist Party mayor elected in Mayaguez before 1914 and his report on the city's affairs indicated his affinity for modern reform because it emphasized public sanitation. Ashford's marriage placed him among prominent members of the island's elite who were modernizing reformers.

---

[13] "Por razón de negra honrilla se ha traicionado a la ciencia...Aquí, no hay fiebre amarilla, hay fiebre de...independencia."

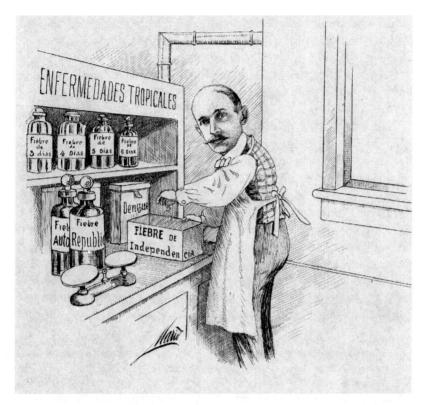

Figure 3. "La Fiebre de Ahora", Drawing by Mario Brau de Zuzuárregui (La Democracia, 17 November 1915).

These associations helped Ashford cultivate his role as an interpreter of U.S. medicine and U.S. colonial authority.

The campaign's broad promise centered on curing anemia, a condition we know today is caused by a variety of diseases, including malnutrition. Of the many ways the campaign participated in manipulating the meaning of politics, the use of aggrandizing claims was perhaps most indicative of Ashford's political and professional authority. The campaign mobilized a dominant narrative about anemia that increased its influence among planters, peasants, and the U.S. colonial administration. For instance, in his 1904 report to the President of the United States, Governor Hunt claimed Ashford and King "successfully treated anaemia" rather than hookworm disease (1904: 28). Despite the existence of other causes of anemia on the island, the first commission's report was accordingly titled "Anemia in Porto Rico" (Commission for the Suppression of Anemia in Porto Rico,

1905). The second "Porto Rico Anemia Commission" reproduced this association. The 1906 act creating a Permanent Anemia Commission similarly
erased the distinction between "Tropical Anemia or Uncinariasis" (Porto
Rico Anemia Commission, 1907). The campaign's broad claim to cure anemia undoubtedly contributed to its prestige and authority.

The broad claim to cure anemia was used by both U.S. colonial administrators and the U.S. medical community to justify colonization. A 1905
editorial in the Journal of the American Medical Association applauded
"work...accomplished by American sanitarians in the various tropical
countries that came under the domination of our government...If the
Spanish-American war brought no other benefits in its train than those of
the saving of life and suffering...it would have been well worth the cost of
men and money it occasioned" (Editorials, 1905: 924). The ostensibly
"humanitarian" intervention not only displaced Puerto Rican physicians'
previous emphasis on hunger and social conditions, but also justified a
form of U.S. medical colonization centered on medical research and treatment. The Puerto Rico hookworm campaign held particular promise for
demonstrating the broader significance of medicine:

> In Porto Rico, the characteristic anemia, which for at least a century has
> been sapping the life and energy of the people, has been studied as never
> before, its true cause recognized, and the proper treatment for it evolved...
> This will be the first time in the history of medicine that a disease affecting
> practically a whole people and easily transmissible has been successfully
> combated. (Editorials, 1905: 924)

The campaign displaced a paradigm that associated anemia with malnutrition in favor of microscopic examinations and medical treatment. As a
result, the island's scientific and medical communities were increasingly
drawn into the international development of tropical medicine. Ashford's
reports were profiled in journals on tropical medicine. The campaign's
work became a model for many others that followed in Latin America. Its
work particularly gained prestige through the Rockefeller Foundation,
"arguably the world's most important agency of public health work" before
the World Health Organization was founded in 1948 (Farley, 2004). As one
of the Foundation's scientists credited, "To Porto Rico belongs the honor
of being the first country in the New World to conduct a campaign against
the greatest of tropical scourges, Uncinariasis" (Hill, 1925: 11). The Puerto
Rican hookworm campaign created an international medical and scientific community that stimulated medico-scientific development and
brought many native physicians and scientists together throughout Latin
America (Ashford, 1934; García and Quevedo, 1998).

The Puerto Rican hookworm campaign's role in ostensibly depoliticizing the island's medical practice and promoting its Americanization has other parallels. For instance, scholars who analyze hookworm campaigns have focused particularly on the Rockefeller Foundation and the programs it introduced through its International Health Board (IHB). These scholars share the conclusion that the United States exported its theories on public health and its practices by shaping and accommodating national politics. Anne-Emanuelle Birn and Armando Solórzano (1999) demonstrate how IHB's programs initiated in the 1920s swayed Mexican political leaders, peasants and business interests, prepared regions for industrialization, and befriended potentially hostile peoples and governments. They point to how the IHB's work was based on medical technology that increased laborers' capacity for hard work while the campaign itself worked to reinforce the principles of North American democratic liberalism, further the Mexican government's ability to monitor revolutionary forces and promote the United States-Mexico relationship. In these analyses, U.S. medical science was inextricably related to imperialism. Tropical medicine in Puerto Rico was similarly tied in ambivalent ways to empire.

The hookworm campaign was embedded in the island's political economy, which meant it overlapped with the insular government and U.S. colonial administration in important ways. The campaign began at a local level and brought many municipal physicians into its work. Through insular funding, local physicians found new revenue streams for remuneration and in order to compensate for weak municipal finances. The campaign's administrative changes also increased Puerto Rican physicians' prominence in the insular government. Two years after it began local work, in 1906, the campaign became a "Permanent Commission" under the U.S. colonial governor's authority. By 1908, the campaign was reorganized as the Anemia Dispensary Service, which brought its work under the insular government's Department of Health, Charities and Corrections. The following year, the campaign's research expanded to a broader set of diseases when it was again reorganized as the Tropical and Transmissible Diseases Service (TTDS). Dr. Pedro Gutierrez Igaravidez, the Service's director, introduced new competitive examinations for participating physicians and integrated municipal sanitation officers into the campaign's work. By 1911, however, the TTDS was dissolved and its work was assumed by the newly-established Sanitation Service.

The Sanitation Service marked the patterned limits of Puerto Ricans' leadership and autonomy within the public health administration because the new Service fell under the direction of Dr. William F. Lippitt, an

American. Ashford lobbied for the resumption of the campaign's work and the Institute for the Study of Tropical Medicine that formed in 1912 fell under Lippitt's administration. Two years later, in 1914, the Institute regained administrative independence as a research body that reported directly to the U.S. colonial governor (Yager, 1919: 28). Like the Sanitation Service, the Institute was subordinated to U.S. colonization vis a vis medical institutions, in this case Columbia University in New York in 1926. The island's medical school only gained administrative independence as the School of Medicine of the University of Puerto Rico in 1949 as the island and the world was decolonized following World War II.

The campaign's trajectory was important for two basic reasons. First, it demonstrated the limits of Puerto Rican physicians' professional autonomy relative to the colonial administration. The Superior Board of Health (SBOH) began licensing examinations in 1900 and the campaign's administrative development similarly expanded to include exams for civil officials. These developments reflected physicians' atypical professionalization through the U.S. colonial administration and distinguished it from the United States, where physicians gained professional autonomy from the state through the American Medical Association. In early-twentieth century Puerto Rico, the meaning of professional autonomy was restricted to developing professional prestige *vis à vis* the U.S. colonial administration.

The campaign's trajectory also reflected how, despite native participation and leadership, Puerto Rican medicine and the island's public health administration was subordinated to U.S. institutions. The Sanitation Service was unpopular under Lippitt's direction because he promoted aggressive methods for implementing sanitation legislation amidst an outbreak of the plague. This contrasted Ashford's methods that that tpromoted local and native influence through the campaign. Ashford also grew resentful of Lippitt's decreased attention to the campaign's work. Through Ashford's influence with the U.S. colonial administration, the Institute for the Study of Tropical Medicine reintroduced native participation (Gutiérrez Igaravidez, Gonzalez Martinez, and Francisco J. Hernandez) in the campaign's research work.

As the campaign demonstrated, Puerto Rican medicine was Americanized through an insular government whose decisions were heavily influenced and often controlled by the U.S. colonial administration. Ashford shared the administration's belief the fight against disease should not be contaminated by political agendas and, in this way, normalized American values and political structure. The annual governor's reports demonstrate how this ethnocentrism worked to consolidate colonial power. Despite changes in individual governors, U.S. colonial administrators continually reproduced a discourse that infantilized native politics. In contrast, "administration" was most often associated with the unquestioned assumption that "American customs and policy" were equivalent to fairness and good government (Davis, 1900b: 10). For instance, Governor Allen listed differences between both political parties on the island, but summarized this distinction with the dismissive claim that "the principal issue between them appeared to be that one was in and the other was out" (1901: 45). His discussion emphasized "the lack of clear-cut issues between the parties," protests regarding the election as "seldom specific and often frivolous," and a primary distinction based on acceptance of "American control of the island in good faith." Although Allen's discussion described the Federal Party in unflattering terms, his characterizations, overall, failed to concede any legitimacy to claims against U.S. colonial authority.

The Changing Meaning of Professional and Political Autonomy

Through the insular government, the U.S. colonial administration controlled municipal government and reshaped the meaning of political autonomy. As it had been in the nineteenth century, the significance of municipal autonomy was associated not only with self-government, but also with defining the limits of colonial authority. The changing significance of municipal government was also informed by the island's long and arduous struggle for political and administrative autonomy under Spanish colonial authority. This anti-colonial struggle was successful and resulted in the 1897 Autonomic Charter. The U.S. government failed to recognize the Charter and many native elites viewed a reduction in municipal autonomy as the re-imposition of colonial rule.

Aside from infantilized constructions of native politics, another way U.S. colonial administrators dismissed Puerto Ricans' political claims was in the ways they validated or failed to legitimize or even mention these claims in their annual reports to the U.S. President. Military General Davis observed:

> municipal government in all Latin countries appears to have been the Roman municipium. This latter, once independent, was...incorporated into the Roman commonwealth...and admitted to a more or less ample participation in the rights of citizenship, retaining... their own distinct organization and political division, and their own magistrates, legislatures, and judicatories. (Davis, 1899: 62–63)

While Davis considered this form of administration inefficient, he summarized his brief statement on native objections to consolidating municipal governments as "various and some of them have weight" (Davis, 1899: 63). He presented a consolidation plan recommended by "one of the political parties" and concluded his report on municipalities by referencing thirteen reports, all of which were authored by U.S. military officials (Davis, 1899: 64). Consolidating municipal governments clearly involved the colonial administration's interest in increasing efficiency. The consolidation also demonstrated the colonial administration's authority, partiality in representing native politics at the insular level, and their indifference to increased taxation and loss of representation at the municipal level. The consolidation implied a reduction in services at the municipal level, although U.S. colonial administrators insisted beleaguered budgets were the result of corruptions and political patronage.

For a variety of colonial administrators, particularly under U.S. Governors William Henry Hunt and Beekman Winthrop, consolidating municipalities represented an efficient way to expand colonial authority. The U.S. military government initially retained a structure instituted under Spanish colonial authority, but eventually restructured the SBOH to promote its authority over municipal governments. The Board's authority over legislation and inspection enhanced its influence at the local level, but was limited by a lack of infrastructure and a budget to compensate for these limitations. Consolidating municipal governments would promote the Board's ability to monitor and regulate them.

The United States believed the first step in replacing Spain's ineffective administration was to understand the problems it left behind. As a result, President William McKinley commissioned Henry K. Carroll to conduct a survey of the "civil, industrial, financial and social conditions" of the island (Carroll, 1899: 7). Carroll began his survey in October 1899. With little direction from the U.S. federal government, U.S. colonial administrators' perceptions of the problems with municipal government were informed by Carroll's report, which identified three problems involving municipal governments. First, it drew attention to municipal appointments and described the Spanish Governor as a "master of the destinies of the country" who held supreme power within civil government and "conducted civil affairs, whether insular or municipal, according to his own pleasure" (Carroll, 1899: 15). According to Carroll, this meant municipal governments produced a "system of representation which was at bottom completely false...[the Spanish Governor] appointed all municipal employees, naming arbitrarily every employee" (1899: 15). Second, Carroll's report recognized municipal appropriations included medical attention for the poor but noted the poor distrusted "town doctors...[who] would not visit the sick poor without pay" (1899: 34)[14] This problem was intensified by limited medical facilities on the island, but Carroll blamed physicians when he asserted "scarcely one in a hundred of the poor who die has the attendance of a physician" (Carroll, 1899: 34).

In a separate and disconnected section, Carroll's report focused on the structure of municipal governments. He acknowledged administration was made difficult in larger municipalities with "a large scattered population" (Carroll, 1899: 18). The report also referenced incomes and expenses involved in municipal administration. Despite his attention to financial and infrastructural constraints, the report failed to explain the obvious implication: municipal governments were heavily in debt and frequently unable to pay salaries for its officials (Hunt, 1903: 31). The U.S. colonial administration similarly ignored how the governmental structure it recreated through several administrative changes reproduced problems at the local level and in rural areas, which compromised services, including medical attention to the poor.

The third problem that Carroll addressed, and the one that U.S. colonial administrators responded to, was sanitation. Despite structural problems in medicine and Puerto Rican's "general disregard, hitherto, of the primary principles of sanitation," Puerto Ricans were reasonably healthy. Carroll found it a "matter of wonder that the scourges of Puerto Rico have been so few." The threat of another scourge, akin to the events following the 1899 hurricane, threatened U.S. capital investments and colonial administrators' interest in promoting the island's prosperity. This prosperity was narrowly defined in relation to U.S. interests. In particular, the SBOH indicated the desirability of a centralized insular administration, but medical attention for the poor was a matter U.S. colonial administrators used to criticize municipal governments and physicians' self-interest and corruption. U.S. colonial officers fostered improvements in sanitation and infrastructure to promote the development of capitalism on the island. These efforts

---

[14] Although mayors identified the poor through lists given to municipal physicians, in practice, it was the latter who often determined who was entitled to municipal charity. Physicians could charge for their services when they fell beyond official duties and they argued many patients could pay for the medical services they [patients] "demanded." Municipal physicians also argued municipal governments made unreasonable demands, which were confirmed by U.S. colonial administrators who noted the lack of municipal resources to pay local officials' salaries.

would primarily benefit the interests of U.S. capital, which included developing a more productive labor force to carry out development projects. In other words, the U.S. colonial administration favored the interests of U.S. capital at the expense of the poor.

The persistent problem of municipal finances resurfaced in 1902 when Governor Hunt called for the elimination of many officers and the consolidation of municipalities. Disregarding previous struggles over municipal autonomy in 1900, Hunt also called for insular auditors who would "see that municipal accounts are kept according to a uniform system, to be prescribed and approved by the auditor and treasurer of the island" (Hunt, 1902: 345). Both positions were held by U.S. colonial officers. These sentiments were expressed in a set of laws passed in 1902 that eroded municipal autonomy in favor of expanding colonial authority. The laws further reduced municipal autonomy on sanitation issues, finding them "without adequate experience in such matters" (Rowe, 1901: 236). Leo Stanton Rowe, a commissioner appointed to revise laws for the island, argued Puerto Rico required "more careful administration of sanitary regulations than is necessary in northern latitudes" (1901: 236). Local commissioners' (*comisarios*) duties and responsibilities of policing rural areas remained the same, but "emphasized sanitary and hygiene surveillance" (Carrasquillo, 2006: 37). Governor Hunt noted that "it does not depart too radically from what was good in the former system, but blends with it much that is American of an approved character" (Hunt, 1902: 58). The Americanization of sanitation involved centralizing what was then considered public health under a governor-appointed Insular Director of Sanitation (Porto Rico Legislature, 1902a). The Director would be the ex-officio President of the SBOH, which became an advisory board. This meant broader authority for medicine was centered on Director, while the Superior Board of Health controlled licensing and authority to practice medicine on the island. The imposition of these standards under U.S. colonial authority was greater than those in effect in the United States (Starr, 1984). Meanwhile, unlike the United States, Puerto Rico lacked a medical school.

Despite the law, the administration of sanitation remained organized at the municipal levels and physicians were still appointed by mayors. This had two significant implications. First, it politicized public health and medical attention for the poor. Municipal officials lost their role as intermediaries and instead became community leaders who organized political demands. Mayors and "comisarios de barrio...became important links between [political] party leadership and country people...[and]

helped the party recruit members" (Carrasquillo, 2006: 37). Second, organized at the municipal level, public health became increasingly contentious as municipal physicians did not always have formal medical training and licenses. The laws failed to provide a measure of professional autonomy from municipal governments (Hunt, 1903: 31). Where the latter were also sanitation inspectors, they came under the authority of an insular Director who took over these appointments in January of 1903 (Quevedo Báez, 1949: 67). The act concerning municipalities also limited health officers' salaries (Porto Rico Legislature, 1902b). The Americanization of municipal governments indicated a simultaneous erosion of local political and professional autonomy.

The same year, physicians organized themselves as the Medical Association of Puerto Rico (*Asociacion Medica de Puerto Rico*, or AMPR). The earliest reforms it requested from the insular government came shortly after its establishment when the AMPR argued that the insular government should administer sanitation. Its initial efforts were directed at the recent legislative changes and long-standing problems with municipal physicians. The AMPR sought to cultivate its political clout independent from established political parties. It lobbied the colonial administration to amend legislation giving municipal governments control over matters related to health and sanitation.

The AMPR's desire for reform was only partially successful. After the Director of Sanitation took over the appointment of sanitation inspectors in 1903, U.S. colonial administrators made a critical administrative decision that stabilized the colonial order and profoundly altered Puerto Rican medicine. These decisions were made as the Federal party reorganized as the Unionist Party, consolidated a variety of political agendas, including factions of the Republican and labor parties, and began pressing for territorial autonomy, i.e., statehood or independence. This administrative decision consolidated the office of prisons, the office of charities and the SBOH, thereby creating the Office of Health, Charities and Corrections, which became known as the *Consolidado*. A brainchild of then-Auditor Regis H. Post, the new office was an attempt to appease what he saw as Puerto Ricans' "natural desire to prove that they were capable of administrative work." Governor Post later confirmed this paternalism when he claimed Puerto Ricans "were actuated by a very natural desire to prove that they were capable of administrative work, and it appealed very strongly to their pride and wish to show their administrative ability" (Post, 1904).

The appointment of the *Consolidado's* first Director was indicative of how U.S. colonial administrators understood the relationship between their own authority and its relationship to native administrators. Specifically, the Attorney General's protests surrounding the appointment demonstrated the limitations placed on native administrators even at the insular level. On the one hand, Post associated the Office with his broader effort to promote efficiency among administrative offices.[15] As a result, a member of the Executive Council who was not already charged with the administration of an executive department would head the Consolidado. The Council member originally appointed to lead the new office was a member of the pro-American Republican Party favored by the U.S. colonial administration, Dr. José Gómez Brioso. On the other hand, Attorney General William Sweet argued the appointment discriminated against U.S. citizens.[16] He argued the office was illegal because its head could increase their power *while in office* and would remain independent of U.S. Presidential authority (Sweet, 1904).[17] Sweet argued the new department meant the popularly-elected House of Representatives could develop bodies over which it would have sole jurisdiction and could "go on and create new departments, the responsible heads of which should not be required to report to any department at Washington and yet disburse large sums of money – in short, perform all of the functions of a department head and

---

[15] Post saw the responsibilities to be assigned to the new head as additional service to the Government and underscored the reduction in administrative costs. The increasing status of the medical profession was implicated in the debate insofar as it impinged on the Director's salary.

[16] Dr. José Gómez Brioso's short administration demonstrated the power that colonial administrators such as Sweet exercised to maintain power in the hands of U.S. officials. Brioso was informed, along with Mr. Guzmán Benitez, that their terms had expired on Dec. 14th of that year. The meeting minutes demonstrate both Benitez and Brioso understood Sweet influenced their dismissal. They targeted the discriminatory underpinning of the dismissal by contrasting the example of an American officer who was allowed to continue in his position despite an expired term. General Elliott's term had similarly expired, but he continued to be paid, without protest from Sweet, to the date of his dismissal. Executive Council members agreed that it was a discriminatory precedent. Benitez distinguished the federal and the colonial "attitude of the local administration" in his protest. See also minutes and letters between Post and Brioso subsequent to the assembly. Post sided with Sweet and informed Brioso his term had expired and he was *not* allowed to continue service until a replacement was found. He then appointed Del Valle as *Acting* Director of Health, Charities and Correction "until such time as the Governor may appoint a Director from among the members of the Council" (in Meeting of the Executive Council, Minutes of Dec. 14, 1904, in National Archives, Record Group 46, SEN58A-F19, Box 80).

[17] As quoted by Sweet, Article 1 stipulated: "No Senator or Representative shall, during the time for which he was elected, be appointed to any civil office under the authority of the United States, which shall have been created, or the Emoluments whereof shall have been increased during such time; and no person shall have been increased during such time; and no person holding any office under the United States, shall be a member of either House during his Continuance in Office."

yet escape that responsibility to the President and Congress which rests upon the head of every other department" (Sweet, 1904).[18] Sweet's arguments demonstrated colonial administrations' concerns about administrative and economic self-governance. He proposed greater federal control over colonial affairs and suggested that if Congress desired to adopt the legislation as their own, they could do so. In contrast, if native members as "heads of departments with the power to approve the disbursements of money" were to be appointed, Sweet (1904) felt "they should apply to the President."

Post countered Sweet's arguments by pointing out U.S. colonial administrators controlled the *Consolidado's* Director, who, being appointed by the President and controlled by the Executive Council, was additionally subject to the Governor's supervision. Post also reminded Sweet the Executive Council would serve as a check and balance on every decision the Director made and would monitor his financial decisions over supplies, salaries and staff. The new office would, after all, bring "these important branches of the government" into closer contact with the Executive Council. True to the paternalism inherent in his creation of the administrative post, Post pointed to positive precedents supporting "the policy of placing a native at the head of this bureau."[19] He also pointed out there was no provision "which forbids a native member from doing some work to earn his salary" because the new office would also provide "more work" for one of the native members.[20]

Post's limited faith in the Puerto Rican's administrative abilities prophesied physicians' doubts about the "morality" of the new Office's appointments and allusions to its political bias (Asociación Médica de Puerto Rico, 1908: 2). The AMPR blamed the office's ineffectiveness on

---

[18] Sweet was particularly concerned about the economic and political power held by the new office. He feared continued consolidation of bureaus would take administrative responsibilities and budgets from officers sent by the President and under the authority of Congress. He pointed out the 1900 Foraker Act also stipulated salaries for the heads of six departments, i.e., members holding administrative duties, were set by the U.S. Congress. The Legislative Assembly was responsible for the other five "native inhabitants," but the Foraker Act fixed the latter's duties and delimited their authority to legislative, not executive, power. Although the House could select the new department head, its choices were constrained to members of the Governor-appointed Executive Council. Similarly, the salary could only be appropriated by an executive council member (Sweet, 1904).

[19] (in Meeting of the Executive Council, Minutes of Dec. 14, 1904, in National Archives, Record Group 46, SEN58A-F19, Box 80).

[20] Post justified the bill by pointing to amendments made by the Committee of Public Institutions and Property. (in Meeting of the Executive Council, Minutes of Dec. 14, 1904, in National Archives, Record Group 46, SEN58A-F19, Box 80).

limitations imposed by a colonial government rather than some inherent native deficiency for effective administration. In letters sent to the House of Representatives in November 1908, AMPR members pointed out the office lacked enforceable laws and regulations and indispensable personnel (Quevedo Báez, 1946: 122).

At the insular level, the hookworm campaign continued to fuel influence for the Unionist party. In 1908, the bill that would eventually create the Anemia Dispensary Service and remove municipal responsibility for hookworm treatment was held up in the Legislature. An article in the newspaper explained:

> The fight was in reality over the anemia bill, or rather that part of it which provides for the appointment of a doctor in each municipality that will have charge of the anemia work. The House insisted that the Director of Health, Charity [sic] and Corrections should appoint them. This was a clever political move and it meant that the $35,000 provided by the bill would be used for Unionist politics. The [Executive] Council held for the appointment of the doctors by the Governor which would remove this work from the politics.[21]

Despite the fact that municipalities lost local authority under the Olmstead Act, Unionists managed to maintain Puerto Ricans' control over the hookworm campaign. This control was soon dissolved, however. Four years later, the Executive Council passed legislation that subordinated Puerto Rican physicians to the Sanitation Service. Similarly, by 1912, the Service subsumed the Puerto Rican *Consolidado*.

U.S. military officers rejected the Spanish colonial regime, which they claimed promoted fraudulent elections, a lack of initiative at the local level, the subservience of town councils, and the consolidation of administrative and political control by "the will of the governor." Despite this frequent and repeated criticism, U.S. military governors repeatedly exercised their own ability to introduce new military orders and influence the development of civil codes. On the one hand, military governor Davis

---

[21] The Unionist party held a secret session. When it was ready to adjourn, "it had determined in secret not to give into the Government." If Unionists "could not have their way on the anemia bill they would not go ahead." The newspaper relating the session concluded that "the Council agreed to give in to the House and the doctors will be appointed by the Unionist Director of Health and not by the Governor of Porto Rico" (Newspaper article dated September 18, 1908, titled "Deadlock In Legislature Over the Anemia Bill: House Stands Pat Holding Irrigation Project Bill Over the Head of Government-Council Gives in," among Bailey Ashford's personal papers, University of Puerto Rico-Recinto Ciencias Medicas).

recognized the Autonomic Charter accorded municipalities with "the power to frame its own laws regarding public education, highways, public health, municipal finances, as well as to appoint and remove its own employees." On the other hand, after finding "in every town...an entire disregard of the simplest laws of cleanliness and hygiene," he appointed the Superior Board of Health to develop sanitation measures. The SBOH proposed "a large number of measures...submitted to the military governor for his action" (Davis, 1901). Although many became law, he ultimately decided which regulations involved changes "so radical and so contrary to the general customs and habits of the people that their approval was delayed or withheld." Despite native membership in the SBOH, it was dominated by U.S. military and medical officers who asserted an ironically superior knowledge about "the general customs and habits of the people." In this way, military governors reproduced the same absolute authority they claimed was a legacy of the previous colonial administration.

The Puerto Rican hookworm campaign became critical to legitimizing U.S. colonial control. The United States reasoned the character of its involvement in Puerto Rico was a humanitarian eradication of Spanish colonialism. In its place, the United States promised to build democratic citizens and government. As a result, many of its initiatives involved Puerto Ricans as civil officers. For instance, the U.S. colonial administration reinstated municipal governments' responsibility over matters related to sanitation and public health. To resolve the contradiction between local authority and the rejection of Spanish colonial government's inadequacy, the U.S. colonial government revised the insular government's supervision over local autonomy. The hookworm campaign was one way of promoting direct local contact with a U.S. colonial administrator, i.e., Ashford. Struggles between the insular and local governments and between the insular-native and colonial administrations also demonstrated how Americanization influenced the development of medicine and an intellectual elite, native professionals, and peasants embedded in the coffee industry.

CHAPTER THREE

COLONIAL INTERVENTIONS ON PUBLIC HEALTH
AND THE BIFURCATION OF PUERTO RICAN MEDICINE

Poverty and hunger were dominant themes in the early U.S. colonial administration's narratives about Puerto Ricans. In his analysis of the middle-class values shaping policies developed during the U.S. military occupation, Henry Wells notes officers "found themselves in a society that seemed to abound in precisely those things which their own culture had taught them to disvalue most highly; poverty, illiteracy, and disease... stark inequality in the social order; dishonesty in government; and both massive nonparticipation and passionate antagonism in politics" (Wells, 1969: 79). Americans' beliefs about poverty and hunger were tied to the ideal of individualism, work, and local government, which guided the colonial administration's interventions in public health. The U.S. colonial administration's influence over the administration of public health was part of how the United States sought to compete with other empires in colonizing populations. "The American style of colonial public health exemplified one area where its scientific elite *had* excelled prior to 1900, namely, administration" (Tomes, 2009: 274). In Puerto Rico, the administration of quarantine, a compulsory smallpox campaign, and sanitation were designed to Americanize the island's society and politics.

In Puerto Rico, the U.S. colonial administration's values were mediated through a relationship that relied on local native labor, organized through insular and municipal governments, but consolidated order under U.S. colonial control. These values extended to a prominent member of the U.S. colonial administration, Bailey K. Ashford. Like the colonial administration, he was critical of municipal governments as a legacy of Spanish colonialism and believed local administrations were corrupt and sacrificed public health to political interest. Like other colonial administrators, he judged Puerto Ricans' politics as self-seeking. Although he also shared the American value of individualism, unlike the colonial administration, he did not blame Puerto Ricans for being lazy of for a lack or "incentive to labor" (Wells, 1969: 77). Instead, he associated his struggle against the hookworm with a fight against bad government and to increase workers' productivity.

Ashford's early efforts to develop a campaign against hookworm disease corresponded with native physicians' interest in developing their influence and prestige. Under the Spanish colonial administration, physicians lacked opportunities for medical training on the island and professional autonomy from local governments. The campaign responded to both concerns as it integrated native physicians in its mission. Although both the colonial administration and the campaign relied heavily on native physicians, the colonial administration imposed regulatory interventions and used native physicians to implement coercive quarantines, a compulsory smallpox campaign and sanitation inspections. In contrast, the hookworm campaign attracted patients. It integrated local and elite physicians, giving them status and influence over building public support for the campaign and promoting its popularity. The campaign also gave native physicians an opportunity to develop professional autonomy, their medical training, and ultimately to negotiate the meanings and implications of public health and colonial difference.

Although native physicians were central to the hookworm campaign's development, their control over the administration of public health was illusory. Instead, local doctors were enlisted in colonial priorities. The development of public health under the colonial administration was embedded in a broader struggle for political autonomy. The hookworm campaign similarly reflected this trajectory insofar as it circumscribed physicians' authority and reproduced a division between public health and science. On the one hand, it narrowly defined physicians' autonomy in relation to treating hookworm infection. On the other hand, it offered professional prestige by associating physicians' participation in tropical medicine with medico-scientific progress and an international scientific community. As some native physicians gained prominence and developed their research and practice as scientific endeavors, they fostered a separation of preventative and curative medicine on the island that had already been institutionalized in the United States (Ramírez de Arellano and Seipp, 1983). By focusing on medical treatment, they minimized the role of "an insufficient or improper diet" and the socioeconomic and cultural circumstances in which anemia was embedded (Ashford, undated).

In this chapter, I explain how public health interventions differed between the colonial administration and the hookworm campaign. I begin with a discussion of the military administration's interventions on smallpox and sanitation to explain the limits in the colonial definition of public health. Then I discuss the hookworm campaign's development to explain native physicians' interests in promoting public health. I conclude with a discussion of the bifurcation of public health work that corresponded with the development of U.S. medicine on the island. This analysis demonstrates how shared interests in public health and the island's progress were ultimately undermined by colonial discourse.

When his forces invaded Puerto Rico in July, 1898, General Nelson Miles proclaimed their objectives were "to give to this beautiful Island the greatest degree of liberty... to bring protection, not only to you, but also to your property, promoting your prosperity and bestowing upon you the guarantees and the blessings of the liberal institutions of our Government" (Berbusse, 1966: 79).[1] As the U.S. government worked to justify the Spanish-American War to both U.S. citizens and Puerto Ricans, the military administration echoed Miles' claim by emphasizing its interest in developing the island's prosperity and capacity for self-government. After U.S. troops established themselves on the island in October, military officers' efforts to direct sanitation in San Juan were conducted as emergency measures. Their concern over soldiers' health increased as soldiers became ill, which they associated with unsanitary conditions in areas bordering the barracks (Gillett, 1995; Silvestrini, 1982). The U.S. military administration commissioned Dr. George G. Groff to survey conditions on the island and he recommended a complete sanitation survey of Puerto Rico (Greenleaf, 1898). He enjoyed the support of other U.S. physicians who argued army officers "knew little of the methods of sanitation" and pointed to "conditions of the majority of the military camps in our own country" to demonstrate army officers' work in regard to sanitation had not been successful (Lee, 1899).

The military occupation that followed the Spanish-American War lasted eighteen months, from 1898–1900. By November 1899, however, the administration reduced its military presence by over 85% (Estades Font, 1988). The military administration was concerned about Puerto Ricans' expectations for increased political autonomy and its own need to promote an efficient administration that would not reproduce similar dynamics of colonial authority. As a result, it developed a variety of interventions that were implemented by Puerto Ricans. The orders and regulations passed by military administrators nonetheless established order and consolidated authority under U.S. colonial control. These interventions were

---

[1] President McKinley, however, had advised colonial administrators to plan "with a view to the future welfare of the island and the improvement of the state and condition of their people as *Dependencies of the United States*" (McKinley in Carrion, 1983: 135–136).

guided by two primary objectives. First, they sought to introduce modern methods for arranging "the population in ways that simplified the classic state functions of taxation, conscription, and prevention of rebellion" (Scott in Willrich, 2011: 373). Second, they promoted the policing of a new subject population that included a rebellious and inaccessible rural population.

The shape of the U.S. colonial relationship was illustrated in Governor Davis' reflection on the military administration and first report on the civil government. He noted the U.S. administration did not understand Spanish laws, which governed the island and were "a constant source of discontent to the natives...and a permanent cause of social and economic unrest" (Davis, 1900). Military governors wanted to simultaneously implement administrative and legislative reforms and avoid the impression it imposed military order and reproduced Spanish colonial authority. As a result, the U.S. military administration implemented reforms through "the most interested, best informed, and prominent Puerto Ricans" (Davis, 1900). Military officers developed an administrative structure that supervised municipal government's autonomy in order "to permit American customs and policy to take root in this island." In this way, Davis tied municipal governance simultaneously to political autonomy and cultural assimilation, or Americanization. In response to Puerto Ricans' queries about when the military occupation would end, Davis explained wrote "the time when territorial autonomy could be instituted... depended solely upon the people themselves; that the people should demonstrate their capacity for the most important and sacred of all duties of citizenship by furnishing examples of towns well governed...[and] rights extended alike-to the rich and the poor, the learned and the ignorant, the strong and the weak" (Davis, 1900b: 10–11). Davis suggested U.S. colonial control over granting autonomy and other social and political privileges, which he made contingent on demonstrating adequacy and fitness for self-government through public health. As the rest of the 342-page report demonstrates, public health was largely defined through colonial interventions directed toward charity (medical care for the poor) and sanitation (cleanliness and public hygiene).

The United States believed the first step in replacing Spain's ineffective administration was to understand the problems it left behind. Carroll's report included recommendations on improving sanitation and public health, but the Foraker Act passed the following year did not include related provisions when it structured a civil government under U.S. colonial authority. The only health concern it explicitly addressed was limited to quarantine activities. Several years later, then-Auditor Regis H. Post commented the omission was not an error but an assignation of responsibility for public health matters to the local legislature (Post, 1904). As a result, regulatory interventions passed under the military administration had singular influence on the trajectory of public health. Their significance was not only legislative, but critically tied to negotiating colonial authority and native influence over public health.

The U.S. military administration established a structure that reinstated local municipal responsibility over the administration of sanitation and charity. Local autonomy seemed to affirm Puerto Rican authority and contradicted the move away from Spanish inefficiency, but the military administration attempted to resolve this contradiction through legislation developed by a Superior Board of Health (SBOH) it formed in July 1899. The SBOH maintained insular control over municipal governments insofar as the latter's activities related to monitoring disease and conducting sanitary inspections. Although the SBOH became an advisory board and its work was consolidated into the Office of Health, Charities and Correction on April 1, 1904, its administration of sanitation remained centralized and largely independent. Its regulations were unpopular because they did not consider input from local health boards (Aguerrevere, 1908). Its annual reports to the Governor also reflect consistent objectives through 1911 when the "Insular Board of Health [became an] advising and controlling body of the Sanitation Service" (Yager, 1915). The Service reflects the administrative development of the island's modern-day Department of Public Health. Aside from the more stable administrative apparatus, the military administration instituted quarantine measures and developed a compulsory smallpox vaccination campaign.

Quarantines served two basic purposes. First, they protected commercial relationships by monitoring incoming shipments through ports. By inspecting shipments of cargo, passengers, or an entire ship, quarantine officers could prevent the importation of infectious diseases. Where quarantines failed to prevent the spread of epidemics, subsequent news of plagues typically meant shipments would be delayed or not received, causing merchants to lose revenue. As a result, quarantines fit within a broader expansion of capital and trade. For the United States, they represented an important way of protecting trading relationships between itself and its partners, including Cuba, Panama and Puerto Rico. Second, the U.S. Marine Hospital Service (a precursor to the modern-day Public Health Service) also established quarantines on the island to protect the mainland U.S. population's health. The bodies of U.S. soldiers represented an uncontrolled border capable of transmitting disease between the island and the U.S. mainland. Fears of contagion were shared throughout the administration. For instance, Groff concluded his report noting a complete sanitary survey of Puerto Rico was also needed for "people of the states" (Greenleaf, 1898). Quarantines were targeted at transmissible diseases, namely, yellow fever, smallpox, malaria and the plague (Glennan, 1899).

Quarantines and sanitary inspections designed to minimize Americans' risk of being contaminated by Puerto Ricans were motivated by early constructions of native difference. In the United States, quarantines were similarly influenced by nativist fears that immigrants would "contaminate" the U.S. body politic (Kraut, 1994; Stern, 1999). They reflected the use of law and police powers to segregate and confine urban migrants and the poor (Buckingham, 2002: 5). The military government also used quarantines to define problems and introduce new methods of managing a subject population. For instance, Captain Lorenzo Paul Davison explained "ten lepers are now in a temporary hospital well guarded, furnished with rations, and are being attended to by the health officer." Davison not only relied on a common method of isolating lepers, "in accord with the latest scientific methods," but also associated his work with the mission of ongoing and permanent colonization. Through visits he made in February, he insisted on "absolute isolation...and steps looking toward permanent colonization of these unfortunate sufferers" (Davison, 1899b: 639).[2]

A means to impose colonial order, quarantines and sanitary inspections met native resistance. For instance, through "a careful search through the city," the U.S. Military Hospital Service Surgeon Arthur H. Glennan "discovered" cases of leprosy "hidden in out-of-the-way places." He argued "a systematic method of quarantine procedure is disregarded either through ignorance or design" (Glennan, 1899d). He insisted cases involved "leprosy and not syphilis, as claimed by the patient" (Glennan, 1899d). In this way, the colonial desire for order and segregation were undermined by municipal mayors and physicians who assigned alternate diagnoses in order to avoid having patients quarantined and removed from their homes and families. Glennan contrasted his intention with municipal mayors' lack of cooperation. His repeated complaints about resistance from mayors,

---

[2] Lepers had already been quarantined under the Spanish administration. In 1883, a wooden building was constructed and located behind a jail in the poor section of San Juan, Puerta De Tierra. Lepers could come and go voluntarily (See Arana-Soto, 1974: 512; Levison, 2003).

patients and sanitary officers, and the SBOH complaints about conditions at the leprosarium, suggest quarantines established by the military occupation were not popular in Puerto Rico (Levison, 2003: 233–234).

The difficulties U.S. military officers encountered with isolating the sick influenced their administration of a compulsory smallpox immunization campaign. The campaign was initiated in January 1899 amidst what officers viewed as an epidemic outbreak of smallpox following the occupation and to deal with its possible spread to soldiers. As Major John Van R. Hoff (1900) explained, the smallpox campaign was a part of "the 'White Man's Burden'." Unlike smallpox in the United States that was concentrated in urban areas, Hoff emphasized the "immense task" of vaccinating an entire population that was dispersed and "scattered" throughout the island. To "search out" the population over large and often inaccessible regions, Hoff divided the island into five areas, each with a managing medical officer under his supervision. Through this organization, the campaign marked "the Army's first co-operative civil public health program" (Hoff, 1900: 799; Wintermute, 2011: 143). Azel Ames, the architect in charge of the campaign, explained it was "always *in name*, a civil undertaking," because it was carried out by municipal mayors and paid for by insular and municipal funds, but ordered under military supervision and authority and "organized and directed wholly by medical officers of the Army."[3] A compulsory campaign organized and directed by the U.S. military shows 790,000 people were vaccinated in three months, which marked the fastest-recorded rate of vaccination in world history up to that time.[4]

The campaign claimed its success partly by representing the prior Spanish administration as ineffective (Rigau-Pérez, 1989). Hoff claimed he found a "mass of administrative confusion and disorder...[there was] not a record, nor a book in which to keep it, not a desk, nothing, indeed, which would furnish any information about the existing organization of the medical department or the number, names, and location of its personnel" (Gillett, 1995). This concern was shared by Glennan who noted in a 1899 Mayaguez sanitary report "an attempt was made to destroy the public records, quarantine and otherwise, and what remained in fragmentary way I gathered up and brought back to the San Juan office for examination

---

3 [emphasis in original] Ames reflects on how the military order indicated "how very difficult it sometimes was, to keep distinct, in thought, speech and action the military and civil functions of the Military Governor, in whom, for the first time in the history of the United States, under such conditions, they were peculiarly combined." (Ames, 1903: 302).

4 National Archives, Record Group 112, Entry 26, #43656.

and file" (Glennan, 1899b). Officers emphasized the legacy of Spanish colonialism in terms of native indifference to both the disease and sanitation in general. Hoff argued the decline of Spanish authority meant sanitation laws were not always enforced and, as a result, had doubled mortality on the island. Ames asserted the legacy of indifference to underscore the broader significance of the smallpox campaign as an "object lesson" to both the United States and the world. As military officers used the Spanish smallpox campaign to reflect the failure of the Spanish colonial administration, they also associated disease with bad government.

Unlike their Spanish predecessors, the U.S. military occupation documented their vaccination program and constructed their success as the innovation of a new and effective colonial government. The campaign represented the first demonstration of U.S. administration's medical expertise on the island and the unique role of Army medics in promoting broader political interests. For instance, Ames referred repeatedly to Great Britain in his discussion of the campaign as an "object lesson." He suggested British vaccination policies had not only "emasculated" their campaigns, but also increased distrust and antagonism for similar campaigns within the United States. The Puerto Rican smallpox campaign therefore served a dual purpose. On the one hand, it demonstrated U.S. military agency in relation to a disease that held "first place in the list of preventable, readily-disseminated, contagious diseases, common to all parts of the habitable globe" (Ames, 1903). Ames associated the smallpox campaign with an "object lesson" for the largest Empire in the world, U.S. audiences, the medical profession, and the world. On the other hand, the campaign was also a demonstration in the interest of Americanizing sanitation in Puerto Rico. Davison suggested letting the military administration "once show them what can be done by a judicious expenditure of money in this direction, and they will begin to realize the conditions, and ultimately carry on the work from their own educated sense of necessity" (Davison, 1899c).

Hoff worked closely with Puerto Rican leaders to implement the compulsory smallpox vaccination campaign. He relied on municipal mayors' support, as well as their knowledge of and access to communities. Local physicians carried out the campaign and conducted a majority of the vaccinations. Puerto Rican physicians were experienced in administering smallpox vaccinations. Despite native physicians' collaboration, Hoff claimed the campaign was "possible only through military agency."[5] The

---

[5] The primary challenges faced by the campaign as the difficulty in accessing the population for a lack of adequate roads, the consequent difficulty in providing fresh vaccine,

U.S. military administration insisted Puerto Rican physicians had to be trained because their efforts against smallpox had been ineffective and underscored its administrative superiority in hygienic terms and claimed native physicians "had to be impressed with the necessity for washing their hands frequently with soap, water, and a nail brush, and then soaking them in a bichloride solution. They also had to be trained to wash each arm with soap, water, and a bichloride solution before breaking the surface of the skin for the vaccination" (Gillett, 1995).

As with quarantines, compulsory vaccination met native resistance. Even before the campaign began, a December civil order made a vaccination certification a pre-requisite for employment. Puerto Rican adults had experienced smallpox and developed immunity, however, and the majority of cases involved youth (Wintermute, 2011). Families resisted having the sick removed from their homes and concealed cases that could have been smallpox (Davidson, 1899c).[6] By the time the smallpox campaign ended, the SBOH required evidence of vaccination in order to access social services. Additional regulations passed in October 1899 required all civilians over the age of six months to be immunized and required mayors to deny access to schools, theaters, and public transportation to persons who hadn't been immunized (Gillett, 1995). The SBOH carried on the "work, searching out the 'submerged' 200,000 who escaped in the grand attack and vaccinating the infants before they reach the age of six months" (Hoff, 1900: 799). In these terms, the smallpox campaign appeared a military operative against Puerto Ricans carried out by the SBOH.

As physicians became part of the U.S. colonial administration, they began participating in U.S. colonization "to permit American customs and policy to take root in this island" (Davis, 1900b: 10). The United States established its administrative and medical superiority over the Spanish legacy of colonialism and ineffectiveness. Training vaccinators in the smallpox campaign involved not only methods for sanitized vaccinations, but also for the maintenance of their personal hygiene as physicians. The basis of its colonial power was tied more broadly to associating public health with a need for effective administration and sanitation as a means for progress and prosperity.

---

and the "fatalism" of Puerto Ricans which led them to conceal their sick rather than risk having them removed from their homes and families (Gillett, 1995).

6 Captain Davison conducted an investigation and reported that 50 cases of smallpox were found in "a detached frame structure being used as a hospital. About 10 more were being isolated in their homes" (1899c: 549).

The U.S. military government had left much of the municipal structure unchanged. In July 1899, however, the Board of Health in San Juan was reorganized as an insular Superior Board of Health. It was composed of Hoff as the Board's first president, Glennan, F.E. Wieber, a U.S. Navy surgeon and Groff as one of the three civilian physicians. The other two civilian physicians were native physicians, Drs. Ricardo Hernández and Gabriel Ferrer. In his report to the Governor as President of the Board, Hoff commented native physicians were "of acknowledged reputation" and noted Hernández as his successor (Hoff, 1901: 8). Despite the board's inclusion of native members, it adapted public health measures developed in the United States (see, for instance, Hunt, 1902: 294–295). At least some prominent physicians considered SBOH members "incompetent," a judgment that centered on Hernández because Ferrer had passed away in 1900 (Aguerrevere, 1908). Its structure and regulations demonstrate how Americanization affected the Board's unpopular approach to public health and sanitation.

The SBOH affirmed the centrality of native support to establish a stable public health administration. As in the smallpox campaign, however, the Board maintained authority over other municipal boards of health and reproduced U.S. control. The implication of this influence was a persistent and invasive emphasis on sanitation that involved public space, housing, and colonial constructions of native difference. For instance, Glennan associated bad government with urban design and crowded living conditions when he explained "the ground floors of the walled houses upon close and narrow streets are damp, crowded, and as many as ten to fifteen people sleep in a single small room. This is due to the fact that the military authorities under the old régime compressed the population within the city walls" (Glennan, 1899c). Overcrowding only intensified administrators' sense Puerto Ricans "have been living in filth so long that they have become habituated to its results" (Davison, 1899c).

Sanitation involved different, but overlapping, conceptions of hygiene and prosperity. For colonial administrators,

> the one grand goal constantly before us was to make these people realize that good sanitation meant the saving of life, that it meant an increase in the value of their property, that it meant a greater demand for the goods upon their shelves and the produce of their fields, that it meant an influx of intelligent capital, and work and good wages for the laborer; in other words, that it meant prosperity, that without good sanitation prosperity could not be permanent (Davison, 1899b).

The island's prosperity was an ideal shared by the colonial administration and the native elite. In 1886, under Spanish colonialism, Dr. Francisco del

Valle y Atiles' *Cartilla de Higiene* was implemented for use within primary school hygiene education (Quevedo Báez, 1946: 385). Prominent native physicians shared the idea a civilization's advancement was effected through hygiene. The definitions of hygiene shifted under the SBOH and reshaped ideals of cultural progress. In particular, it developed regulations surrounding sanitation "based upon the codes of the more advanced States" (Hoff, 1900: 798).

The SBOH was based in San Juan and compiled vital statistics, drafted annual budgets and published health bulletins. It established license examinations for physicians, physician assistants (*practicantes*), pharmacists, dentists, midwives and nurses, which increased SBOH control over medical practice on the island. Its principal functions included sanitary investigations, planning and supervising aqueducts and sewers to improve water quality and supply, and establishing programs to protect food and drug supplies. By appointing sanitary inspectors and through a chemist appointed to its new laboratory, the SBOH became embedded in policing a changing society. A similar local structure had existed under the Spanish as a Royal Subdelegation of Medicine, but the SBOH expanded its administrative emphases and developed new regulations governing housing, business and individual behavior.

Vital statistics were collected by municipal sanitation inspectors, but military officers occasionally filed reports from neighboring areas. By developing its relationship to municipal governments and relying on supervised local autonomy, the colonial administration attempted to regulate a new subject population through surveillance statistics. Spain had collected similar data, but the SBOH presented an illusion of local autonomy through public health administration. This cooperation generally guided U.S. colonial governance in local areas despite clear instances of local and public resistance to policing.

The SBOH was authorized to formulate rules governing sanitary measures that would be implemented by the local boards of health.[7] Sanitary regulations codified U.S. dominance over standards governing buildings and individual actions. SBOH regulations were also distinguished by their attention to individual behavior. Through the President-appointed Director of the Interior, U.S. colonial control over the SBOH's work encoded culturally-specific standards governing individual behavior as legal standards of hygiene. For instance, Juan Alvarez experienced the change first-hand when his "littering...on a daily basis" in front of his

---

7 National Archives, Record Group 46, Sen58-A-F19, Box 80.

house resulted in a fine.[8] The boundaries of "decency" were also policed by explicit reference to the level of "civilization" within Puerto Rican culture. Regulations constructed Puerto Rican bodies as potential sources of filth, which invited modern interventions in the form of inspections and policing. What made an individual's behavior punishable by law was ultimately defined according to colonial standards. For instance, General John R. Brooke wanted the population to appear "clean," and "to the extent possible," "worthy" of being visited by external travelers.[9] As a result, among his earliest general orders issued in December 1898, the military governor attempted to govern "decency in the dress of men, women and children." Governor General Davis' standards of decency and worth similarly reflected the condescending and intrusive terms of colonization in which colonial elites simultaneously infantilized Puerto Ricans and attempted to Americanize their behavior. Americanization was imposed as fines were assessed for infractions. Where fines could not be collected, the order required the mayor set jail sentences (Henry, 1898).

The sanitary inspector was a unique character who negotiated the relationship between the insular administration and the island's residents. The municipal sanitary inspector was often a "health officer" and a municipal physician.[10] The colonial administration's concern for sanitation made this function of particular importance. The military governor ordered each municipality to make an allocation in its annual budget to contract doctors and *practicantes* (physicians' assistants) to attend to the public.[11] Brooke suggested vesting the newly-established municipal posts of health officer and sanitary inspector with police authority "as may be necessary to gain the end sought by all good citizens."[12] This perspective

---

[8] Archivo General de Puerto Rico, *Documentos Municipales*, San Juan, Leg. 107, Exp. 160.

[9] President of the *Consejo de Secretarios to the Honorable Presidente del Ayuntamiento de San Juan,* Letter, Nov. 8, 1898, Archivo General de Puerto Rico, *Documentos Municipales,* San Juan, Leg. 125½, Exp. 147.

[10] See *Laws of Porto Rico*, Approved March 1st, 1902. Section 46 stipulated that "No person shall be eligible for appointment as health officer who is not a physician duly licensed to practice his profession according to the law." Other documents emphasized the primacy on appointment of a physician, *where possible.*

[11] General Orders No. 67, San Juan, March 29, 1900, National Archives, Record Group 350, #848, Doc. #6.

[12] "the municipal government should create the position of health officer and sanitary inspector and clothe him with such police authority for sanitary inspections as may be necessary to gain the end sought by all good citizens, and in view of this the suggestion is presented for the consideration of the city government." Brigadier General, Letter to Mayor of San Juan, Nov. 14, 1898, in Archivo General de Puerto Rico, *Documentos Municipales*, San Juan, Leg. 125½, Exp. 147.

was shared by Groff who argued sanitary inspectors should have punitive powers, and at a minimum, should avail themselves of the penal system to enforce sanitary legislation. This authority was granted prior to 1902, where it was referenced by the SBOH. Municipal medicine therefore expanded physicians' and inspectors' political influence as they enforced new sanitary regulations, primarily through inspection. Their inspections were, at times, conducted by force.

Municipal physicians had additional significance because their responsibility included preserving public health. They were at the center of a debate to define government's responsibility to the poor. Because the mayor appointed him, the municipal physician shared an interest in policing the use of municipally-budgeted resources. In municipalities where the municipal physician was also the sanitary inspector, changing insular legislation gave him additional responsibility and power to enforce new regulations. The military occupation redefined medicine's legal functions, especially in the area of urban population management. In San Juan, for instance, municipal physicians could aid judicial proceedings. They aided police and the courts by identifying criminals, producing reports and conducting autopsies. So long as they did not relate to his office, the municipal physician could charge independently for his services. His public service and private practice created a conflict of interest and introduced a potential for corruption.

Local physicians were responsible for providing a monthly report of complaints to the insular government against the municipality. The extensive administrative responsibilities attached to the position were evidenced by the higher fines attached to physicians' failure to fulfill their duties. Physicians, veterinarians and pharmacists who failed to carry out their functions, "without prejudice to the legal proceedings," were fined five to ten *pesos*. All other civil employees could be fined anywhere from one to five *pesos*. Mayors were responsible for warnings and fines and municipal boards were authorized to make decisions about firing officials.

Sanitation inspectors were an extension of government and provided access to businesses, and increasingly, individuals' homes. They were tasked with exercising "constant personal vigilance" over places which could be sources of insalubrity or unwholesomeness. Governed spaces included cemeteries, stables, slaughterhouses, markets, sewers, latrines, patios, schools, public and private colleges, markets, factories, jails, hospitals, "etc., etc." This meant sanitation inspectors had broad powers and police authority for enforcement. The sanitation inspector was also ordered to visit places where food was bought and stores, cafés, taverns, candy stores, liquor distilleries and bakeries. Particularly in large cities, like San Juan, the sanitation inspector was aided by a veterinarian who supervised cow slaughter on a daily basis and identified any contagious diseases within the stable or among the animals. In order to protect public health and eliminate disease from contaminated food, the sanitation inspector also shared the task of destroying rotten or unhealthy food with the veterinarian, although the latter was more narrowly ordered to supervise the destruction of meat. The sanitation inspector and veterinarian were aided in the work of food inspection by a laboratory chemist, who analyzed suspicious meats, fats, wines, liquors and vinegars. The chemist also supported the port inspector by analyzing drugs and medical substances and in order to quarantine shipments.

The development of an administration surrounding sanitation centered colonial public health on policing populations. Justified in terms of protecting public health, the construction of filth underscored the need for modern U.S. intervention. For the U.S. colonial government, the broader goal of discovering and identifying threatening populations hidden beyond urban areas required modern and effective methods to eradicate the sources of threat. Sanitary regulations were important steps in not only monitoring and regulating threatening populations, but also establishing modern forms of administrative intervention.

The most substantive and comprehensive sanitary legislation targeted public spaces where people converged.[13] The broader public interest, the best interests of the country and the "public good" were all ways of representing responsibility for public space. Sanitation regulations emphasized these spaces and underscored individual responsibility. They turned spaces into a matter of public concern that had formerly been considered private, namely, homes.[14] In urban areas, increasing attention was paid to waste disposal and hygienic housing conditions. The SBOH developed a variety of regulations that ordered homeowners to adequately dispose of waste products like feces and dirty water, to paint their houses and make

---

[13] In distinction from private space, the meaning of that public space, its boundaries, origin, and possibility that it has ended in our contemporary reality has been widely debated elsewhere. Here, however, I want to use the term "public space" to refer only to those places physically visible, accessible, and therefore "knowable" by government and other individuals. National Archives, Record Group 350, Townsend Report on Plague Measures.

[14] These regulations became particularly strict with the 1912 plague, where a comprehensive effort was made to rat-proof homes at the expense of home and land owners.

other structural improvements, and to vacate houses inspectors found unhygienic.[15] As the U.S. colonial government attempted to scrub away the legacy of Spanish ineffectiveness, it increasingly regimented individuals. Sanitation officers issued fines and enforced violations through imprisonment.

Individuals resisted municipal officers who enforced the SBOH regulations and saw the latter as colonial impositions. Sanitary inspectors, many of them municipal physicians, issued fines for violating an expanding array of regulations including littering in public or adulterating milk by, for instance, adding water.[16] Regulations centered on food became particularly contentious as costs increased and as inspectors struggled to police a variety of practices, including preventing mothers from watering down scant milk supplies in order to meet their households' needs. Some felt it was "impossible" to comply with sanitation regulations that involved food. For instance, in Mayaguez, Dr. Jose Maria Muñoz prevented the slaughter of what some municipal residents considered "superior cattle." One resident testified Muñoz had refused a bribe and "they were going to denounce Dr. Muñoz for asking money of them, although it is not true, as it was impossible to comply with the laws of the Americans, and that in that manner he would be discharged and another appointed whom they could fix by giving a sum every month."[17] Municipal physicians' role as intermediaries between the colonial state and its subjects was clearly an uncomfortable position, particularly because it seemed thankless and poorly remunerated. Dr. Muñoz's annual salary was only $600 in 1901, which was equivalent to about $16,000 in 2011 dollars and just barely above poverty guidelines for a single person in the same year (Parke, 1901).

---

[15] Ironically, in the same report Davison both affirms his inability to draft sanitary regulations and declaration of "nuisances" in public space. He writes that "so far it has not been practicable to formulate the code of sanitary regulations" because it "requires an amount of judicial inquiry and of time which I have been unable to give." In describing the "methods of house sanitation," however, he relates declaring the "worst places" needing "cesspools cleaned" a nuisance. He also details the adequacy of collecting fines, only two of which were outstanding and he believed the mayor would be able to collect (Davison, 1899b).

[16] The adulteration of milk was a practice that colonial officials decried as alternately greed or ignorance. Vendors watered down milk in order to reap greater profits from selling it. Archivo General de Puerto Rico, *Oficina del Gobernador; Correspondencia General, Clemencias Ejecutivas*.

[17] For months afterwards, there continued to be complaints that Dr. Muñoz would not allow the slaughter of superior cattle. AGPR, Oficina del Gobernador; Correspondencia General, clemencias Ejecutivas, Publicaciones (Sanidad), Julio 1903–1907 Caja 226, "Expediente relative to Conduct of Dr. José Maria Muñoz, of Mayaguez" (sept. 1902).

Meanwhile, by 1903, salaries for municipal physicians were capped by revisions to colonial policies structuring the municipal administration.

The destruction of food by sanitation officers continued to be a persistently politicized activity. As indicated by Figure 4, many Puerto Ricans felt the SBOH were callous in developing regulations around food. A man casually rests on the ground supported by the multiple regulations governing many aspects of everyday life. The man wears a jacket and striped pants that were often used to symbolize Uncle Sam. He uses his telescope to watch bread, or *pan,* fly away in the distance and beyond anyone's grasp.

Despite civil officials' critical role in negotiating a difficult transition to a new colonial administration, U.S. military officers like Davison interpreted native resistance and "open opposition" as "dilatory tactics" and obstacles that hampered the work of sanitation. He believed "natives require careful handling and *constant supervision*. They have no initiative and little persistency or what they have of either is the wrong sort"

Figure 4. "Pan", Drawing by Mario Brau de Zuzuárregui, in Colección de Dibujos de Mario Brau (1904–1915). Reproduced with permission from Colección Puertorriqueña del Sistemas de Bibliotecas, Universidad de Puerto Rico, Recinto de Río Piedras.

(Davison, 1899b). He associated native opposition with the "history of these people" who didn't share his hygienic standards (Davison, 1899b).

> lower floors of more pretentious buildings were occupied by a poverty-stricken and indescribably dirty mixed population, living in absolute violation of all civilized rules. Much of this nastiness was due to a lack of water and lack of proper sewer system. If, however, the inhabitants had carefully studied the question of how to avoid healthful conditions, they could not have done worse. The main trouble was that these people did not realize their dirty condition and had no sympathy with the efforts of the department commander to put the city in a sanitary state (Davison, 1899b).

In San Juan, for instance, the work of the SBOH to improve sanitary and health conditions in San Juan continued with competing visions of its "success." In 1901, Dr. William Fawcett Smith, Secretary of the SBOH, wrote Governor Allen to report the Board had improved sanitary conditions in San Juan. He suggested the perception of improvement depended, however, upon the "intelligent citizens" rather than the "lower classes" whose "moral qualities" were "lax." Ironically, the perception of success was also disputed within the administration. Only one month before Smith's report, E.B. Fink claimed general sanitary conditions in San Juan were bad.[18] The divergent claims was a broader reflection of how the colonial administration's efforts and success in implementing sanitation standards were limited by their emphasis on urban areas and, more specifically, in public spaces accessed by the city's elite in San Juan and Ponce. Sanitation had not dramatically improved in urban spaces that were shared by U.S. soldiers and the poor.

Legislation set forth by the SBOH in an attempt to secure basic sanitation was not always comprehensive and left a significant degree of responsibility with the municipality, which meant sanitation was carried out inconsistently. Municipal resistance to implementing insular legislation reflected political tensions between insular legislators and municipal administrations. Even within San Juan, Davison, who was the Ex-Officio President of the SBOH in 1899, complained sanitation officials paid little or no attention

---

[18] National Archives, Record Group 94, Entry 547, #284 and #284A (San Juan Post). The qualification in Smith's March 1901 letter contrasts the city's elite and its poor. Fink also focused on "lower classes, [their] sexual promiscuity, and [their] venereal disease," which he was particularly concerned about because of conditions surrounding soldier's barracks in the city. As Ogden Rafferty explained in his letter to the Chief Surgeon, Dept. of the East Governor's Island in NY, dated July 8, 1906, the high rate of VD in the barracks was "due to the situation of the different barracks in the heart of a city where the moral qualities of the lower classes are very lax." The SBOH represented its success as shared across the island.

to requests from the insular Board and blamed the system of municipal government for the lack of advances in sanitation (Davison, 1899d).

What distinguished U.S. colonialism as a modern form of colonial rule was its use of local physicians and inspectors in forming a new, and uniquely colonial, public sphere (Kalpagam, 2000). U.S. colonial administrators supervised local government through ideas about administrative efficacy that used native physicians to impose public health interventions. Despite the centrality of native physicians to public health work, the colonial administration claimed exclusive credit for the "success" of medical interventions. This failed to satisfy native physicians' interests in greater professional autonomy and prestige.

Puerto Rican physicians were not professionally evaluated for their expertise. Instead, U.S. colonial administrators insisted on the incompetence of what they saw as physicians whose work had been compromised by the Spanish legacy and political subordination. As the U.S. civil government consolidated its authority over the island, Puerto Rican physicians lost political influence and found themselves in a position not unlike that of their sick and vulnerable patients. They may not have shared the colonial administrations' ideas on incompetence, but elite physicians agreed municipal physicians lacked status and power within municipal governments. An influential physician argued "a *majority* of the time, [municipal physicians] disobeyed orders that implied a great social benefit because of mayors' imposition" (Quevedo Báez, 1949: 53–54). Business owners also capitalized on municipal physicians' reputations for corruption to evade new sanitation legislation, which many viewed as a foreign imposition.[19] This reputation for corruption appeared to have some legitimacy. At times, sanitation inspectors collected fraudulent taxes from food vendors. When inspectors met opposition, they had legal authority to destroy goods.

Speaking from a different structural location, elite physicians' arguments reinterpreted those of the U.S. colonial administration. They used Carroll's criticism of conditions existing under Spain to explain the inferior condition of medicine in municipalities. They argued against local political autonomy that undermined municipal physicians' work. For elite physicians, local autonomy had corruptive effects on otherwise politically neutral and scientific medical practice in the public interest. In 1902, elite physicians organized themselves as the *Asociación Medica de Puerto Rico*

---

[19] "Expediente relative to Conduct of Dr. José Maria Muñoz, of Mayaguez," Sept. 1902, Archivo General de Puerto Rico, Oficina del Gobernador; Correspondencia General, clemencias Ejecutivas, Publicaciones (Sanidad), Julio 1903–1907 Caja 226.

(AMPR) a professional medical society founded to protect the interests of the "medical class." Among its first efforts were responding to recent legislative changes and long-standing problems with municipal physicians. They argued that the insular government should administer sanitation and lobbied the colonial administration to amend legislation that gave municipal governments control over matters related to health and sanitation.

The AMPR's original plans for reform were only partially successful. At the end of 1902, in his inaugural address at the AMPR's first assembly, a co-founding member mourned the position of any physician who remained "an instrument of all political egoisms." Manuel Quevedo Báez had supported autonomy under Spain and, although affiliated with the Republican party in favor of U.S. statehood, would gradually come to support the island's political independence. He worried what he saw as the lamentable state of physicians who had to haggle over compensation for medical services and remained a class enslaved to society and the political power of others. The solution, according to Báez, rested on winning professional authority first and confidence later. At the same time, the AMPR elected to meet with Ashford regarding his proposals for a campaign against anemia in rural areas (Quevedo Báez, 1949).

In 1903, Báez demonstrated his awareness of the potential that X-rays had to make opaque bodies visible. Although they had been discovered in 1893, Puerto Rico did not have an X-ray machine available for medical research until 1911. In lieu of advances in medical technology, U.S. colonial administrators made a second critical administrative decision in 1904 that profoundly altered the way Puerto Rican physicians came to see their medical interventions and magnify the significance of their work under the colonial administration. After Governor Hunt approved funds for expanding the hookworm campaign into rural areas, an increasing number of physicians participated in its "scientific" work. They saw the expanded use of the microscope in diagnosis as a method for developing their professional legitimacy and as a way of promoting their autonomy from municipal governments.

The Hookworm-Anemia Campaign as Public Health

Dr. Bailey K. Ashford, an American Army Medic, arrived in Puerto Rico in 1898 during the military occupation. Originally charged with treating U.S. military forces, his focus shifted after Hurricane San Ciriaco hit the island in 1899. The hurricane claimed more than 2,200 lives and so thoroughly devastated food crops that the Army fed as many as 183,000 Puerto Ricans a day. Ashford headed a provisional tent hospital as part of the Army's relief effort. His narrative on admitted patients began with the presumption that, "fully three-fourths of those admitted were suffering from anemia," but provided no basis upon which he established this diagnosis. He initially treated his patients' "pallor" by feeding them iron-rich meat, but claimed the change in diet gave them diarrhoea. He tried arsenic, which similarly failed to produce results. He ruled out common explanations for what Puerto Rican physicians considered widespread "pernicious anaemia," including "malaria, climate, lack of hygiene," poor diet and poverty. Instead, he used a microscope to examine his patients' blood. He noticed "a decided and rather general eosinophilia" and remembered other investigations that tied the observation to parasites (Ashford and Gutierrez Igaravidez, 1910a: 25).[20] His November 25, 1899 letter to the U.S. Army Surgeon General noted the predominant cause of anemia on the island was "worms in the faeces."[21] This diagnosis and his subsequent research on anemia upended traditional local discourse regarding peasants' health and catalyzed a campaign that transformed public health and medical training in Puerto Rico.

Dr. Ashford is credited with discovering the true cause of the rural peasants' debility: anemia. Ashford titled his autobiography *A Soldier in Science,* alluding to the multiple struggles he confronted as a U.S. Army medic working among rural laborers and Puerto Rican physicians. His battle to convince these groups he had discovered an explanation for the inefficient production of the Puerto Rican peasant, a significant obstacle to economic progress, ultimately rested on proving it was the hookworm, a microscopic parasite, that was responsible for Puerto Rico's "most significant" health problem.

In his autobiography, Ashford proclaimed his passion for science and his resentment of clinical observation.[22] Ashford sought to pursue his passion for science and a military career in the U.S. Army Medical Corps and explained (in third person), "he realized now that the government of the freest country on earth had given certain men the power to command because those men knew more than the rank and file" (Ashford, 1934: 13).

---

[20] The details of discovery vary among Ashford's different narratives (Palmer, 2009).

[21] Ashford, 1899, University of Puerto Rico, Recinto Ciencias Medicas, Ashford's Personal Papers.

[22] He complained of his medical training because "there was much teaching of half-truths, much unconvincing argument, much stuffing of heads with intellectual refuse, and, above all, too much 'clinical eye'" (Ashford, 1934: 15).

As a U.S. Army medic, Ashford's claim to specialized knowledge implied a new set of power relationships that extended beyond the "rank and file" of a U.S. citizenry. The "government of the freest country on earth" became an imperial power at the end of the Spanish-American War. Although the U.S. both looked to and rejected European models of colonial governance, medicine continued to inform an idea that economic progress was part of its new and unique colonial responsibility.

The birth of "tropical medicine" as a new specialty in U.S. medicine and its definition of "tropical diseases" reflected a geopolitical interest in securing professional prestige relative to other empires. Even within the U.S. administration, professional competition surrounding tropical medicine was reflected in Ashford's relationship with his Georgetown University professor, Dr. Charles Stiles. At the Army Medical School, Ashford had been influenced by a broader medical emphasis on bacteriology and the search for specific causal agents. His helminthology professors lectured on parasites, including those found only in tropical environments. These lectures would eventually cast doubt on Ashford's claim. Ashford gave Stiles specimens of the Puerto Rican *uncinaria* he had "discovered" and Stiles described and classified two hookworm varieties as *Ancylostoma duodenale* and *Necator americanus,* literally, American killer. Stiles took Ashford's samples and credit for discovering the hookworm in the southern states. He was supported by U.S. journalists who insisted Stiles mentioned the possibility of hookworm in the southern states and the tropics during an 1896 lecture. Stiles enjoyed legitimacy with the Rockefeller Foundation who, upon hearing of his reports, subsequently earmarked $1,000,000 to found a Sanitary Commission for the Eradication of Hookworm Disease on October 26, 1909. Ashford persisted in defending his claim over the discovery a couple of weeks after the Rockefeller Foundation rewarded Stiles for his work and argued that the media was wrong. He went to great lengths to set the record straight in his version of the events. Asserting his specialized knowledge, he attempted to distinguish himself as a physician uniquely qualified to make characterizations of diagnoses or symptomology (Ashford, 1909).

Ashford referenced other European scientists' work to underscore the economic importance of scientific research for developing a healthy, efficient and productive labor force. From the outset, the hookworm had broader implications for scientific prestige and economic development. For instance, in 1904 he noted the campaign's work "was attracting the curious attention of all civilized nations, and the fate of thousands of laborers could not fail to excite a lively interest and initiate professional research" (Commission for the Study and Treatment of Anemia, 1904: 20). In this way, Ashford implied medicine's potential to manage labor.

A discourse on the uniqueness of the "tropics" implicated not only a unique medical specialty based on the idea that Puerto Rico was scientifically distinct but also a patient that was somehow different by virtue of that climate. Despite his research that established the hookworm as the cause of rural peasants' debility, a medical claim, Ashford reproduced the idea tropical environments delimited mental capacity and interest in assuming hygienic norms. His ideas reflected his ambivalence about the effects of climate on racial degeneration.

The ways native physicians negotiated the racial implications of tropical medicine were apparent in the ways the campaign contrasted descriptions of the indigenous Tainos and European Spaniards. The campaign's work disrupted the Spanish conception of sixteenth-century natives that explained death as a result of a "weak constitution." On the one hand, the campaign's directors medicalized this constitution and "weak complexion" as symptoms of disease. On the other hand, they challenged the idea of a "weak constitution" by asserting native survival despite a history of decimation through "grinding slavery, imported plagues, and separation of families." The contradiction between explaining and rejecting native weakness reflected an ambivalent sense of the Puerto Rican native as white, black, or other white. If the native was white, but compromised by a "hot, humid climate," tropical medicine could restore "white prestige" (Ring, 2009: 307). If the native was black, his complexion would persist despite U.S. colonization. Native physicians were committed to studying hookworm scientifically, partly because the campaign observed, and subsequent studies confirmed, whites were particularly susceptible to infection (Coelho and McGuire, 2006). The campaign's ideas about race also reflected its ambivalence about whiteness, which became increasingly associated with defining Spaniards as a separate race under the U.S. colonial administration. Many Anglos believed Spaniards were lazy and therefore not white. Campaign directors challenged the idea of Spaniards' inherent laziness by pointing to the latter's conquests throughout Latin America (Ashford and Igaravidez, 1911: 4–7).

The practice of tropical medicine through the hookworm campaign involved a variety of strategies that included developing local clinics for treating anemia, influencing local municipal politics and modernizing the degenerate *jíbaro* as a productive worker. Although the U.S. colonial project has been depicted as a process of Americanization, the campaign was ultimately founded and developed through the premise that native development of Puerto Rican medicine could promote the island's progress.

The silences in Ashford's narrative allowed him to highlight "science" and establish a basis upon which to develop the authority of an emerging discipline, U.S. tropical medicine. In his exclusive focus on hookworm as the cause of anemia, Ashford failed to engage other explanations dominant in Puerto Rico, including starvation, poor food, malaria and climate. Ashford's exclusive focus on a specific causative agent, what Rene Dubos calls "the doctrine of specific etiology," obscured the possible importance of these other social causes (1959; see also Tesh, 1988). The doctrine of specific etiology, when applied to disease prevention, has generally been a conservatizing force because it locates the cause of disease in germs. The resulting intervention leads toward a search for a cure and away from programs of broader social change.

Ashford pushed Puerto Rican medicine toward his new scientific emphasis on the hookworm, he could not exactly describe how the *uncinaria* caused anemia (Commission for the Suppression of Anemia in Puerto Rico, 1905). The first anemia commission simply reverted to the idea that the mere presence of the worm itself was an "affection...marked by profound anemia and degeneration of vital organs, leading to chronic invalidism and often results in death" (Commission for the Study and Treatment of Anemia, 1904: 17). By 1906, the second anemia commission reverted to a mid-nineteenth century hypothesis that the hookworm produced anemia by releasing a "poison" qualitatively changing the *jíbaro's* blood. The Commission wrote the hookworm's:

> effect is manifested by certain notable disturbances in the functions of vital organs. While frequently the symptoms are confined to a general reduction in strength, dizziness, and vague pains in chest and stomach, without noticeable pallor, it is only too common to observe a more or less grave alteration of the blood...(Commission for the Suppression of Anemia in Puerto Rico, 1905).

The hookworm gathered ferocious physical power, not only to debilitate and kill the *jíbaro*, but also to change him physiologically.[23] As the worm increased in explanatory power, it also increased in scientific significance. In his early papers, Ashford minimized the role of "an insufficient or improper diet" because "we as medical men may deplore but cannot help such conditions wherever they may exist" (Ashford, undated). Ashford's

---

[23] Ashford wrote that his original research was stimulated by Brown's observation of "prominent strawberry-looking eosinophiles" in the blood.

medical man could offer the *jíbaro* what seemed to them much more important. After all, they believed the parasite was the sole source of, and solution to, an anemia that some Puerto Rican physicians had previously declared "beyond their power to cope with."

For instance, in Figure 5, the anemia campaign used a picture to represent the "State of Nutrition." The full face in the picture contrasts with the image of an emaciated patient, thereby downplaying the role of hunger and malnutrition in anemia. The picture emphasizes the patient's face as an example of edema and notes the patient's case is severe. The emphasis on the patient's face, rather than his bare feet, also associated his anemia with other markers within the picture, such as those that indicated his class, work, and racial difference.

One could see Ashford's limited research as part of a mission to redirect the political energies of Puerto Rican medicine toward developing "scientific" cures. While Ashford undoubtedly sought to gain the attention and support of Puerto Rican medicine, he did not necessarily believe all

SHOWING STATE OF NUTRITION IN SEVERE CASE REPORTED BY DR.
ROSES ARTAU.

Figure 5. State of Nutrition (Ashford and Gutiérrez Igaravídez, 1911).

physicians could lead the way toward a new scientifically-based progress. A variety of groups resisted Ashford's theories, but he insisted on his scientific training. When Puerto Rican physicians and politicians challenged Ashford, he attributed this resistance to their ignorance and political involvements. Ashford engaged in an all-out war to win their attention and support to establish a new, and seemingly apolitical, scientific foundation to the anemia problem.

The Puerto Rico anemia campaign, initially led by Ashford, went through several stages that transformed it from relief work to the foundation of public health and medical training on the island. The first stage was characterized by developing a framework for popular and professional support for the campaign's work. Ashford returned to the United States after the relief efforts concluded, but was reassigned to care for troops in Ponce in 1902. There he met Walter W. King, the port's Public Health Officer and assistant surgeon of the U.S. Public Health and Marine Hospital Service. They began a survey of 100 cases at the Tricoche Hospital that year that concluded with an article estimating hookworm "affected approximately ninety percent of the rural population" and was "a most important economic question in the betterment of the island" (Ashford and Gutiérrez Igaravídez, 1910a: 27).

The 1902–1903 survey was followed by two Anemia Commissions. The first was particularly significant because it consolidated and expanded public and professional support and international visibility for the Commission's work. It began in Bayamón, where the director of the Bayamón Hospital and health officer of the town, Dr. Pedro Gutiérrez Igaravídez, joined the Commission as one of its directors. The Bayamon station was directed by Dr. Agustín Stahl. Through these appointments, native physicians creolized the campaign (Scarano, 2012). Its public support was also indicative of how the hookworm campaign shaped emerging meanings of public health. From Bayamón, the first Commission extended its efforts to Utuado in 1904 and Aibonito in 1905 and included substations in many surrounding towns. As the campaign expanded, it gained support from municipal governments such that "in four of our ten stations the town offered to bear all the expenses if we would administer the work and furnish the medicines" (Ashford and Gutiérrez Igaravídez, 1910b: 1760). Utuado and Aibonito were critically tied to national interests. More specifically, Utuado was a town at the center of coffee-production, criollo (island-born creoles) influence and native resistance (Picó, 1981, 1993). Similarly, Aibonito was "symbolically and deeply linked with jíbaro society and culture" (Scarano, 2012).

The second Commission, in 1906, reflected native physicians' leadership over an institutionalized campaign. It was a permanent commission formed by three 'original members' of the first campaign with Igaravidez as its president. Noted physicians Isaac Gonzalez Martinez of Mayaguez, who is credited with discovering bilharzia on the island, and Francisco Sein y Sein, a municipal physician of Lares, continued to participate in the Commission. Ashford and King returned to regular Army duties. This second and Permanent Commission expanded the campaign's work to the towns of Rio Piedras, Mayaguez, and Lares. By 1907, the Commission's reports demonstrate several cases of station directors who participated in the campaign without pay and companies that paid physician's salaries.

A second phase of the campaign's work, following the two anemia commissions, was characterized by its institutionalization in the insular government in 1908 when a law established the Anemia Dispensary Service under the Department of Health, Charities and Corrections. Igaravidez continued to direct the campaign and expanded treatment to include other diseases, fighting tuberculosis and improving sanitation laws. A 1909 Act reflected this development and reorganized the campaign's work as the Tropical and Transmissible Diseases Service. The new Service introduced competitive examinations for participating physicians and "efforts of all kinds were made to secure competent doctors to take charge of the work... among all the inhabitants of the rural districts, but in spite of all efforts made," only two physicians could be contracted (Colton, 1911: 269). It appeared impossible to secure physicians "to take charge of the work in the rural districts" (Colton, 1911: 269). Sanitation officers took over the direction of the anemia dispensaries in 1910 and "rendered their services gratuitously" (Colton, 1911: 269). They were civil servants charged with other duties related to sanitation and appointed by the municipal mayor, but that year a draft bill proposed a new director of civil service under the Department of Health who would appoint sanitation officers with the governor's approval.[24] The bill centralized authority related to health and sanitation work on the island under the colonial administration and reduced local political autonomy.

---

[24] Secretary of War, "A Report Made by the Secretary of War Upon Conditions Existing in Porto Rico," *House Documents,* 61st Congress, 2nd Session (Washington: Government Printing Office, 1910), 8 (Regarding the appointment of sanitary officers, see Willoughby, 1909). The officer's sanitarion duties included "inspection of meat, bread, milk, and articles of food...corals, stables, pens...butchers, breadmakers, cigarmakers, etc." (Ashford and Igaravidez, 1911: 17).

The final stage in the campaign's early development was characterized by a bifurcation of its work between public health and medical training and research on tropical diseases and anemia. In 1911, the Tropical and Transmissible Diseases Service was taken over by the newly established Sanitation Service under the direction of Dr. William F. Lippitt, an American. The campaign's hookworm work appeared suspended until 1912, when an Act established an Institute for the Study of Tropical Medicine that soon became the Institute for Tropical Medicine and Hygiene. The Institute brought Lippitt, Ashford, Gutiérrez Igaravídez, Gonzalez Martinez, and Francisco J. Hernandez together in resuming the campaign's work (Yager, 1913).

Ashford's vision for the hookworm campaign contrasted with what he saw as the political corruption within Puerto Rico's medical profession. He believed the campaign responded to the previously ignored medical needs of the island's rural peasants. His vision may have been shared by some physicians working with the campaign, but was challenged by a broader political context that involved a national struggle for autonomy. The Unionist Party also claimed to address the needs of a nation whose autonomy was compromised by the colonial administration. As the first anemia commission developed, the Unionist Party built solidarity among many formerly oppositional classes including labor, many Republicans and the Federal Party. Feeling threatened by their imminent electoral success, Governor Hunt granted Ashford $5,000 for the campaign's work.

Political tensions between colonial domination and native desires for autonomy were reflected within the campaign. For instance, Ashford characterized the Puerto Rican stationed at Bayamón, Dr. Agustín Stahl, as a medical scientist who came to the camp "seemingly, in order to make impromptu speeches filled with complicated eloquence in the Spanish language to the wall-eyed populace seeking a sign, not a reason." Ashford resented Stahl, who would later serve as the AMPR's second President (1905–08), for being a "hard talker" and unresponsive to the needs of poor patients. He related an incident in which Stahl reacted in anger to a patient's request for a medical visit to his bedridden wife. According to Ashford, Stahl "suddenly veered round in a purple rage and, after cursing him skillfully in English and German, did an exceptionally complete job in Spanish, even going so far as to 'mention his mother' to his face" (Ashford, 1934: 55). Ashford contrasted imagery of the docile, vulnerable and needy patient, like the bedridden wife, with Stahl's neglect. He implied that Puerto Rican physicians subordinated the common good to their personal and political interests.

Ashford favored native physicians who had influence but less explicit political involvements, such as Dr. Gutiérrez Igaravídez who began working with the campaign at Bayamón. Ashford distinguished Dr. Gutiérrez Igaravídez in terms of his sacrifice, rather than making claims about the value of his work. Ashford explained Igaravídez severed "all of those professional relations which would have made him to-day the wealthiest physician in San Juan." Ashford noted Igaravídez's association with the first Porto [sic] Rico Anemia Commission invited "the criticism and even the ridicule of those who constituted the society in which he lived" (Ashford, 1934: 56). Igaravídez also distinguished himself from a tradition of social medicine on the island that was disrupted by U.S. colonization. In 1918, as director of the Institute for Tropical Medicine and Hygiene, he refers to himself as a "missionary of medical science" and his speech emphasizes the institution's research rather than the problem of anemia or public health (Gutiérrez Igaravidez, 1918). Claims about public interest seemed political instruments that were not necessarily indicative of a particular physicians' work.

Through the hookworm campaign, Ashford promoted not only a broader political agenda but also presented the clinic as a bureaucracy reorganizing municipal physicians' civil service. At the rear of the Bayamon Municipal Hospital, Puerto Rican physicians had "an opportunity to observe the practical work and the results of treatment" (Ashford, 1910). The hookworm campaign appealed not only to municipal physicians' who wanted to develop public health, but also to their interest in reforming municipal governments. Although Ashford saw himself as bringing medical attention to remote and isolated rural areas, he nevertheless reproduced the organization of the campaign's administration in urbanized municipal centers. From the town's center, Ashford claimed to counter jíbaro's isolation, but ultimately emphasized his interest in cultivating public favor.

Because of its local organization, the campaign exerted widespread influence on medical practice. In particular, both Commissions influenced public health and standardized physicians' work. In its first two years, the Commission developed and recommended methods to fight hookworm infection, which were subsequently taken up by the SBOH (Commission for the Suppression of Anemia in Puerto Rico, 1905). It developed a station/sub-station model to centralize and standardize physicians' clinical methods across units dispersed throughout the island. The central station in Aibonito was established in June of 1905 and substations in Lares, Utuado, Guayama, Coamo, San Sebastian, Comerio, Barranquitas and Barros soon followed in July and August. On August 31, 1905, the team invited physicians of certain towns, the majority of whom had already petitioned the Governor for a substation of the Commission in their own municipalities, to study the methods employed in Utuado (Ashford, 1905; Ashford and Gutierrez Igaravidez, 1911). During the days they spent there, they were taught standard uses of the microscope and methods for registering and taking clinical histories. Physicians were also trained using unpopular methods. For instance, they performed autopsies so unpopular among rural peasants that one "had to be done in a considerable hurry at the graveyard" (Ashford, 1934: 73).

Through this training, the Commission institutionalized King's military methods of identifying hookworm infection cases. King's methods introduced new ways of classifying rural peasants that simultaneously tracked their behavior. He applied methods of categorizing Puerto Ricans he had developed during the military occupation to police local banditry (see Figure 6). These cards recorded clinical histories that included information about patients' skin color, social standing, trade and use of a latrine. Campaign physicians maintained these cards and lists of patients. The histories monitored individuals over time and served as a form of surveillance over their activities.

The clinics included tent hospitals, an office, a dispensary and a laboratory. The primary function of the laboratory was to render a "definitive diagnosis" of hookworm disease and to collect data that could be used to monitor infection. Ashford insisted on the use of the microscope as the only true and reliable way to observe the hookworm and diagnose anemia. As a result, the Commission sent microscopes to all the stations in order to facilitate data collection and monitor the modes of infection re-infection. By 1908, the campaign deemed the microscopic examination of patients' feces the only way to positively diagnose *uncinariasis* and institutionalized its use through the law establishing the Anemia Dispensary Service.

The laboratory also helped build a broad basis of both professional and popular support for the hookworm campaign. Private practice physicians had begun setting up their own labs and saw the broader use of microscopes as part of medico-scientific modernization. Ashford similarly noted the clinic's "strange instruments," blood exams, urine and fecal analysis were novelties that promoted the campaign's popularity. The microscope and the clinic promoted the separation between doctors and their patients. By reinforcing their reliance on the microscope for diagnosis, physicians' increasing distance from the lived experience of their patients limited their understandings of the social context in which anemia was embedded.

```
┌─────────────────────────────────────────────────────────────────┐
│              PORTO RICO ANEMIA COMMISSION.                        │
│                                                                   │
│              CLINICAL CARD.          STATION OF ............      │
│                                      RURAL DISTRICT........       │
│                                      FARM..................       │
│  No...................Name.....................................   │
│  Date...............Color.........Age.........Sex.........Social standing.........  │
│  Trade...........Privy..... ...... Clinical form of uncinariasis ⎱ Very light   │
│                                                              ⎰ Light           │
│                                                              ⎱ Medium          │
│  Mazamorra..................Were infected. ................... ⎰ Intense       │
│                                                                Very intense    │
│  Parasites, (Uncin.) (Ascar. lumb.) (Tric. dispar.)... .........................  │
│  Prominent symptoms...............................................................  │
│  ......... .............. ......... ...............................................  │
│  Complications and intercurrent ⎱ ......... ......................................  │
│                      diseases ⎰                                   │
└─────────────────────────────────────────────────────────────────┘
```

Figure 6. Clinic Card (Ashford and Gutiérrez Igaravídez, 1911).

Medical arguments over the nature and cause of anemia overlapped and at times contradicted themselves. Small wonder, then, that the campaign's arguments remained platitudes largely independent of Puerto Ricans' experience of anemia. Even as late as 1915, physicians who emphasized patients' subjective experiences of disease challenged Ashford's findings. Dr. Luis García de Quevedo, for instance, argued against Ashford's emphasis on the *uncinariasis* as the only intestinal parasite causing anemia, pointing out that anemia persisted despite comprehensive rural education programs, widespread medical treatment and the efforts of the anemia stations. He encouraged Puerto Ricans to explore other causes and pointed, for instance, to the role of constipation in anemia. Upon questioning patients at the stations, García de Quevedo had found that they thought being *well* (of the stomach) meant to not defecate for 2 to 3 days (García de Quevedo, 1915). Ironically, constipation is a symptom of iron-deficiency anemia. Had this hypothesis been pursued, it would have led to an emphasis on nutrition. Other physicians also continued to assert the role of other gastro-intestinal problems in later anemic outcomes, such as other tropical parasites, hunger and malnutrition, bad hygiene, or a combination of all of these factors.[25] Eventually, by the time

---

[25] The statistics within *Public Health Reports* on gastro-intestinal diseases are significantly higher than any other disease on which statistics were systematically collected. Dr. Jesus Maria Amadeo y Antonmarchi refuted the prevalence Ashford attributed to

of his 1934 biography, even Ashford conceded alternate explanations for anemia and wrote: "There is even good reason to believe that a true anaemia of a pernicious type can and does develop out of a nutritional unbalance under the stress of tropical climate" (Ashford, 1934: 380).

Beyond the clinical distance introduced by the laboratory, the campaign failed to criticize the context in which the rural laborer lived. Instead, it emphasized the patient as an individual. The campaign's economic relevance was a direct reflection of the broader interests of colonial capital in creating a productive labor force. Campaign physicians believed they had the potential to regenerate what they saw as lazy rural peasants into a stable and productive labor force.

The campaign located itself in municipal centers and worked to influence local politics. It gave local physicians a greater degree of independence from municipal mayors. The campaign's popularity also influenced politicians' decisions and support for public health-related matters. In this way, the campaign became a part of colonial discourse that reflected the administration's claims of success. Unlike the slow development of sanitation under the U.S. colonial administration's authority, the hookworm campaign attributed its success to native physicians, like Gutiérrez Igaravídez. The participation of native physicians in the hookworm campaign reflected their role as intermediaries in establishing new forms of U.S. colonial governance (Ashford and Gutiérrez Igaravídez, 1911: 3).

The campaign's interventions paved the way for future public health efforts to address hygiene education and sanitary regulation and inspection. In this way, the campaign's development accommodated not only colonial priorities, but also an interest in progress and modernity that preceded U.S. colonization. In essence, bodies became a basis for reshaping a modern island. The campaign distinguished itself from British tropical medicine by promoting interventions that focused less on direct control over parasites than on hygiene education and self-discipline. Although the campaign's discourse depoliticized anemia, through hygiene education, native physicians also promoted individual responsibility in the interests of public health. For instance, by the second Anemia commission, the campaign emphasized the role of individuals in transmission and infection:

---

anemia and pointed to other diseases and parasites that produced anemia in Puerto Rico (Amadeo, 1904). Dr. José Gómez Brioso's work emphasized the role poor mastication had on cavities, which in turn led to intestinal infections that weakened intestinal walls and resulted in pernicious anemia (García de Quevedo, 1915).

It must here be categorically emphasized that every ovum produces but one worm, if it hatches out, which it sometimes does not do. Ovum laid must pass on to its full development, as an encapsulated larva, outside of the human body. This means, of course, that multiplication of *uncinariae* contained in an infected individual is impossible, and that, if a man has one hundred such parasites, he will never have any more until he is infected from without. This is the most important and the saving clause in the prevention and treatment of the affection, and is in sharp contrast to other infectious diseases commonly known (Commission for the Suppression of Anemia in Puerto Rico, 1905).

The "saving clause" reflected tropical medicine's influence on the campaign and reflected its politicized emphasis on the environment. Although the campaign emphasized medical treatment, it suggested hygiene could promote modern progress. By focusing on rural peasants, physicians joined in the colonial task of promoting individual responsibility and Americanization toward eventual self-government and political autonomy.

The campaign reflected an opportunity to intervene in what colonial administrators and native physicians saw as an impenetrable rural environment. It emphasized medical treatment. As a result, the broader construction of latrines, inspections of latrines and homes and "soil-pollution" laws were later developments pursued by the colonial administration and its public health authorities. By 1909, the campaign separated activities related to sanitation and education from its emphasis on science. Part of its distance from direct contact with patients seemed reflective of his failed sanitary education. For instance, Ashford wrote a letter to Major Charles Lynch of the Army Medical Corps in 1909 and insisted treatment, "after trying every known means of combating the disease from a sanitarian's standpoint...[was] the only true way to exterminate *uncinariasis* from among a whole people" (Ashford, 1909). The campaign treated medicine as the sign of modern progress. It was the sign the campaign offered and Ashford believed patients searched for on the dispensary line. Medicine was the sign Ashford used to displace ostensibly self-interested physicians like Dr. Stahl and a symbol of what the latter failed to provide.

The Puerto Rican hookworm campaign was unique in its emphasis on regenerating Puerto Ricans' vitality and modernizing public health. Its success remains a dominant narrative. Puerto Rico's first medical school attributes its origins to the campaign. Puerto Rican historians include the campaign within a narrative about public health improvement. Historians of science and medicine include the campaign in a narrative about the scientific triumph over the Puerto Rican hookworm. Main streets in the tourist center of Puerto Rico's capital city bear Ashford's name. As hookworm work expanded through local municipal-level governments, however, it laid the foundation for later developments in public health institutions, interventions and discourses. The dissemination of anemia discourse occurred not only through academia and practicing doctors, it also played critical roles in the development of professional medical societies and journals, as well as in the training of sanitation officials after 1911. Anemia discourse and work, therefore, affected every aspect of the early development of public health in Puerto Rico.

The importance of anemia work is that it underscores the relationship between the "domination of others" and "technologies of the self." Tropical medicine had an important role in global imperialism and played a critical role in European colonization. In Puerto Rico, tropical medicine was distinguished by its emphasis on patients. While European tropical medicine attempted to control disease by eradicating parasites, tropical medicine in Puerto Rico emphasized native physicians who claimed they could effect a cure by promoting individual interventions. The campaign's intervention nonetheless obscured the economic, political and social conditions leading to anemia. This discourse became critical within professional circles and influenced the ways a new U.S. colonial government understood problems related to the social conditions of Puerto Rican life (Ashford, 1899). Puerto Rican medicine was ultimately Americanized by promoting "tropical medicine" and professional prestige.

Ashford's later writing evidences a "colonial ambivalence," a colonialist's subjective paranoia resulting from a conflict between "the reforming, civilizing mission" and the native's threat to the static "boundaries of truth" he constructed (Bhabha, 1994: 95, 123, 142). Ashford had at least partly "gone native" by marrying a Puerto Rican woman. Ashford's colonial ambivalence was also reinforced by the frequent failure of U.S. science to recognize his scientific contributions and his sense of "belonging" within the Puerto Rican medical community. By the time of his 1934 biography, it seemed apparent that Ashford had displayed his ambivalence by partly conceding to alternate explanations for anemia. He wrote, "There is even good reason to believe that a true anemia of a pernicious type can and does develop out of a nutritional unbalance under the stress of tropical climate" (Ashford, 1934: 380).

CHAPTER FOUR

NATIONAL PHYSICIANS AND PROFESSIONAL PRESTIGE

In many ways, the discourse on anemia and the hookworm campaigns it developed were only indirectly about rural patients. Time would demonstrate that the campaigns had limited efficacy in preventing patients from being re-infected by the hookworm. Time would also prove other parasites were more prevalent, and other diseases more pronounced, than hookworm infection. Subsequent medical findings on hookworm did not so much indicate the early Puerto Rican hookworm campaigns had been "wrong" as they represented the development of medical science on the island. Time was also implicated in a generational shift between an older generation of liberal-elite physicians and a newer generation of professionals. The hundreds of pages furthering the discourse on anemia and documenting the hookworm campaigns' work remain analytically useful because they tell the story of how medical needs were constructed in relation to shifting political and professional interests. These texts demonstrated how the hookworm campaign became a vehicle for dissociating anemia from the colonial relationship and a new generation of professionals labored to produce these documents and came to develop tropical medicine as an attractive, modern and exportable resource. Their texts demonstrate how a new breed of medical scientists emerged to promote their political influence and professional prestige and modernize the colonial relationship.

In this chapter I trace the development of Puerto Rican physicians' professional authority relative to the U.S. colonial administration. At the end of the nineteenth century, Puerto Rican physicians were involved in politics and conceived their mandate broadly in terms of promoting the "moral and material" interests of society. By 1911, however, those same physicians conceived their mission more narrowly in terms of protecting and promoting the interests of the medical profession. Through the development of a unique medical association in 1902, the *Asociacíon Medíca de Puerto Rico* (AMPR), and subsequent incorporation of AMPR in the American Medical Association (AMA), Puerto Rican physicians hoped to gain influence within the colonial administration and generalize their construction of Puerto Ricans' broader interests.

I begin with a brief discussion of professional status, physicians' relationship to the rural countryside and Puerto Rican medicine under the
Spanish colonial administration. The U.S. colonial administration's observations about the existing medical infrastructure on the island provide a
context for elucidating the shifting meaning of medical practice. Medicine
was stratified under both colonial administrations. In the late-nineteenth
century, an older generation of liberal elite physicians represented an
important component of the native political and intellectual elite. They
both overlapped and were distinct from a professional and scientific elite
that emerged after 1898. This generational difference was not determined
by age or support for bacteriology. Instead, this new generation emerged
through the hookworm campaign and transformed the state's relationship to municipal residents and rural populations. Physicians' relationship to urban spaces also shifted as a result of improved transportation
and their professional activities were increasingly organized around the
city of San Juan, which was a space they shared with the U.S. colonial
administration. Despite their increasingly urban concentration, the U.S.
colonial administration encouraged expanding professionals' interventions in rural environments. These interventions became a basis for lodg-
ing status claims for professional recognition.

My analysis of the hookworm campaign reveals how the idea of penetrating the tropics became critical to developing professional prestige at
both domestic and international levels. The campaign provided a method
for colonizing rural areas and accommodating a variety of interests, including the development of scientific medicine, the insular administration, and
broader imperial projects. This discussion suggests physicians' previous
emphasis on the colonial relationship and greater political-professional
autonomy was displaced by the hookworm campaign, which instead
focused on developing an infrastructure for a public health administration.
The apparent dichotomy between politics and administration did not mean
the campaign was not political. Instead, this dichotomy served to displace
the growing influence and authority liberal elite physicians had
cultivated in the late-nineteenth century. As the campaign colonized rural
areas, it provided clinical material for the development of tropical medicine
and delimited the terms of professional autonomy.

Professional Status

Puerto Rican physicians' struggle for professional prestige was undoubtedly
distinct from their U.S. counterparts who engaged in intra-occupational

competition to distinguish their profession and negotiate a unique social position. In the United States, developing professional status involved gaining legitimacy and cultural authority by acquiring a monopoly over a market of clients and achieving control over a jurisdiction (Abbot 1988; Larson 1977; Starr 1982). In order to secure professional autonomy, this negotiation involved practitioners in persuading the state that they served the public interest, which implied exclusive authority over the profession and control over the content of their work (Friedson 1970). As physicians gained professional status, U.S. medicine came to typify experts' expanding social influence. U.S. medicine enjoyed a degree of power, prestige and autonomy unparalleled elsewhere in the world during its so-called Golden Age (Brandt and Gardner, 2003; Burnham, 1997; Tomes, 2001).

Although the early twentieth-century Puerto Rican physician resembled his American counterpart in several important respects, the former had a much more intimate relationship with ideas of a "nation" and state power than the latter.[1] Under Spanish colonial rule, many physicians were prominent members of the island's liberal elite. Most of these practitioners were educated in the medical schools of a politically-tumultuous Spain, which led them to envision a broad social regeneration based on scientific principles (Nouzeilles 1997; Scarano 1996; Trigo 2000). Their version of modernity and education furthered their political authority on the island. They worked to expose Spanish colonial authority as an obstacle to modernization and a source of isolation and decay at both individual and institutional levels. Liberal-elite physicians used their status to justify their political involvement and social leadership. As leaders of a struggle for greater political autonomy under Spanish colonial rule, physicians articulated an identity that treated the political and the professional as inseparable.

After 1898, under U.S. colonial rule, Puerto Rican physicians' political strategy and professional identity shifted. Physicians' status and leadership were undermined by a U.S.-directed modernization that questioned Puerto Rican physicians' professionalism, doubted their qualifications, and found everything Spanish, including the political-professional role that Puerto Rican physicians had crafted, prone to corruption and political self-interest. Many physicians strategically asserted their difference as

---

[1] There were a few Puerto Rican women who had completed a formal medical education and obtained a degree, including Ana Janer Palacios, Maria A. Seixas, Lola Pérez Marchand and Palmira Gatell. Most female healers were alternate medical practitioners (Azize Vargas and Avilez, 1990).

Puerto Ricans to promote their professional authority and political influence. When this approach failed to mobilize a collective identity among physicians across the island, elite physicians revised this strategy, abandoned the independence of their recently developed professional association, and narrowed their emphasis to pursue professional, rather than broader political, autonomy.

Status in Urban and "Threatening" Rural Spaces

In the late nineteenth century, elites compared the urban areas where they lived with their political, professional and intellectual ties in Europe and Latin America. Liberal elite physicians sought to modernize urban areas and eradicate illness, which they viewed as having physical, social and moral expressions. Although they wanted to actively intervene to eradicate urban social ills, their attitude toward the countryside was more complex.

Liberal elite physicians saw rural areas in the interior mountainous regions of the islands as geographically and socially isolated because Puerto Rico lacked a developed infrastructure of roads. For instance, in his biography, Dr. Jose Angel Franco Soto explained he departed from Mayaguez to Sábana Grande by horse carriage at noon, but the trip involved a host of difficulties that allowed him to *palpar muy de cerca* (closely feel) the whim, ignorance and sword of colonial life (1949: 19). They began the second leg of their trip to Ponce the next day at 5 am and spent eight hours covering approximately 35 miles. As a result, although rural production was tied to urban markets and drew a variety of groups into urban areas, the lack of adequate roads linking urban and rural environments limited reciprocal exchanges.

The hazards of travel had two implications for liberal elite physicians' relationship with rural environments. On the one hand, they had a romantic fascination with Puerto Rico's tropical environment. Rural areas seemed removed from the path to modern progress that the elite envisioned and ripe for developing their authority through discursive interventions. They saw the *jíbaro* as the backward, lazy victim of Spanish colonialism, incapable of promoting his own well-being or supporting Puerto Rico's modern progress, but this caricature also reflected elite physicians' distance from the lived experience of rural peasants. On the other hand, elite physicians shared a disdain for work in rural areas, which they imagined were filled with swamps and disease. They were apprehensive about what they experienced as rugged, hazardous travel. They were also worried about catching diseases they believed were concentrated in a rural tropical environment. Elite physicians saw rural areas and the people who lived within them as sources of contagious diseases they felt ill-equipped to control. They were unlikely to conduct house calls in rural areas to mediate the difficulty of transporting sick patients. As a result, in late-nineteenth century Puerto Rico, academically-trained physicians' relationships to the rural interior regions of Puerto Rico was conceptually abstract.

Many physicians' perception of a tropical rural interior shifted in the early twentieth century through the hookworm campaign. Dr. Bailey K. Ashford illustrated how these areas became ripe for colonization when he related a story about travel through this ostensibly dangerous landscape. In his biography, Ashford immediately follows-up a narrative about the ambivalent role of military physicians by narrating his trip from San Juan to Ponce via Mayaguez and San German. He explained that the rains made travel more difficult and suggested the woods facilitated an ambush by *Aguila Blanco*, The White Eagle.[2] Ashford contrasts his own bravery with the driver's cowardice in running off. He tells his wife to inform the bandits of his military title and his prominent father-in-law "who would make it hot for them if anything disagreeable happened" (1934: 33). This element of the narrative reflected the significance of both U.S. colonial authority and class status in penetrating rural environments. Ashford ultimately associates his victory in navigating the incident and evading death, with his own wits: he claimed he tricked one of the bandits into calling on the aid of the Cavalry Commander at Yauco. Ashford concludes the narrative in terms that demonstrated how his "friends at Yauco were old Indian fighters" who were could not capture the White Eagle because the latter "knew the *monte* [mountainous rural interior] better than our crowd did." In this narrative, the rural interior became a place to be conquered by "authorities" in the interest of reducing violence. Both authorities and bandits were associated with this violence, but U.S. colonial authority (personified by Ashford) wanted to direct "Indian fighters" in reducing lawlessness. His narrative implied that Ashford understood his role as one

---

[2] White Eagle has at times been solely associated with José Maldonado Román and at other times with a band. In either case, popular narrative and historians dispute whether he/they were bandits, Robin Hoods, or revolutionaries who favored the island's liberation (Bryan, 1899; Marín, 2006; Picó, 2004). In Ashford's narrative, White Eagle was a band of intoxicated "bandits" (1934:32).

that complemented the U.S. military's objective of consolidating control over inaccessible rural space. His narrative helped move physicians' away from an intellectual relationship with the rural interior to one that was directly engaged with the enemy: the hookworm.

Medical Practitioners in the Late Nineteenth Century: One of Many

Under Spanish colonialism, elite Puerto Rican physicians tied their professional identity to their class position. The island lacked medical institutions, such as schools and laboratories, which made their work indistinguishable from many other practitioners, including non-elite physicians trained outside of Europe, pharmacists, surgeons, *practicantes* (medical and surgeon assistants), *parteras* (midwives), *curiosos* (those curious about solutions), and *curanderos* (folk healers). Their work also overlapped with that of other specialists who used various forms of medicine, including blood-letting, leeching, cupping, and caustic healing, although these methods declined in popularity by the end of the century. The diversity of medical practice meant that institutional associations, limited opportunities for medical training, and licenses to practice did not consistently distinguish practitioners or foster a collective identity.

Among this amorphous group of medical practitioners, academically-trained physicians had the highest social status. At the top was a relatively small elite group who had been trained in Europe and primarily in Spanish medical schools. Most of these physicians worked in urban areas on the coast where they had private practices catering to a wealthy clientele. Some were employed by the municipal government. Less affluent physicians obtained their medical training in Cuba, Santo Domingo, Venezuela or the United States, since travel to these countries was less expensive. Like other academically-trained physicians, these less affluent doctors sought out wealthy clients, but most worked with the urban middle class through their private practices, in urban charitable institutions, or in towns within smaller municipalities.

Medical training formed an important means for establishing professional associations and status. For instance, Table 5 identifies physicians who held a formal administrative position in Ponce during the first decade of the U.S. colonial administration. At least half were trained in Spain, but the other half trained in the United States, Europe or Latin America. Elite physicians who were trained in Spain developed their

Table 5. Physicians in Ponce around 1898.[1]

Physician	Medical Degree Conferred In:
Alfredo Ferran	Cuba
Jose Gomez Valencia	Spain
Julio Ferrer Torres	Spain
Jose Julio Henna	United States
Luis Aguerrevere	Venezuela
Manuel Zeno Gandia	Spain
Pedro Hernandez Y Santiago	Spain
Pedro J. Salicrup	United States
Ramon A. de Torres	1884, Brussels; 1897, Habana
Vicente Santoni	France
Victor Gutierrez Ortiz	Spain

[1] (Data abstracted from Arana-Soto, 1966a, 1968).

political and professional associations in their schools, through travel or by visiting exiles in France. Other academically-trained physicians promoted their political activity on the island through regional networks organized around cities, particularly Ponce, Mayaguez, and San Juan. Ponce facilitated communication between elite physicians, including Manuel Zeno Gandia, Felix Tio Malaret, Jose Julio Henna, and Jose Gomez Brioso.

Outside of Puerto Rico, other physicians working toward professional status similarly fostered a collective identity through institutions like medical schools. Unlike American doctors, however, Puerto Rico lacked a medical school, consistent opportunities for medical training and a developed structure of modern bureaucratic institutions, such as medical schools, hospitals and clinics. A select group of elite physicians offered courses at the *Ateneo Puertorriqueño*, but their efforts were short lived (Arana-Soto, 1978b, 1978c). Medical students had to leave the island to complete their medical education. Other institutions they could have used to define and maintain their professional identity, such as hospitals, required significant structural improvements and could neither project physicians' competence nor promote a modern, scientific presentation for the profession. These factors had several significant consequences. First, they meant there were few academically-trained physicians on the island. For instance, the ratio of trained physicians was approximately 1 for every 7,500 persons (Guerra, 1998: 68). Second, these factors limited physicians' ability to establish a professional identity, a division of labor, or their autonomy from colonial government. As a result, physicians' family background and class location defined their status more than any attempts to restrict entry into the profession.

Because elite Puerto Rican physicians felt reasonably secure in their class position, and because they could not control the medical profession's boundaries or membership through medical training, they were likely to collaborate with other medical practitioners. For instance, Puerto Rican physicians relied on *curanderos* as assistants during the cholera epidemic of 1855 (Arana-Soto, 1978b). Medical and administrative texts frequently referred to *practicantes* and *curiosos* in the late-nineteenth century, which indicated their regularized apprenticeships with academically-trained physicians. The most-important source of competition for all practitioners came from pharmacists, but even in these instances, physicians like Dr. Manuel Quevedo Báez fondly recalled these relationships in his text on the history of Puerto Rican medicine and surgery (Quevedo Báez, 1949). Similarly, as demonstrated in Figure 7, his advertisement indicated the reciprocal and collaborative nature of his practice and a physician's storefront. He notes requests for service could be directed to the pharmacy of Francisco and Domingo Martinez.

Pharmacists prescribed and prepared medicine without a physicians' prescription, despite Spanish legislation that prohibited this practice. Pharmacists also ignored Spanish authorities' attempts to control the secret compounds used in preparing medications, including poisons, opiates, and abortifacients. They also performed illegal procedures, including abortions, deliveries, and caesarians (Quevedo Báez, 1949: 501). The performance of these illegal practices indicated the lack of control Spanish authority exercised over informal medical practice. As a result, many Puerto Ricans avoided physicians and their fees altogether by buying drugs and obtaining medical advice directly from pharmacists.

Geography organized medical care and promoted urban physicians' status by limiting competition. Most elite physicians, located in growing urban areas on the coast, established private practices that catered to a wealthy clientele who could afford their services. Some academically trained, non-elite physicians also sought out wealthy clients in urban areas, but most worked with the urban middle class in towns. *Curanderos* served the poor and, because trained physicians had little incentive to visit the sick of the countryside for little or no pay, they were often the only medical practitioners available in isolated rural environments. *Parteras,* women who were perhaps the least segregated of the medical

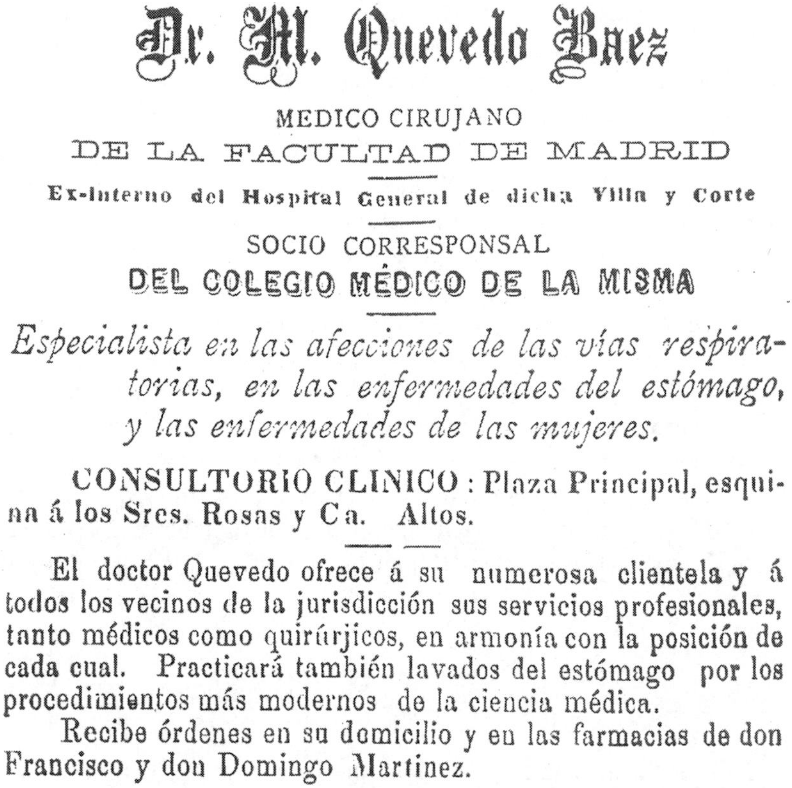

Dr. M. Quevedo Baez

MEDICO CIRUJANO

DE LA FACULTAD DE MADRID

Ex-Interno del Hospital General de dicha Villa y Corte

SOCIO CORRESPONSAL

DEL COLEGIO MÉDICO DE LA MISMA

Especialista en las afecciones de las vías respiratorias, en las enfermedades del estómago, y las enfermedades de las mujeres.

CONSULTORIO CLINICO : Plaza Principal, esquina á los Sres. Rosas y Ca.   Altos.

El doctor Quevedo ofrece á su numerosa clientela y á todos los vecinos de la jurisdicción sus servicios profesionales, tanto médicos como quirúrjicos, en armonía con la posición de cada cual.   Practicará también lavados del estómago por los procedimientos más modernos de la ciencia médica.

Recibe órdenes en su domicilio y en las farmacias de don Francisco y don Domingo Martinez.

Figure 7. Advertisement: Physicians and Pharmacists. (Morel Campos, 1896).

practitioners, aided other women in their deliveries. The gendered character of work meant deliveries were poorly remunerated and were less interesting to trained physicians. Rather than competing with academically trained physicians for the same clients, alternative medical practitioners served a diverse client base and practiced in areas trained physicians found undesirable.

Regional associations characterized a prominent phenomenon of how many physicians organized their medical practices. Physicians tended to practice in more than one area within a region and they developed regional associations. For instance, the AMPR's assembly listed physicians who were regional delegates representing other prominent physicians in surrounding areas. Dr. Mariano Ramírez, the municipal physician in Mayaguez, represented Drs. Nicolas Gimenez Nussa from the same municipality and Miguel A. Hernandez Comas from nearby Aguadilla. Dr. Felipe Vizcarrondo from Fajardo represented Drs. Miguel Veve and Jose A. Vazquez from the same municipality. Many physicians also practiced in two or three areas within a region simultaneously or over their career trajectory. For instance, Dr. Jose Daussa y Castro practiced in Patillas in 1890, in Maunabo in 1912 and Yabucoa in 1913 (Hafner 1993). These towns were all located in the southeastern corner of the island, within 15 miles of one another. Dr. Felix Tio Malaret was a municipal physician in both Adjutas and Sabana Grande, two towns in the southwestern region of the island that are roughly 35 miles from one another. Although San Juan would become a nucleus for the medical profession after 1910, in the first decade of the twentieth century, many prominent physicians were clustered around Ponce or Mayaguez. The regional shift was tied to physicians' collective identity. The AMPR claimed to represent the island's physicians, but it was centered in San Juan. It unwittingly tied professional status to San Juan and participated in an inequitable distribution of medical resources on the island (Mountin, Pennell and Flook, 1937; Torres-Gómez, 1999).

Municipal Physicians and State Competition: Spain

Under both Spanish and U.S. colonial rule, there was no clearer evidence of state competition than the case of municipal physicians. Under Spanish colonial rule, elite physicians saw their municipal counterparts as a significant obstacle to their professional status and attempts to gain autonomy from the state because municipal physicians were appointed by the Spanish governor (Hoff, 1901). Although the nature of the problem changed with the change in sovereignty, elite physicians' inability to control municipal physicians' appointments, work, and compensation consistently compromised their ability to negotiate on the profession's behalf and to gain professional autonomy.

Like other academically-trained practitioners, municipal physicians with medical qualifications from Spanish medical schools predominated within the group. This dominant group practiced in larger municipalities like Fajardo, Mayaguez, Ponce and San Juan and was tied into a surrounding regional network of professional and elite associations. Another group of physicians with a subordinate status were not highly integrated in these networks and practiced outside of the main urban areas or in smaller towns in more remote rural areas.

Table 6 distinguishes dominant features of the group.[3] Some municipal physicians were part of the intellectual elite and this membership was marked by publishing poems, biographies, autobiographies, or other literary works like theatrical plays. Some were politically involved at local and insular levels and campaigned to occupy a political position under Spanish or U.S. colonial authority. A few became involved with the hookworm campaign. Fewer were interested, involved or participated independently in publishing medical science research, which also indicated the lack of an institutional structure that could support the scientific development of the profession. Ultimately, however, most shared an interest in professional development, which was demonstrated by their membership in the *Asociación Medica de Puerto Rico* (AMPR) after 1902.

Municipal government physicians were another amorphous group of practitioners because some had not completed medical training.[4] The small number of academically-trained physicians meant some municipal governments had to resort to practitioners with questionable qualifications whose training was incomplete or was obtained through informal apprenticeships. For instance, Francisco Aguirre y Federico was the municipal physician of Hatillo in 1901, but did not obtain a license to practice under the Spanish colonial government (Arana-Soto, 1966). Similarly, Dr. Gregorio Santo Domingo Gonzalez practiced in Barros, a small rural municipality in the mountainous interior of the island now called Orocovis. He had obtained his medical degree at the University of Santiago in Spain but experienced difficulty having his credentials recognized by the Spanish colonial government in Puerto Rico, which occurred more generally when there was a misspelling of a physician's name on their degree (Arana-Soto, 1966). In the following years, he was also forced to rely on the courts in order to collect payment for his medical services.

---

[3] This table identified municipal physicians in 1901, under U.S. colonial authority. It seems a valuable proxy for municipal physicians under Spanish colonial authority because the year preceded many administrative changes to municipal government structure introduced under U.S. colonial authority. In essence, the U.S. colonial administration inherited a municipal government structure and was focused on mayors rather than other employees. Many physicians in this table, particularly in smaller municipalities, also had stable residences and were probably appointed under the Spanish colonial administration. To the extent Spanish physicians left the island with the change in sovereignty, however, there is probably an alternate profile of municipal physicians prior to 1898.

[4] See, for instance, the case of Francisco Ramos who was allowed to practice in Ciales as a "*curandero o curioso*" in 1855. Ramos became secretary to the Ciales mayor and mayor of Yauco, which suggests the legitimate political participation of *curanderos* (Arana-Soto, 1974: 405). See also Arana-Soto's (1978c) discussion of doubts surrounding Dr. Francisco Oller's medical training.

Table 6. Municipal Physicians in 1901.[1]

Physician	Municipality	Professional (PR)	Political (PO)	Intellectual (IN)	Scientific (SC)	Involved in Hookworm Campaign
Celso Caballero Balbas	Adjuntas					*
Felix Tio Malaret	Adjuntas AND Sabana Grande		*	*		
H.C. More	Aguadilla					
Julian Benejan	Aguadilla	*				
Jose Florencio de Santiago y Colon	Aibonito					
Francisco Maria Susoni Abreu	Arecibo	*	*			*
Julio Lopez Gaztambide	Arecibo					
Juan Trujillo Piza	Arroyo	*				
Gregorio Santo Domingo Gonzalez	Barros					*
Agustín Stahl y Stamm	Bayamon	*			*	*
Enrique Rodriguez	Bayamon	*				
Alfredo Fernandez Blanco	Cabo Rojo					
Fernando Gonzalez	Caguas					
Jose Marti Cuyar (Cuya)	Caguas					
Felipe B. Cordero y Escalona	Camuy	*				*
Arturo Cabrera Soler	Carolina					
Fernandez B. Clemente (Clemente Fernandez)	Carolina AND Loiza					
Manuel Muniz	Catano					
Jose Chacar	Cayey					
Victor M. Flores Arrieta	Cayey	*				
Jose Ciriaco Marcano de Rivera	Ciales	*	*			*

Table 6. (*Cont.*)

Physician	Municipality	Professional (PR)	Political (PO)	Intellectual (IN)	Scientific (SC)	Involved in Hookworm Campaign
Manuel Blanquez (Blasques, Blazquez)	Ciales	*				
Leonardo Igaravidez y Landron	Coamo	*				*
Miguel Herrero	Corozal	*				
Antonio Goicuria (Goicurria)	Dorado	*				
Diego Roman y Diaz	Fajardo					
Esteban Lopez Gimenez (Giminez, Jimenez)	Fajardo	*		*		
Jose A. Vazquez	Fajardo					
Venancio Abella	Fajardo					
Alfredo L. Marquez y Valdivrelso	Guayama					*
Joaquin Sabater	Guayama					
Mariano Duran y Cottes	Gurabo					
Francisco Aguirre y Federico	Hatillo	*				
Rafael Cestero Molina	Juana Diaz	*				*
Jose Barreras	Juncos					
Pascual Vuoni	Lajas					
Francisco Sein	Lares	*				
Valeriano Asenjo	Lares	*				
Juan Garriga	Manati					*
Luis Oms	Maricao	*				
Antonio Jose Amadeo	Maunabo					
Enrique Pina	Mayagüez	*				

(*Continued*)

Table 6. *(Cont.)*

Physician	Municipality	Professional (PR)	Political (PO)	Intellectual (IN)	Scientific (SC)	Involved in Hookworm Campaign
Joaquin Martinez Guasp	Mayagüez					
Jose Maria Munoz	Mayagüez					
Mariano Ramirez	Mayagüez	*				
Nicolas Gimenez Nussa	Mayagüez					
Jose Francisco B. Basora	Mayagüez			*		
Hipolito Aparicio	Naguabo	*				
Francisco Rendon y Camacho	Ponce				*	
Jose Gomez Valencia	Ponce					
Pedro Hernandez Y Santiago	Ponce	*				
Vicente Santoni	Ponce					
Sicinio Vizcarrondo	Rio Grande					
Alfonso Paniagua	Rio Piedras	*				
Luis P. Orcasitas	Rio Piedras	*				
Alejandro Giol Texidor	Salinas					
Victor Gutierrez Ortiz	Salinas	*	*			*
Eleuterio Quinones Cardona	San German	*				
Euripedes Lopez	San German	*				
Aurelio Lassaletta	San Juan	*				
Jose M. Cueto Rodriguez	San Juan	*				
Narcisco Dobal (Doval) Espiet	San Juan	*				
Rafael Velez y Lopez	San Juan	*	*		*	
Miguel Rodriquez Cancio	San Sebastian	*				
Jose Angel Franco Soto	San Sebatian			*		*
Antonio Estruch y Martinez	Sanitary Physician, Guayanilla					

Table 6. (*Cont.*)

Physician	Municipality	Professional (PR)	Political (PO)	Intellectual (IN)	Scientific (SC)	Involved in Hookworm Campaign
Luis Garcia Paredes	Santa Isabel					
Jesus Maria Amadeo y Antomarchi	Toa Alta				*	
Jose Reguero Feliu	Toa Baja	*				
Adrian Cueto y Rodriguez	Utuado		*			
Julio R. Audinot	Utuado					
Jose H. Amadeo	Vega Baja	*	*			*
Guillermo Carreras y Iglesias	Vieques	*				*
Henry Reading Heydecker	Vieques					
Antonio Dapena	Yabucoa					
Jose Dausa (Daussa Y Castro)	Yabucoa					
Julio Atilio Gaztambide	Yauco			*		*
Rafael P. (A.) Gatell (y Garcia de Quevedo)	Yauco	*		*		*

[1] (Data abstracted from McLeary, 1901).

The difficulties in securing trained physicians to serve in municipal governments meant that although many had political status, they lacked professional legitimacy. Two factors contributed to this paradox. First, because the Spanish Governor controlled appointments to municipal government posts, and therefore those of municipal physicians, at least some of these appointments were politically influenced. Second, the circumstances surrounding municipal physicians' qualifications, training and appointments meant that their work was often criticized for being politically corrupt and not responding to municipal residents' demands.

These criticisms were rooted in the relationship between physicians and municipal governments.

Municipal physicians had an ambivalent position and mediated multiple and competing demands by residents and the colonial state. Municipal physicians conducted sanitation investigations, performed autopsies and testified in court cases as forensic experts, which embedded them in the colonial administration. They were also responsible for providing medical attention to the poor who were identified through lists the mayor gave them or by using their own discretion. Where a mayor had not appointed a physician, under Spanish law, other physicians were obligated to provide care. A municipal appointment increased the likelihood a physician would be paid for these services. At the same time, a municipal physician could charge patients who were not considered poor. Although a municipal appointment was probably not a particularly attractive option for many elite physicians, other rank-and-file practitioners who had completed their medical education probably saw municipal appointments as a way to expand their client-base. For instance, in Figure 8, Dr. Adolfo Marti prominently advertises both his medical services and his position

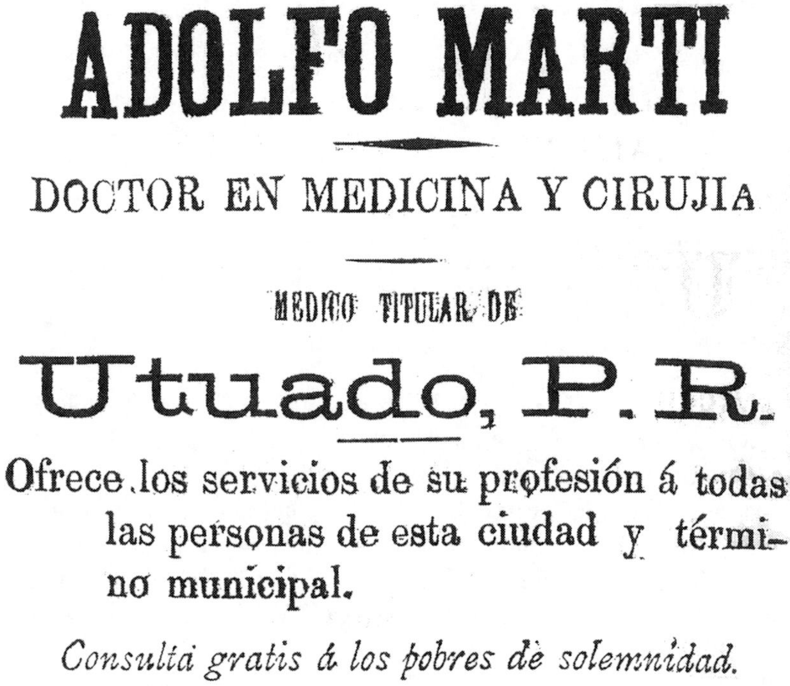

ADOLFO MARTI

DOCTOR EN MEDICINA Y CIRUJIA

MEDICO TITULAR DE

Utuado, P. R.

Ofrece los servicios de su profesión á todas las personas de esta ciudad y término municipal.

Consulta gratis á los pobres de solemnidad.

Figure 8. Advertisement: Municipal Physician. (Morel Campos, 1896).

as a municipal physician (*medico titular*) who offers free consultations to the poor.

Despite the benefits, municipal physicians most often resented the multiple demands of the position and the lack of remuneration. They were paid the "wages of a dock laborer" and they were often paid late, if at all (Hernandez in Allen, 1901: 338). Their work was subordinated to Spanish colonial government, which undermined their autonomy. In particular, municipal physicians resented Spain's control over appointments for several reasons. First, they saw mayors not only as political instruments, but also authoritarian instruments. Municipal physicians believed that mayors turned their work into instruments of capricious whims, thereby undermining their ability to protect the public's health. Second, because Spain controlled municipal appointments, including those of physicians, they believed Spain undermined their professional authority. Third, physicians felt that Spanish control over municipal physician appointments undermined their professional legitimacy because the appointments were politically motivated and included at least some *curiosos*. Finally, physicians resented municipal governments' control over their work because they saw its demands as unreasonable. They insisted that they were general practitioners and resented the expansion of their work to forensic medicine, particularly because municipalities often failed to reimburse physicians for performing autopsies or for traveling to court proceedings. They were poorly paid by municipal governments and argued that they had to pay out of their own pockets to practice medicine. As a result, municipal physicians described the conditions of their service under the Spanish government as deplorable.

A major goal for physicians' professional autonomy was administrative autonomy from municipal governments. The law that required physicians to provide medical attention to the poor meant physicians could not control their work. The lack of a concerted effort to enforce this law indicated not only the lack of medical attention for the poor, but also problems with physicians' ability to represent themselves as having a collective orientation. Municipal appointments undermined physicians' broader professional legitimacy and status. Physicians' inability to control appointments also limited their ability to wage their status claims with many other rank-and-file members. Elite physicians envied mayors' ability to appoint municipal physicians because it represented a form of autonomy from colonial authorities and within municipal governments. At a minimum, all physicians shared an interest in securing their salaries at levels that reflected their training and sacrifice.

Licensing and State Control Under Spanish Colonial Authority

To exert control over the highly heterogeneous collection of physicians that practiced on the island, Spain created a governmental body, the *Real Subdelegación de Medicina,* in 1841. Its primary role was to organize municipal physicians and to implement various regulations, including obligating mayors to forward copies of all the degrees of practitioners practicing within their municipalities. It also attempted to develop regulations to license medical practitioners; these were unsuccessful for several reasons. First, those who worked autonomously from the government had greater flexibility in their practice and could therefore escape governmental regulations. Second, the *Real* could not successfully regulate the amorphous groups of medical practitioners whose practices overlapped. For instance, Spain had also created a *Real Subdelegación de Farmacia* in 1839 to regulate pharmacists' practice by requiring physicians' prescriptions to prepare and dispense medicine. Pharmacists nonetheless continued to dispense medicine directly and they used compounds and performed procedures the *Real* declared illegal (Quevedo Báez, 1946: 407). Third, demands for medical attention, which could not be met by the number of existing physicians, undermined Spanish legislation making particular practitioners and their practices illegal. Although Spanish legislation made *curanderos'* practice of medicine illegal, for instance, it made exceptions. Spanish law gave many *curanderos* legal permission to work as physicians' assistants performing small operations, "*sangrías, ventosas, sanguijuelas,* etc." (bloodletting, cupping, leeching, etc.) during the cholera epidemic in 1855 (Quevedo Báez, 1946: 406). Finally, because many of these practitioners occupied distinct niches in the market, competition between them was limited.

For their part, elite physicians were more concerned about expanding opportunities for medical education on the island than they were about reducing the presence of *curanderos* in rural areas. Although they were very concerned about fraudulent medical practices, controlling medical practitioners was not a priority. Their medical practices also varied as much as those of *curanderos.* Puerto Rican medicine experienced dramatic growth in the second half of the nineteenth century, however, which made academically-trained practitioners increasingly uncomfortable with the overlap between their work and that of the *curanderos.* Trained physicians argued that *curanderos* used irrational methods and represented a threat to the public's health. They insisted that *curanderos* were lazy witch doctors who, rather than work, cheated the innocent and sick poor.

Among his personal papers of 1895, for instance, a local physician related the story of a well-known *curandero* who relied on an assistant to diagnose the "waters" (urine) of the patient (López Giménez, 1998). This is a common practice even by current standards, but in the late-nineteenth century, trained physicians sought to establish the authority of their clinical observations. In the local physician's narrative, the *curandero's* assistant interviewed patients regarding their symptoms, medications they had taken, etc. Meanwhile, the *curandero* listened through the wall of an adjoining room. When the interview was concluded, the *curandero* would go out the back door, come around through the front entrance, study the patient's waters and recite everything he had heard "in academic tones." Privileging his own authentic academic practice in his narrative, the academically-trained local physician ridiculed the *curandero* as a fraud, a quack. The physician explained the *curandero* would charge the patient for developing a potion that would allegedly cure the malady, but the potion was a vermifuge (medicine for the expulsion of intestinal worms) mixed with rum and water, and, at times, dog feces, cricket legs or cockroaches (López Giménez, 1998: 179–182).[5] This narrative was [un/intentionally] ironic. At a time when the efficacy of medical treatment was largely limited to antiseptics and anesthesia, his narrative indicated other practitioners commonly used vermifuges and nutritional supplements. Unlike many other medications, vermifuges were innovative treatments that are now alternately called antihelmintic medications. Their use would gain international credibility in treating hookworm infection in the years that followed, including through their popularization by the hookworm campaign in Puerto Rico. In other words, Lopez Giménez' narrative suggests the hookworm campaign's medical treatment may not have been so novel for many practitioners and their patients after all. Instead, the packaging of the medication changed and the clinical setting distinguished the new hookworm campaign's practitioners.

Elite Physicians' Ideas about their Imagined Community (the Nation)

Medical practitioners lacked a collective identity at the end of the nineteenth century, but academically-trained physicians had established

---

[5] This narrative indicates that Spain and the medical profession were unable to regulate the sale of medications whose contents were unknown. Also known as the golden age of patent medications, this problem was shared in the United States (Tomes, 2001).

clearly articulated political and intellectual positions in relation to Spanish colonialism. During the last two decades of the nineteenth century, physicians' collective identity was closely related to their class position. Although they were professionals, many physicians identified with other Puerto Rican elites who strove to reform their long-standing status as colonial subjects. Within their struggle for greater political autonomy, physicians became notable actors because their education afforded them greater social status and access to political networks and activities. For instance, many elite physicians, such as Drs. Francisco del Valle y Atiles, Manuel Zeno Gandia, and Cayetano Coll y Toste, strongly influenced other reformist elites through their literary and historical writings. Other physicians cultivated intellectual influence by publishing, editing or providing written contributions in many of the island's newspapers.

Physicians shaped important features of the political elite. For instance, some physicians, like Drs. José Gómez Brioso and Santiago Veve y Calzada, distinguished themselves through their work within the Autonomist Party. Dr. Celso Barbosa led a faction of Autonomists and refused to negotiate the terms of political autonomy through pacts with established political parties in Spain. Other physicians demanded more radical political reforms as exiles. For instance, Dr. Ramón Emeterio Betances represented a separatist strain of the political elite. He led political mobilizations surrounding the 1868 *Grito de Lares* rebellion, which almost gained autonomy for Puerto Rico as a concession from the Spanish colonial state. Exiled in New York, Drs. José Julio Henna and Jose Francisco B. Basora advocated the island's independence through the Cuban Revolutionary Party.

Liberal-elite physicians' political involvements were rooted in an attempt to mediate Spain's tumultuous transition to a modern state by localizing political control within the colony. They considered colonialism antithetical to their own economic, political, and professional autonomy. For example, they argued that, "to stay far from that struggle was an indignity for those who considered that politics was a *science* for the men of good faith" (Pedreira 1937:39). They construed political involvements as both professional and patriotic duties. They defined their healing mission broadly and considered themselves social servants whose responsibilities included promoting Puerto Ricans' "moral and material" interests, which they associated with education, cultural development and economic progress. They caucused secretly with other elites to strategize against Spanish colonialism and exercised political influence within these meetings.

A notable example of these secret caucuses within Puerto Rico involved Dr. Félix Tió y Malaret and the subversive society known as *La Torre del Viejo*, or *secos* [born in Puerto Rico, *criollos*] *y mojados* [peninsular Spaniards in Puerto Rico]. Through his attendance at the Ponce Assembly of the Autonomist Party in 1887, Tió y Malaret learned of and joined the society. Written communications were expressly forbidden by the society and he was sworn to secrecy by its members, but well after the change in sovereignty, Tió y Malaret wrote about its meetings and repression by the Spanish colonial government. He explained the society's objective was to promote a boycott against peninsular Spaniards that would force *mojados* to leave the country or concede their exclusive control over business and commerce. The relationship between politics and medicine was also reflected in his ideas about modernization as it was defined by his contemporaries: he developed the island's first civil (secular) cemetery and lectured on medicine's potential ability to cure criminality (Jiménez Malaret, 1985).

Liberal-elite physicians used their education to position themselves as a vanguard within the autonomist movement, but this education also made their vision of broad social reform more radical than that of many other liberal reformists.[6] Impelled by late-nineteenth-century scientific advances, many believed they could use their education to organize Puerto Rico along scientific principles and cure social ills (Martinez-Vergne 1999). For these physicians, eradicating social ills meant defending society against broader moral decay that included alcoholism, masturbation, suicide, homicide, and robbery. They used the concept of disease to articulate what they saw as the consequences of colonialism and believed that, by reforming the political environment, they could eradicate illness and regenerate Puerto Ricans as modern and productive citizens fit for equality with their Spanish counterparts. In guiding Puerto Rican society's regeneration, physicians saw themselves as playing a central role within a broader social transformation.

As liberal-elite physicians struggled for political reforms, they not only generalized their own interests to all Puerto Ricans, but they also promoted their vision of modernization. For instance, beginning in the 1870s,

---

[6] Liberal-elite physicians were mobilized by their educational experiences in revolutionary and Restoration Spain, where there was an "overwhelming sense that a society is being rapidly constructed, consciously and from scratch, in all its institutions, and that simultaneous participation in many cultural orders is vital in this project" (Ríos-Font, 2005: 341).

physicians like Drs. Francisco Hernandez Baralt, Manuel Alonso Pacheco, and Francisco R. de Goenaga Olza, pushed for institutional reforms in what was then called the insane asylum (*Casa De Beneficencia*). The asylum represented a site where both physicians and the Spanish colonial state promoted modernity in Puerto Rico. Physicians sought to modernize the asylum by introducing changes, such as administrative shifts that classified and separated patients, including women, children, and the poor. Physicians used their local autonomy and status to "finish the asylum, organizing it under scientific principles, to offer a hope of healing the unfortunate that inhabit it" (Quevedo Báez, 1946: 474). In urban areas like San Juan, liberal-elite physicians' discourse reflected their desire to control modern institutions, stratify urban social boundaries, distance themselves from elements within it they saw as threatening, and place themselves at the top of a social hierarchy (Martinez-Vergne, 1999). For this group of physicians, eradicating illness was a metaphor for how they viewed their attempts to cure Puerto Rico's lack of modernization.

Independence movements in Cuba and Santo Domingo left a weakening Spanish empire increasingly concerned about separatist activities in Puerto Rico. Puerto Rican physicians saw Spanish attempts to monitor and prevent their assembly as an obstacle to developing science. For example, Ferrer and Baralt's brief attempt to train practitioners in anatomical dissection at a cemetery was considered illegal and interrupted by a judge, which represented the influence of Spanish government on the profession. Physicians viewed governmental interference with medical education and Spanish colonialism, in general, as obstacles to progress.

Ideas about the Nation: From Spanish to U.S. Colonization

Puerto Rican physicians had profound, but conflicted ideas about the nation and state power. Their work was directly influenced by Spanish colonialism, which controlled medical licensing and the local organization of medicine vis à vis municipal physicians. Their inability to control their work, i.e., their lack of professional autonomy, compelled many Puerto Rican physicians to oppose Spanish colonial authority. Physicians projected their concerns onto the nation. They saw the professional as political, defined their healing mission broadly, and treated political activity as part of their work. In the late-nineteenth century, many physicians had secretly met with other members of the liberal elite to strategize against Spanish colonialism; their advocacy for greater political autonomy contributed to the development of the Autonomic Charter of 1897.

Despite gaining political autonomy under Spain, many physicians joined other elites in welcoming the U.S. military's arrival in Puerto Rico in 1898. They shared a widespread belief that U.S. intervention would eradicate colonialism, foster democratic liberalism and promote their vision of the island's modernization and progress. Physicians responded positively to a U.S. President-commissioned survey of conditions on the island in 1899 and complained about Spanish colonialism to Henry Carroll, the report's author. Although they joined a broad cross-section of Puerto Ricans who also responded to Carroll's interviews, physicians seemed confident that their ideas for reform would be crucial to planning Puerto Rico's future development and that U.S. intervention would bring about the modernizing reforms they had envisioned for medicine.

Puerto Rican physicians' initial enthusiasm quickly dissipated. Their status was undermined by the U.S. colonial government and its representatives in several ways. They began competing for legitimacy with U.S. physicians who came to the island. They found themselves almost immediately marginalized in decisions regarding the compulsory smallpox campaign. Their authority was usurped by U.S. military officers who worked directly with municipal mayors to organize the campaign. Their competence was undermined even though they had performed smallpox vaccinations throughout the nineteenth century (Arana-Soto, 1974; Rigau-Perez, 1989). Their work in the campaign was selectively appropriated by U.S. military officers who did not give physicians' credit, but instead believed the near-impossible administrative task was made possible only through military agency (Gillett, 1995). Meanwhile, they were drawn into unpopular work by compulsory smallpox campaign. Puerto Rican physicians were also derided for what was essentially a structural problem: the lack of medical attention on the island. They were blamed by U.S. colonial administrators for being self-interested and, therefore, undeserving of professional status.

The U.S. colonial administration imposed its vision for physicians' roles onto Puerto Rican medicine. U.S. colonial administrators insisted that a professional, specifically a physician, should perform a single specialized task and serve the public without personal interest. Although Puerto Rican physicians shared this vision and they certainly saw themselves as "men of good will" who promoted Puerto Ricans' interests, U.S. colonial administrators persistently reinterpreted and denigrated native physician's political involvements as self-serving attempts to gain power

(Negrón-Portillo, 1990: 31). As with reformers in the United States, U.S. colonial administrators reproduced the dichotomy between politics and public administration as "a strategic tool for bringing about fundamental change in the nation's political leadership" (Rosenbloom, 2008: 58). Within the new bureaucracy, U.S. colonial administrators set up an all-or-nothing proposition for medicine and political involvements.

Physicians' disappointment with the U.S. military government coincided with other threats to their market position and professional status that followed in the wake of the San Ciriaco hurricane of 1899. Their market of wealthy and middle-class patients were destabilized by the subsequent economic crisis because many patients were unable to pay physicians' fees and turned to alternative practitioners who charged less. Physicians who had completed a formal medical education at considerable expense now found their competition increased with a heterogeneous group of medical practitioners who migrated to urban areas in search of work. These developments increased trained physicians' sense of competition and they increasingly viewed alternative medical practitioners as a threat.

Here the story of Puerto Rican physicians took a decidedly distinct turn. The rest of this chapter relates these fundamental shifts by explaining two important changes that occurred within the medical community. One of the changes implicated all Puerto Rican physicians on the island. The question of professional status hinged on physicians' relation to the state, which was reflected through both licensing and municipal physicians' uncomfortable negotiation with local governments and the U.S. colonial administration. These changes involved native physicians in the work of developing a separate medical association that fostered important debates about medical training and professionals' involvement in formal electoral politics. The *Asociacion Medica de Puerto Rico* (AMPR) eventually reconciled itself with incorporating into the American Medical Association (AMA). Another set of changes focused on a related problem: professional presentation. As formally-trained physicians developed a strategy for recovering their reputations, three physicians were of significant consequence. Drs. Luis Aguerrevere, Pedro Gutiérrez Igaravídez and Agustín Stahl y Stamm reflected many important factions within an embattled medical community. They illustrate the shifting meanings of professional status under U.S. colonization. I now turn to a discussion of these changes in turn: one explicitly involving the public health administration and the other implicitly intending to mediate the effects of a stigma and spoiled status identity (Goffman, 1963).

Licensing and State Control Under U.S. Colonial Authority

Not only did Puerto Rican physicians face increasing competition from alternative practitioners after the 1899 hurricane, but they also faced a new threat in the form of licensing. In both the Spanish and the U.S. colonial contexts, the colonial administrations controlled the profession's regulatory functions and licensing remained outside of Puerto Rican physicians' control. Elite physicians were re-established as colonial subjects under the U.S. military government that reorganized and renamed the *Real Subdelegación de Medicina* as the Superior Board of Health (SBOH) in 1899. The only Puerto Rican members of the SBOH, Drs. Gabriel Ferrer and Ricardo Hernandez, were appointed and subject to the U.S. colonial administration. Seeking a greater degree of control over regulating medical practice, the SBOH introduced a new system of licensing medical practitioners in 1900. For U.S. colonial administrators and the elite physicians of the SBOH, licensing was a way of controlling the "quackery of every conceivable sort" that flourished as a "natural consequence" of the medical profession's lack of institutional development and the low salaries paid to municipal physicians (Hernandez in Allen, 1901: 338). Hernandez considered quackery a traditional and endemic problem that could be resolved by the administration. He distinguished an elite market of patients who relied on licensed physicians from a popular market of "ignorant people" driven by "prejudices, customs or superstitions" who relied on a variety of practitioners (Hernandez in Allen, 1901: 338).[7] In this way, he reproduced a discourse about the poor to advocate political positions. Despite Hernandez' purported concern for public health, however, other prominent physicians considered his administrative decisions politically motivated and arbitrary because they undermined the same SBOH regulations he authored (Aguerrevere, 1908).

Physicians' ability to control licensing and regulate access to the practice of medicine is generally considered a critical step toward gaining professional autonomy from state regulation (Abbott, 1988; Friedson, 1970; Starr, 1982). In this colonial context, however, licensing remained outside

---

[7] "Most of the blindness is produced by maltreatment of new-born [sic] infants by quacks of both sexes whose ignorance is total, but whose influence over the equally ignorant people is surprising. For this state of things it is hopeless to expect a remedy except that of education, and we all know how difficult it is to eradicate prejudices, customs or superstitions that have the sanction of generations at their back" (Hernandez in Allen, 1901: 338).

of Puerto Ricans' control and was in the hands of a colonial administration. U.S. colonial policies were imposed by the SBOH and represented new standards and norms for licensing exams. The first licensing exam, for instance, was modeled on the one in use at New York State University (Hoff, 1901). The SBOH "tolerated" some existing medical licenses, but many physicians who had not obtained a license under the Spanish colonial state faced new regulations along arbitrary standards developed by a small, elite and insulated board of colonial officers and, later, physicians affiliated with the SBOH.[8] Rather than increasing the power of the medical profession, licensing undermined the autonomy of Puerto Rican physicians and placed them under U.S. bureaucratic control. For Puerto Rican physicians, SBOH control over licensing meant they still lacked the power to control access to the profession.

Elite physicians also felt U.S. control over licensing undermined the value of their medical knowledge. They considered the medical qualifications of U.S.-trained physicians inferior to the ones they obtained in Spain and knew there was still little basis for discriminating against their competence. In the United States, for instance, medical education would not be standardized until after the 1910 Flexner Report and many schools were considered degree mills where a title could be purchased rather than earned (Starr 1984). In contrast, many elite physicians, including Drs. Cayetano Coll y Toste, Manuel Guzmán Rodríguez, Pedro Malaret Yordan, Pedro Gutiérrez Igaravídez and Isaac Gonzalez Martinez, received their medical degrees from the University of Barcelona where Dr. Santiago Ramón y Cajal would win the Nobel Prize in 1906 for his work in neurology. Physicians' frustration intensified because neither the SBOH nor the U.S. colonial government made any provisions for helping Puerto Rican physicians meet new licensing requirements: there were no immediate plans to set up a medical school in Puerto Rico.[9] Puerto Rican physicians like Dr. Quevedo Báez, a co-founding member of the AMPR, viewed SBOH attempts to control the medical profession as an affront because it

---

[8] The SBOH used the policy of "toleration...[for] those who had a diploma or other equal evidence of attainment granted by a teaching body, but who had failed to obtain a license for the Spanish Government in Porto Rico", but evaluated new licenses on a case-by-case basis and retained complete authority over evaluating acceptable educational attainment. For instance, the SBOH did not accept Dr. J.K. Konek's licensing examination results from Costa Rica (Davis, 1900: 501).

[9] The House of Delegates made some limited scholarships available to help students study medicine in the mainland United States, which would eventually benefit future physicians like Jose S. Belaval and Octavio Jordan who studied at Jefferson Medical College in Philadelphia.

imposed a "foreign culture, language, and standard of work" that pushed the profession into a "hybrid process...[of] inevitable and fatal crisis... where a conqueror of race, language, laws, customs, and banner constrained...invaded...strikes and implants...all official channels of new and regulated activities" (Quevedo Báez, 1949: 6). Elite physicians began to consider themselves a class whose material interests were eroded by the U.S. colonial administration.

Municipal Physicians and U.S. State Competition: The Public Health Administration

Although physicians were disappointed by the initial changes following the change of sovereignty and the hurricane, the erosion of their professional status was more definitively evident when the 1900 Foraker Act created a civil government structure that seemed to ignore the public health administration. They had hoped an end to the U.S. military occupation would mean a resumption of their recent political victory: elite physicians believed political autonomy could protect their professional status, but the Foraker Act made it plainly evident that Puerto Rico's status was subordinated to U.S. tutelage. Four elite physicians gained formal political positions within the insular administration, but they were subordinated to U.S. colonial administrators and did not control the civil government.[10] Their hopes that the smallpox campaign and improvements in sanitation through new regulations could eventually result in positive developments for their professional autonomy, quickly dissipated when these administrative changes ignored elite physicians' professional authority. They found that U.S. colonial administrators considered their training inadequate and their medical explanations unscientific. Puerto Rican physicians were increasingly alarmed they would not have a significant role in leading medicine's growth because U.S. colonial administrators considered them incompetent and corrupt. They were ridiculed by U.S. colonial administrators for ignoring the health of the island's poor (see, for instance, Ashford's characterization of Stahl in 1934:54–55). Their identity as uniquely-qualified leaders was undermined by a U.S. colonial state that did not distinguish them from other, less qualified, medical practitioners.

---

[10] These physicians included Drs. Gabriel Ferrer Hernandez (died in 1900), Jose Celso Barbosa Alcala, José Gomez Brioso, Manuel Zeno Gandia, and Santiago Veve Calzada.

The local organization of medical care through municipal governments represented an early form of the public health administration on the island. Under the U.S. colonial administration, municipal physicians continued to support the state's need for forensic evidence and testimony, to improve local sanitation, inspect food and provide medical attention to the poor. They were implicated in Carroll's 1899 report that identified three problems surrounding municipal government. First, the report cast municipal appointments under the Spanish Governor as arbitrary. Second, despite legal provisions and municipal appropriations for charitable work (medical attention to the poor), the report noted that many distrusted "town doctors...[who] would not visit the sick poor without pay" (Carroll, 1899: 33). Although physicians saw both problems as a result of their subordination to local government, the report ignored their fundamental concerns about being overworked and underpaid...when they were paid at all. Instead, U.S. colonial administrators used the report to implement policies that further eroded municipal government's ability to control their already severely burdened budgets. U.S. colonial administrators held elite and municipal physicians equally responsible for public criticism and both were summarily dismissed as self-serving and irresponsible practitioners.

The third problem the report addressed, of sanitation in urban areas, had already become an important concern and activity. Carroll found it "a matter of wonder" that Puerto Ricans were reasonably health despite their "general disregard, hitherto, of the primary principles of sanitation" (1899: 10). The U.S. colonial administration's interest in promoting American ideals of sanitation was tied to protecting soldiers' health, promoting infrastructural and institutional development that supported U.S. capital investments, ordering urban space and monitoring interactions within urban areas (Carrion 1983; Negron de Montilla 1975).[11] These ideals were imposed and few Puerto Rican physicians participated in developing the regulations developed by the Superior Board of Health (SBOH); however, the costs and responsibility of sanitation work were ultimately thrust

---

[11] The experience of a typhoid epidemic during the Spanish-American War demonstrated the importance of sanitation to U.S. military officers (Cirillo 2000). Rates of soldiers with VD in Puerto Rico were 467.8 per thousand in 1898, while on the mainland, the 1897 rate was 84.59 per thousand (Garver and Fincher, 1945). Station logs demonstrated U.S. administrators' concerns over soldiers' health, which centered on sexually-transmitted diseases and waste from buildings surrounding military barracks (National Archives Record Group 94 Entry 547). Sanitation was also important to the development of education to support the consolidation of U.S. colonial rule (Montilla, 1975).

on municipal physicians and municipal governments' already beleaguered budgets.

Sanitation provided a means for U.S. colonial administrators to introduce themselves into the native bourgeoisie's pre-existing interest in establishing and policing urban social boundaries. U.S. colonial administrators envisioned themselves as providing object lessons in sanitation and more broadly developing good government on the island. These lessons in self-government took on an increasingly individualized character and municipal physicians were enlisted in the effort to reform medical attention for the poor. This enlistment had mixed results, but not because Puerto Rican physicians were self-interested. As with all social groups, Puerto Rican physicians agonized about their place in the social hierarchy under U.S. colonial authority and did the best they could at negotiating a more comfortable social location. Ultimately, many Puerto Rican physicians could not be enlisted in medical attention for the poor because they were overburdened with multiple and competing demands. Informed by a variety of U.S.-appointed commissioners and other colonial authorities, the insular administration imposed an ever increasing array of regulations onto municipal work, but kept salaries low and subsequently capped them in 1902 as part of a persistent effort to further erode municipal government authority.

Rather than authors of modernization, elite physicians were reduced to respondents within a report that reproduced physicians' subservience to state-directed work. The U.S. military restructured the SBOH, centralizing control over new sanitation regulations, but the latter had trouble enforcing unpopular sanitary laws. Instead of addressing elite physicians' vision of modernization, which included developing municipal physicians' autonomy, the 1900 Foraker Act left the administration of public health in the hands of municipal governments. Elite physicians were inculpated in the failures of SBOH centralization. U.S. colonial administrators, who argued that U.S. tutelage would build Puerto Ricans' self-reliant character, summarily ignored elite physicians' desire for professional autonomy. Instead, U.S. Governor William Henry Hunt insisted "the habit of dependence upon the central government is yet deeply seated in the character of the people" (1902: 57). Aligned with the general premise that local governments were politically immature and not ready for the responsibilities of self-government, the laws passed in 1902 further reduced municipal autonomy on sanitary matters and were justified by U.S. colonial authorities based on the premise that municipal physicians had been found "without adequate experience in such matters"

(Rowe, 1901: 236). The law continued the trend of increasing the less-for-mally trained municipal physicians' responsibilities, which implied a gen-eral erosion of physicians' status. The law passed in March 1902 was the final impetus for the creation of Puerto Rico's independent medical society.

Under the military government, Governor General Davis claimed greater awareness of the "general customs and habits of the people" and denied measures the SBOH proposed (1900: 149). Under the civil govern-ment, U.S. colonial administrators continued to use the SBOH to pro-mote their authority. The SBOH usurped the power of local health boards and limited the influence of local governments, municipal physicians and their sanitation officers, and it selectively enforced sanitation regula-tions (Agueverre, 1908). The SBOH also overstepped its authority and overturned municipal physicians' appointments despite laws conceding this authority to municipal mayors. For instance, the mayor of Ponce questioned why Secretary Charles Hartzell reinstated Dr. Pedro Hernandez as the municipal physician despite the latter's negligence in his duties. Mayor Arias recognized the insular SBOH favored Dr. Pedro Hernandez, but was puzzled about why Hartzell mentioned Dr. Aguerrevere and rejected his [Aguerreve's] appointment (Arias in Aguerrevere, 1908:6).[12] In response, Hartzell clarified it was not only indiscreet of Aguerrevere to criticize the SBOH director, but also prohibited for a person "with a pub-lic charge," i.e., a government-appointed position, to express his opinion about official matters related to the government through the press or even in private communication (in Agueverre, 1908: 11). Hartzell indicated how U.S. colonial administrators worked to silence the most active elements of

---

[12] Criticisms of R. Hernandez may have been shared as there are scant references to him in historical documents and even these are predominantly confined to his signed reports to the governor. As a prominent figure in early sanitation efforts on the island, this silence is deafening. In contrast, there is a much longer history documenting Aguerrevere's work in sanitation, as Director of the prominent Tricoche Hospital in Ponce, and in sup-port of the 1902–1903 hookworm survey. Aguerrevere was part of the assembly forming the Autonomist Party and he collaborated with other politically-active dissident physi-cians, including Dr. Rafael Pujols (Arana-Soto, 1963: 262). In Aguerrevere's estimation, R. Hernandez was overpaid and incompetent. Hartzell suggested Aguerrevere's conflicts with R. Hernandez were motivated by religion and called the former an "enraged catholic" (in Agueverre, 1908:11). In correspondence with Hartzell, Arias insisted Aguerrevere's reli-gion did not influence his work and should not influence how he was evaluated (Arias in Agueverre, 1908:6). A little over a year after the exchange, Hartzell resigned in order to take on another position representing the insular government in legal disputes over church lands valued at $3,000,000 (New York Times 1904).

a group who sought to develop a collective identity as a professional class of politically-active physicians. Through the SBOH, the U.S. colonial administration used public institutions financed by the insular treasury to control the most stable source of income for physicians: municipal appointments.

U.S. colonial administrators gave municipalities' administrative autonomy in 1898 but established the SBOH to maintain legislative control over their public health-related activities. As such, SBOH's control over licensing was not only an affront to Puerto Rican physicians' sense of professional autonomy but also involved a broader politic that underscored physicians' lack of political legitimacy relative to the U.S. colonial administration. In 1902, two events seemed to be the final threats behind the impetus for Puerto Rican physicians to organize a formal and collective response. These events increased insular power over sanitation and radically undermined municipal control over SBOH legislation enforcement.

The Asociación Médica de Puerto Rico: Nationalism, Class and Labor

The AMPR's early years involved professional struggles to secure a better social location. The AMPR worked to develop a collective identity based on shared interests surrounding compensation, controlling their work (professional autonomy) and monopolizing the market of patients. The AMPR also had to cultivate professional status in relation to the state, which involved a much more difficult negotiation of its jurisdiction over political affairs and physicians' rights to maintain active political involvements. On the one hand, many elite physicians wanted to build on their professional associations to recover the status they enjoyed during the late nineteenth century. On the other hand, this status was eroded relative to the growing influence of U.S. medicine on the island. The AMPR found itself competing with the hookworm campaign over the meaning of professional and scientific presentation and the implications of regional differences among physicians' associations.

As the AMPR's first president, Dr. Manuel Quevedo Báez was a spokesperson for many liberal elite physicians. He received his medical education in Spain (Madrid) and became involved in a variety of medical institutions formed after the AMPR's founding, including the Board of Medical Examiners and the *Academia de Medicina*. He helped establish the AMPR's medical journal, the *Boletín de la Asociación Médica de Puerto*

Rico. He also became involved in the insular administration as a physician to the police commission. In addition to his medical involvements, Quevedo Báez participated in a variety of educational and cultural institutions, including *El Palenque de la Juventud,* the *Ateneo Puertorriqueño,* the University of Puerto Rico, the *Academia Antillana de la Lengua* [Antillean Academy of Language], and the *Instituto Universitario José de Diego* [University Institute of Jose de Diego]. In addition to his broader intellectual influence and position among the elite, Quevedo Baez was clearly well-supported by his peers when he made his presentation before the AMPR's inaugural session in at the *Cámara de Delegados* (House of Delegates) in San Juan. In short, Quevedo Baez reflected the social and political commitments many liberal elite physicians maintained in that period.

The AMPR developed an autonomous identity through a set of ethics that were informed and firmly entrenched within established elites' material conditions. In general, ethics allow a profession to establish a collective identity and promote its status, but unlike other codifications to develop domestic legitimacy, the AMPR's *moral médica* explicitly emphasized physicians' control over markets and their interest in social mobility within a changing colonial context. The invitation sent to physicians for a preparatory meeting construed the profession as a class when the AMPR claimed an interest in protecting "the interests of the class in general" (Quevedo Báez, 1949: 13). Rather than a concern over broad domestic legitimacy, the AMPR encouraged physicians to develop their work at the regional level, winning authority first and confidence later. The purposes for establishing the AMPR, therefore, were not directly related to consolidating physicians' domestic legitimacy. These statements reflected the elite's immediate attempt to gain legitimacy within the U.S. colonial administration, to continue pursuing alternate methods for promoting their economic position beyond the U.S. colonial state, and to revive their status through the profession.

Through Quevedo Báez as their spokesman, the AMPR mourned what he saw as the lamentable state of all physicians who had to haggle for compensation and envied the gains laborers had made within the U.S. colonial administration, industrial societies, and commercial trusts. According to Quevedo Báez, physicians had given in to labor's "strong and agitated muscle" to maintain social harmony, but they had to haggle over compensation for medical services and could not control their work or peer over the summits of their position to "breathe the more beautiful air of a life of greater liberty" (Quevedo Báez, 1949: 22–23). Physicians, he argued, remained a class "enslaved" to society and the political power of others (Quevedo Báez, 1949: 23).

The AMPR based its collective identity on class, but elite physicians' location heavily circumscribed the association's identity and impeded its attempts to mobilize other academically-trained, non-elite physicians as rank-and-file professionals. Unlike the labor party, which supported Puerto Rican statehood, elite physicians did not initially promote the AMPR's affiliation with a U.S.-mainland organization like the American Medical Association (AMA). Instead, elite physicians promoted Puerto Rico's political autonomy in much the same way other nationalist politicians called on all Puerto Ricans to put aside their differences, such as class and political affiliation. Elite physicians presented themselves as advocates of rank-and-file practitioners, generalized their interests to the entire profession, and attempted to revive their social position by mobilizing non-elite practitioners' support for professional autonomy.

Although the AMPR attempted to shape a collective identity based on class, Quevedo Báez ultimately advocated a shared paradigm for medicine. His call for solidarity recognized modern medical practices were not decidedly implanted in Puerto Rico and he argued scientific "routinization" should be uprooted in favor of allowing for new methods of observation. This call demonstrated the AMPR's support of bacteriology, but implied it accepted a variety of medical practitioners on the island. Despite this appeal, membership rolls were dominated by allopathic physicians. Quevedo Báez encouraged physicians to set aside alternative paradigms and develop the "medical personality" and "moral condition of their professional class" through solidarity with one another, trusting in the AMPR to guarantee each individual's scientific character (1949: 23). In his inaugural address, Quevedo Báez related Ashford's findings in the context of support for bacteriological research and argued, "in a good clinic," physicians had to explore beyond what the eye made observable and use the microscope to observe not only the manifestation but also the cause of disease (1949: 25). He believed bacteriology would "erase past errors" (Quevedo Báez, 1949: 25).

Intra-professional conflicts were not marked at the time the AMPR was established, but AMPR physicians were alienated from the rank-and-file members of the profession. Their alienation undermined their influence within the colonial government. AMPR-affiliated physicians tied physicians' general alienation from one another to medicine's subservience within municipal politics and seized upon the problem as a focus of mobilization. This strategy reflected several considerations. First, the administration of public health was organized at the municipal level and remained physicians' only legitimate and uncontested link to political power. Second, the lack of trained physicians on the island gave them some degree of immunity from political patronage. Third, elite physicians still did not control municipal appointments, which continued to threaten their professional status.

AMPR physicians turned municipal physicians' location within municipal governments into an opportunity for gaining status and influence under U.S. colonial authority. In his inaugural address at the AMPR's first assembly in December 1903, Quevedo Báez identified the most significant problems facing municipal physicians: their work was subordinated to political influences, they struggled for compensation, and they lacked status. Speaking from a different structural location, their arguments reinterpreted those of the U.S. colonial administration. They blamed the condition of public health in municipalities on municipal governments. He mourned the position of any physician who remained "an instrument of all political egoisms" (Quevedo Báez, 1949: 22). The AMPR insisted municipal control over the public health impeded municipal physicians' work and ability to enforce sanitation regulations. Quevedo Báez argued that "a *majority* of the time, [municipal physicians] disobeyed orders that implied a great social benefit because of mayors' imposition" (Quevedo Báez, 1949: 53–54; emphasis mine).

AMPR physicians wanted to centralize public health, but gain control over its administration. In this way, AMPR physicians could develop their ability to negotiate U.S. colonial policies that influenced the administration of public health and medicine. Physicians inverted the U.S. colonial administrations' discourse on centralized control and administrative and bureaucratic efficiency. Much in the same way the Foraker Act centralized political control under the U.S. colonial administration, physicians sought to gain greater control over municipal physicians' appointments. They argued that, as physicians, they were uniquely qualified to direct the work of public health and its administration. AMPR physicians transformed U.S. colonial discourse about the hazards of political patronage as impediments to medical progress. They dissociated municipal politics from its associates' explicit political involvements. The AMPR's physicians hoped to gain independence from local and colonial government and redirect their political participation from a privileged space of professional sovereignty. Despite its efforts, by the time Quevedo Báez wrote his book on the history of medicine and surgery in Puerto Rico, he noted that municipal physicians' "abstruse and misunderstood problem" persisted as late as 1948 and continued to make the medical profession suffer (Quevedo Báez, 1949: 67).

Much in the same way the Foraker Act centralized political control under the U.S. colonial administration, AMPR physicians sought to gain greater control over municipal physicians' appointments and develop their ability to negotiate U.S. colonial policies that influenced the administration of public health and medicine. AMPR physicians transformed the U.S. colonial discourse about the hazards of political patronage as impediments to medical progress by dissociating municipal politics from its associates' explicit political involvements. The only debate at the AMPR's inaugural session involved the association's jurisdiction over political affairs and its associates' rights to maintain active local and regional political involvements. Although AMPR physicians agreed to maintain the association's jurisdiction, the debate on individual physician's rights "motivated a long discussion" and involved the majority of the meeting's attendees (Quevedo Báez, 1949: 17). This debate put Drs. Jose Esteban Saldaña and Narcisco Dobal (Doval) Espiet, who favored protecting these rights, at odds with the majority that included Drs. Quevedo Báez, Ramon Ruiz Arnau, Francisco Sein, Jesus Maria Amadeo, Jose Carbonell and Rafael Velez y Lopez. Drs. Saldaña and Dobal were unlike the majority in other ways: the former completed his medical degree in Brussels and would affiliate with the Unionist Party, and the latter was a municipal physician. Ultimately, Saldaña and Dobal succeeded in convincing the attendees to protect physician's rights to maintain their significance in local or regional politics. In a vote of 9 in favor and 5 against, the AMPR decided to "substitute" (amend) the article. Quevedo Báez also related that Amadeo left the "abandoned the room" after the vote, perhaps in frustration with the vote's outcome.

The AMPR formed at a legislative assembly meeting on September 21, 1902, at a time when more general demands for political autonomy were organized, including a broader political mobilization in defense of the "Puertorrican personality." This mobilization culminated in the development of the politically-dominant Unionist Party in 1904, although all three of the AMPR's initial officers were members of the Republican party.[13] Like many of his peers, however, Quevedo Báez left the Republican Party to support Muñoz Rivera. Many other academically-trained physicians

---

[13] Drs. Jose Carbonell (Secretary-Treasurer) and Rafael Velez y Lopez ("vocal" or member at large) were Republicans (Arana-Soto, 1961).

shared an increasing skepticism about U.S. colonial authority on the island and concurred with the idea that the "Puertorrican personality" was both unique and threatened. For doctors joining the AMPR, this demonstrating this ascribed personality involved tying the broader struggle for greater political autonomy to professional autonomy. The problem for the AMPR was not necessarily one of having a political position in favor of a broad political autonomy for the island as much as it was that physicians had lost political and social influence under U.S. colonial authority. Many AMPR-affiliated physicians saw direct political involvement as a problem in which physicians had lost power. To re-establish their influence and prestige, AMPR physicians pursued strategic support for U.S. colonial policy. As scientists, they hoped to redirect their political participation from a privileged space of professional sovereignty.

The AMPR's heated debates about physicians' political involvement reflected the challenges they faced in the U.S. colonial context. They wanted to centralize public health, but control its administration. The AMPR ultimately inverted the U.S. colonial administrations' discourse on centralized control and administrative and bureaucratic efficiency and argued that, as physicians, they were uniquely qualified to direct the work of public health and its administration. As Quevedo Báez explained, the AMPR wanted to clarify the "scientific and social problems" corresponding to pathology and hygiene, which indicated it sought to recover its influence over politics and society (1949: 16). Although it was debated within the AMPR, the association's support for the SBOH was likely a part of this overall defensive strategy to protect elite physicians' material interests. The association between political involvement and securing its status was evident when Quevedo Báez noted the AMPR's primary objective and purpose was "none other than the defense of the material interests of the class first, performing as many gestures as necessary for this close to official spheres, and later, to study and discover other means that may exist for this defense" (1949: 16). The AMPR created a strictly hierarchical and stratified structure and required every associate commit himself to absolute fidelity, discipline, and observance of statutes which include support of bodies that could one day help the association (Quevedo Báez, 1949).

The AMPR seemed to realize its goal of centralization when the U.S. colonial administration created the insular position of a Director of Health in March 1902, but the official was appointed by the governor and public health remained under the control of municipal governments and local boards of health (Fernós Isern, 1926). The centralization desired by the

AMPR also seemed to materialize when the Board of Medical Examiners took over licensing from the SBOH in 1903, and the Office of Health, Charities and Corrections (the so-called *Consolidado*) was created in 1904; but the AMPR viewed the *Consolidado* as politically biased and doubted the "morality" of the Office's appointments (Asociación Médica de Puerto Rico, 1908: 2). The AMPR blamed the *Consolidado's* ineffectiveness on the lack of enforceable regulations and indispensable personnel (Quevedo Báez, 1949:122). Even as late as 1948, Quevedo Báez continued to lament municipal physicians' "abstruse and misunderstood problem" that continued to make the medical profession suffer (Quevedo Báez, 1949: 67). The problem was not only about Puerto Rican physicians, but also their unsuccessful competition with U.S. colonial administrators, and U.S. medicine, to represent the public interest. As a result, many elite physicians saw their attempts to gain professional status and autonomy from both municipal and colonial-state governments as largely unsuccessful. In contrast to AMPR affiliates' regional associations, the hookworm campaign accomplished a centralized organization that enabled its U.S. directors to control public statements. Ashford's consistent influence on the campaign, and on Gutiérrez Igaravídez, helped to shape the campaign's dominant image and foster favorable public opinion about its work. The campaign also centralized its physicians' work squarely within the U.S. colonial bureaucracy and was subject only to the Governor's authority. Although AMPR-affiliated elite physicians sought to promote their own interests *vis-à-vis* municipal physicians, these interests were not mutually exclusive from those of rank-and-file practitioners. After some physicians' unsuccessful attempt to develop another association in Ponce, in 1905, the only other option open to non-affiliated practitioners was to participate in U.S.-directed changes within the administration of public health and sanitation (Torres-Gómez, 1999).

By 1905, demoralized by the AMPR's inability to gain control over municipal physicians, some elite doctors began to develop their interest in becoming a part of the U.S. medical community. Their participation in the hookworm campaign and their debates about incorporation with the AMA also reflected physicians' competing ideas and persistent efforts to navigate discriminatory U.S. colonial state interventions.[14] In relation to

---

[14] The AMPR referred to its affiliation with the AMA as "incorporation," but the AMA referred to the AMPR as a "constituent assembly." AMPR physicians approached the AMA on the issue of incorporation as early as 1905, after their political losses and before many

the hookworm campaign, the AMPR worked to expand the physicians' role in promoting Puerto Rico's productive efficiency. Quevedo Báez led the AMPR's new emphasis on the hookworm campaign, seeing it as an opportunity to promote scientific development and professional status. By participating in the campaign, he felt AMPR physicians could play a critical role in the social reconstruction of a nation. According to Quevedo Báez, this regeneration would make labor more efficacious and better suited to enjoy liberty. Quevedo Báez encouraged physicians to work toward developing "the people's" energies to feel liberty because "liberty without fruit and efficacy" was like a "luminous radiance painted on the imagination of brains *somnolientos* [sleepy and drowsy] and sick, visionaries of a conquest they would never possess" (1949: 26). He encouraged AMPR physicians to "use science to give [Puerto Rico] better fruits from labor" (1949: 26).

Forgoing elite physicians' original strategy of forming a "medical body with its own personality," the AMPR struggled with the decision to incorporate itself within the AMA (Quevedo Báez, 1949: 12). Debate among its members reached such heights that the AMPR's activities stopped for a period in 1909. To resolve the stand-off, the AMPR held an extraordinary session in Ponce on August 14, 1910, where its President, sociologist-physician Dr. Font y Guillot, seemed to deliver a eulogy, as he called upon all Puerto Rican physicians to unite, "strong and firm," within a single body because they:

> ... had demonstrated [through] bitter and inconsolable experiences that isolated and individually [physicians] could not maintain respect and considerations that physicians deserved, while united [they] will constitute a great social force, perhaps the most intense of the country, [a] force that will be felt in all public bodies. (Quevedo Báez, 1949: 130)

A "great majority of votes" defeated incorporation in August, but incorporation was approved by a 36 to 5 vote margin only four months later in December, 1910 (Quevedo Báez, 1949: 126, 129). The AMPR's radical about-turn reflected elite physicians' attempts to reformulate their political and professional identity. Through incorporation in the AMA, AMPR physicians sacrificed their original strategy of forming a "medical body with its own personality" and chose a political affiliation in favor of the profession (Quevedo Báez, 1949: 12). Although many physicians considered

---

physicians' involvement in the hookworm campaign (Blasingame, 1959; American Medical Association, 1905).

themselves outside the U.S. government in political, ethnic, and professional terms, they wanted the professional status that Ashford enjoyed, the technological modernity that the microscope represented, and the metropolitan representation that incorporation could afford. Puerto Rican physicians sought to be recognized as equals within the profession and gain representation and status in the United States through the AMA. In crafting their role of social regeneration and forming a healthy nation of effective workers better suited to enjoy liberty, Puerto Rican physicians also cultivated their position as a class of intermediaries between the colonial government and its subjects (Quevedo Báez, 1949: 26). The AMPR's desire for autonomy and its eventual incorporation into the AMA paralleled the increasing political divisions in the period from 1909 to 1912. Divisions within the Unionist Party led most physicians to abandon their hopes for independence, feeling it was no longer politically feasible, while others, like Dr. Manuel Zeno Gandía, worked to establish the independence party.

Professional Presentation and Status

The U.S. military occupation had presented a critical problem for physicians' professional presentation. Their relief efforts were used to undermine native physicians' scientific presentation and competence. To manage the disaster, the U.S. Army set up a provisional hospital directed by a U.S. Army medic, Dr. Bailey K. Ashford. Although many physicians treated anemia during the nineteenth century as a symptom of malnutrition and saw it as a social problem, Ashford almost immediately dismissed their explanations as unscientific (1934: 55). This dismissal directly affected liberal elite physicians, like the award-winning Dr. Agustín Stahl, who explained anemia's origin lay in iron and nutritional deficiencies. Elite physicians' hoped for reforms and shared a vision of modernization with a broader elite, but their claims about anemia were undermined and displaced by Ashford. Puerto Rican physicians' competence was still in question more than thirty years later when Ashford compared it to untrained medical practitioners and asserted "only the bedrabbled old *curandera,* or medicine-woman of the town, with her stringy hair and one remaining tooth, was held competent when it came to curing this terrible disease [uncinariasis]" (1934:67).

As the clouds set in for Puerto Rican doctors under the U.S. colonial administration, one prominent physician took a different approach from associating with a professional organization and instead offered his resources to facilitate Ashford's research on hookworm infection. As Director of the Tricoche Hospital in Ponce, Dr. Luis Aguerrevere was unlike many peers and he eschewed formal membership in the AMPR. He was also unlike many *criollo* physicians in that he was tied to Venezuela; although he was born in Puerto Rico, his father emigrated from Venezuela. Aguerrevere completed his medical training in 1882, at the Universidad Central de Venezuela, and probably maintained social ties to the country. He died in Venezuela in 1920 (Hafner, 1993).[15]

Despite these differences, Aguerrevere was much like many liberal elite physicians. He attended the Ponce Assembly forming the Autonomist Party in 1887. He was politically mobilized through his professional associations and his political involvements aligned him with Drs. Manuel Zeno Gandia and Martin Corchado. His association with Corchado and his position at the hospital indicated Aguerrevere likely supported bacteriology and ideas on antiseptic medical practice (Arana-Soto, 1963). At the hospital, Aguerrevere had also worked with Dr. Rafael Pujals who was a member of the Cuban Revolutionary Party and director of a revolutionary club in Ponce (Arana-Soto, 1966). Aguerrevere supported autonomy under the Spanish colonial regime, but was described as a strong orator and a Pro-American Republican (Arana-Soto, 1963; Ashford, 1934). Aguerrevere exemplified how being a Republican did not necessarily imply rejecting greater political and professional autonomy in favor of annexation to the United States (Negrón-Portillo, 1990). Instead, he demanded both through his significant and sustained conflicts with the SBOH and U.S. colonial administrators (Aguerrevere, 1908).

Agueverre's ambivalent position was indicative of the hookworm campaign that followed Ashford and King's survey of hookworm at the Tricoche Hospital. On the one hand, Ashford legitimated the claim that anemia was Puerto Rico's biggest medical problem, a widely prevalent disease and a significant factor undermining laborers' productivity. On the other hand, Ashford's claims about anemia's prevalence contradicted Carroll's findings that the Puerto Rican population was reasonably healthy, despite their "general disregard for the primary principles of sanitation" (Carroll, 1899). Although there was widespread consensus that both morbidity and mortality increased on the island following the 1899 hurricane, Ashford insisted anemia had a long history on the island. The claims

---

[15] Aguerrevere may have died in Maricao, Puerto Rico, in 1916 (Arana-Soto, 1966).

surrounding anemia implicated the U.S. colonial administration and its vision of a public health administration that excluded physicians' influence in formal electoral politics.

Elite physicians' interventions on Puerto Rican bodies were redirected by a critical administrative decision in 1904 when Governor Hunt lobbied for funds to establish the first Puerto Rico Anemia Commission, thereby introducing a new administration in rural areas. The campaign appealed to many physicians' pre-existing interest in regenerating rural *jíbaros* and, by implication, intervening in a variety of economic and political relationships that were compromised by the hurricane and the change in sovereignty. Ashford, who highlighted the central economic importance of anemia and workers' efficiency within U.S. colonial interests, and emphasized a specific etiology, usurped Puerto Rican physicians' broader concerns about prevalent diseases and social issues (such as hunger and malnutrition) on the island. Elite physicians lacked Ashford's political and professional status and could not compensate for the training opportunities and institutional development that the coordinated and scientific presentation the hookworm campaign offered. Elite physicians found their scientific and professional presentation displaced by the campaign's emphasis on medical treatment and research. Elite physicians' former claims to expertise and authority based on clinical observation were undermined by the campaign's insistence that its physicians use the microscope for diagnosis. They became an extension of the dispensary and were compelled to work in ways that prioritized facework over medical knowledge. For instance, by 1914, the Director of Sanitation, Dr. William Fontaine Lippitt, insisted station physicians "must examine and prescribe for every sick person who consults them. This is the only means by which we can be at all sure of securing attendance" (1914: 112). The campaign could standardize medical practice in way that Puerto Rican physicians could not. Elite physicians worried about how they could mobilize many rank-and-file physicians who worked with the campaign and who were increasingly removed from formal electoral politics.

Elite physicians and the AMPR nonetheless gained significant professional influence through the hookworm campaign. This influence was personified by Drs. Pedro Gutiérrez Igaravídez and Isaac Gonzalez Martinez. Gutiérrez Igaravídez joined the campaign from its inception in 1904, as a member, and was chairman of the second anemia commission. He became the Vice President of the AMPR in 1909 (Torres-Gómez 1999). A member of the AMPR, Gonzalez Martinez was also part of the first Board of Medical Examiners in 1903. He began conducting research through the campaign in 1904 and led the development of the Anemia Defense League in 1905 (*Liga de Defensa contra la Anemia*). Along with Ashford, both Gutiérrez Igaravídez and Gonzalez Martinez were founding members of the Medical Academy (*Academia de Medicina*) in 1914. All three men were young and in their early thirties when the campaign began. They reflected how the campaign cultivated a new professional elite distinct from an older generation of physicians who were members of a political and intellectual elite in Puerto Rico.

The appeal of the hookworm campaign involved not only professional status, but also a response to long-standing concerns about compensation. For instance, in its 1905 report, the second Anemia Commission recommended paying station directors an annual salary of $1800 and assistant directors and physicians at substations, $1000 (Commission for the Suppression of Anemia in Puerto Rico 1905). Meanwhile, municipal physicians were paid an average of $600 or less by most municipal governments in 1901 (McLeary 1901). Dr. Francisco Sein y Sein, a co-director of the Permanent Commission that formed in 1906, earned a salary of $360 as a municipal physician in 1901 (McLeary 1901).[16] Salaries for campaign physicians were disbursed from insular funds and physicians were secure in the knowledge they would be paid for their services. What also distinguished the campaign's medical men from municipal physicians was that the former were employed indirectly by the insular and U.S. colonial government, which reduced local political influences on their work. At the same time, U.S. colonial administrators replaced municipal governments as employers. This meant physicians working with the campaign were paid more than their local counterparts, struggled less for payment from private practice fees, and commanded greater influence and prestige. Physicians employed through the campaign in substations and dispensaries enabled the colonial administration to establish a presence and a public relations image of itself at the local level independently from municipal governments.

A defining aspect of public health in the early-twentieth century, the hookworm campaign reflected the tensions between local autonomy and centralized control. Many municipal physicians did not participate in

---

[16] Several physicians supplemented their income as landowners. For instance, Dr. Sein y Sein owned over 56 acres of land that was put into production in 1914. The 1935 Agricultural Census shows he carried a mortgage on the land that 20 persons lived on, which probably represented many workers or tenant farmers since he did not cultivate the land (Schedules of the 1935 Special Censuses of Puerto Rico: The Agricultural Schedules).

the campaign despite their familiarity with the municipality's *barrios* and its residents (see Table 4.1). For instance, despite the origins of the first anemia commission in Utuado, of its two municipal physicians in 1901, neither was ever involved in the hookworm campaign. The Puerto Rican directors explained it wasn't "logical to consider that the present municipal physician of Porto Rico, in the midst of the pressing duties with which he is already loaded, can be the principal figure in the campaign" (Commission for the Suppression of Anemia in Puerto Rico 1905: 32). The campaign's directors also recognized its independence from not only municipal physicians, but also municipal governments. They explained municipal appropriations for public health were inadequate to meet the problem, "not because the municipality is careless of their [the sick's] wretchedness," but because municipalities lacked funds (Commission for the Suppression of Anemia in Puerto Rico, 1905: 32).

The campaign was born from, and promoted, the centralization desired by the AMPR. The directors reiterated "the necessity for the assumption by the Insular Government of the responsibility for a labor which is really a social and economic problem" (Commission for the Suppression of Anemia in Puerto Rico 1905: 32). Although the campaign's work would be funded by insular government, it would control the hiring of personnel. This gave campaign directors the ability to control the work of health officers, then appointed by the *Consolidado*, because "the work at a dispensary would not be sufficient to occupy a physician's entire time" (Commission for the Suppression of Anemia in Puerto Rico 1905: 35). The campaign became an alternate way of involving rank-and-file physicians in the colonial government's projects, which included dispensary physicians as health officers and "sanitary inspectors attached to each central station" (Commission for the Suppression of Anemia in Puerto Rico 1905: 35). In short, the campaign became an alternate method for a new professional elite to promote professional autonomy at the local level.

The cost of providing personnel, medicine and transportation for the campaign were promoted as insular responsibilities, but the reasons some municipal governments and municipal physicians were ambivalent about the campaign may have represented rank-and-file practitioners' sense that they remained distinct from a new professional elite. For instance, Dr. Miguel Roses Artau was the Utuado station's director. He was a Spaniard and probably the son of a wealthy coffee planter of the same last name in the same municipality (Picó, 1993). His political influence was suggested by his friendship with Theodore Roosevelt (Hernandez Paralitici, 1983).

Ironically, he was one of the few campaign physicians to discuss diet and perhaps the only one to concede some validity to previous medical ideas about anemia. He insisted the commission consider "the views which have been echoing about us for seventy eight years" (Roses Artau in Commission for the Suppression of Anemia in Puerto Rico, 1905: 48). In the debate between these views and "recent and conclusive facts demonstrated" by the first commission's directors, Roses Artau asserted patients must not only be treated, but also nourished because "bad food weakens the resistance of the organism and a debilitated subject is exposed to the gravest forms of the disease. Neglect of preventive measures opens the way for the invasion of parasites in a weakened economy" (in Commission for the Suppression of Anemia in Puerto Rico 1905: 48–49). He recognized the importance of diet and sanitation, which competed with the campaign director's dominant narrative about anemia and emphasis on medication, but Roses Artau nonetheless agreed "it is of prime importance that we unite and support the initiators of the work" (in Commission for the Suppression of Anemia in Puerto Rico, 1905: 49). As a result, Roses Artau's criticisms were couched within a context of overall support for a campaign initiated by U.S. colonial administrators.

Other campaign physicians' narratives also suggested a competitive tension with municipal governments and their physicians based on funding and work. For instance, Dr. Felipe B. Vizcarrondo, a station director at Barranquitas, suggested the campaign alleviated public demands on municipal governments' meager public health resources (less work for municipal physicians) and lowered municipal physicians' salaries (less pay) (Permanent Commission for the Suppression of Uncinariasis in Porto Rico, 1907: 78). Dr. Francisco Izquierdo, the Cayey station director, noted the support and confidence of local authorities and proprietors had been almost nil and they demonstrated "the most complete indifference" to the campaign (in Permanent Commission for the Suppression of Uncinariasis in Porto Rico, 1907: 86). Nonetheless, despite municipal physicians' mixed record of participation in the campaign, many other station directors in Aguadilla, Arecibo, Barros, Cabo Rojo, Cayey, Guayama, San German, San Sebastian, Vieques and Yauco thanked municipal governments for their support (Commission for the Suppression of Anemia in Puerto Rico, 1905; Permanent Commission for the Suppression of Uncinariasis in Porto Rico, 1907).

The sense of distinction between rank-and-file practitioners and an emerging professional elite may have been produced by the campaign's appointments (see Table 7). Aside from the campaign's documents that

Table 7. The Hookworm Campaign's Medical Men (Formal Appointments, 1904–1907).[1]

Anemia Commission Directors		Position
Bailey K. Ashford	1904–1906 (First Anemia Commission)	member/co-director
	1906–1907 (Second Anemia Commission)	honorary member
Walter W. King	1904–1906	member/co-director
	1904–1907	honorary member
Pedro Gutierrez Igaravidez	1904–1906	member/co-director
	1906–1907	President/chairman
Isaac Gonzalez Martinez	1906–1907	associated member
Francisco Sein	1906–1907	associated member
Station Directors		*Municipality*
Acisclo Bou la Torre	1906–1907	Corozal
Agustín Stahl y Stamm	1906–1907	Bayamon
Alfredo Ferran	1906–1907	Ponce
Americo Oms y Sulsona	1906–1907	Las Marias
Buenaventura Jimenez Serra	1906–1907	Aguadilla
Celso Caballero Balbas	1906–1907	Adjuntas
Eduardo Casalduc	1906–1907	Anasco
Espiridion Canino	1906–1907	Aibonito
Eulalio Garcia Lascot	1906–1907	Arroyo
Felipe B. Cordero y Escalona	1906–1907	Manati
Felipe B. Vizcarrondo	1905–1907	Barranquitas
Francisco Izquierdo	1906–1907	Cayey
Francisco Maria Susoni Abreu	1906–1907	Arecibo
Francisco Sein	1905–1906	Lares
Gregorio Santo Domingo Gonzalez	1905–1907	Barros
Guillermo Carreras y Iglesias	1906–1907	Vieques
Isidro Antonio Vidal	1906–1907	Humacao
Jose A. Diaz Y Rodriguez	1906–1907	Fajardo

(Continued)

Table 7. (*Cont.*)

Jose Angel Franco Soto	1906–1907	San Sebastian
Jose H. Amadeo	1906–1907	Vega Baja
Juan Garriga	1906–1907	Aguada
Julio Atilio Gaztambide	1906–1907	Cabo Rojo
Leonardo Igaravidez y Landron	1905–1907	Coamo
Luis Gonzalez Garmendia	1906–1907	Isabela
Martin O. de la Rosa Rodriguez	1906–1907	Comerio
Miguel Roses Artau	1905–1907	Utuado
Pedro J. Palou Gimenez	1906–1907	Juncos
Pedro M. Rivera Pagan	1906–1907	Morovis
Pedro Malaret Yordan	1906–1907	San German
Rafael Cestero Molina	1905–1907	Guayama
Rafael P. Gatell	1906–1907	Yauco
Vicente Roure	1906–1907	Quebradillas
Victor Gutierrez Ortiz	1906–1907	Caguas
Station Assistant Physicians		
Jose Ciriaco Marcano de Rivera	1906–1907	Rio Piedras
Juan Benet Valdes	1905–1906	Aibonito
	1906–1907	Lares
Manuel Dueño	1905–1906	Aibonito
	1906–1907 (RESIGNED)	Mayaguez

[1] (data abstracted from Commission for the Suppression of Anemia in Puerto Rico, 1905; Permanent Commission for the Suppression of Uncinariasis in Porto Rico, 1907).

list station director's names, there was no clear or consistent way to determine how appointments were made. A physician's proximate residence and/or practice area was not a reliable indicator of his appointment. For instance, Dr. Juan Garriga had been the municipal physician in Manati in 1901, but was not appointed as the municipality's station director. Instead, in 1906, he became the station director at Aguada, which was almost 60 miles away. Similarly, Dr. Felipe B. Cordero y Escalona had been the municipal physician of Camuy in 1901, but was appointed approximately 35 miles away as the Manati station director in 1906. Although it was not uncommon for physicians to change residence and/or expand their practice areas over time, they developed regional influence and associations. The campaign appointed several physicians in stations outside of their familiar regions. For instance, Dr. Jose Ciriaco Marcano de Rivera practiced in Utuado in 1899 and had been the municipal physician of Ciales in 1901, but he did not become the station director of either the Utuado or the Aguada station that were both less than 20 miles away from Ciales. Instead, he was appointed as the station director for Rio Piedras, which was over 40 miles away. Similarly, Dr. Luis Gonzalez Garmendia, a Venezuelan who had practiced in Utuado and whose family remained in residence there, directed the station at Isabela over 40 miles away. The campaign directors wanted physicians' professional reputations to reflect positively on the campaign's work, but may have also wanted to disrupt local or regional political associations they considered inconvenient in expanding the campaign's influence.

The distinction between rank-and-file practitioners and an emerging professional elite was also reflected in their ideas about medical practice. Unlike many of the campaign's medical men who promoted sanitation reforms, legislation and enforcement, the campaign's directors emphasized medical treatment. The campaign's work was inconsistent in promoting sanitation through regulations, home inspections or education. The distinction between the campaign's physicians, its central organization and its administrative objectives was personified, for instance, by Dr. Stahl who persistently reminded the Commission of the need for prophylactic measures. Unlike Ashford and allopathic medicine's emphasis on medical intervention and treatment, Stahl insisted prevention was the objective to which all men of science had directed their efforts "in all times and places" (in Permanent Commission for the Suppression of Uncinariasis in Porto Rico, 1907: 81). Stahl lamented the campaign's lack of executive power to enforce sanitation regulations that existed on the island. His assertion of a universal and immutable claim to scientific principle competed with Ashford's emphasis on his status as a physician.[17] Stahl also implicitly challenged Ashford when he contended his support

---

[17] Ashford alternately claimed a status as a physician and as a scientist. For instance, in competition with Charles Wardell Stiles for credit over discovering the clinical effects of Uncinariasis, Ashford asserted his status as a physician. In competition with Puerto Rican physicians who had emphasized clinical observation, Ashford asserted his status as a scientist. In the 1911 report, Ashford explains he did not pursue preventive measures in the form of sanitation regulations because they would have made the campaign unpopular.

for prophylactic measures was not changing theories or vague hypothe-
ses, but the expression of a logic that was evident and scientific (in
Permanent Commission for the Suppression of Uncinariasis in Porto
Rico, 1907: 82).

Several campaign physicians associated hygiene and sanitation reforms
with a competing sense of their role in national progress. Although
Dr. Felipe B. Vizcarrondo helped co-found the AMPR in 1902, he rejected
both its emphasis on professional status and physicians' material interests. As the director of the Barranquitas substation, he felt it was necessary
for physicians to "throw aside professional materialism and...sacrifice
something for humanity" (Vizcarrondo in Commission for the Suppression
of Anemia in Puerto Rico, 1905: 46). He criticized not only physicians' limited emphasis on treatment, but also municipal physicians who did not
take an active part in preventing uncinariasis and claimed the latter's multiple duties and the scarcity of funds were no excuse. Unlike the campaign's overall report that emphasized insular responsibility, his report
asserted that municipal responsibility was "of highest importance...[they]
are in obligation to better the conditions of life of the poor" (Vizcarrondo
in Commission for the Suppression of Anemia in Puerto Rico, 1905: 46).
Vizcarrondo felt municipal governments were in the best position to
supervise sanitation and he recommended increasing their influence and
resources. He also insisted:

> we do not need conferences, assemblies, and grand oratory in those centers
> in which the countryman does not gather and in which all that is done is to
> affect a knowledge of medical science larded with eloquence. To the open
> country, to the barrios, to the hut of the unfortunate countryman we
> must go, and with practical advice which will acquaint them of the danger of
> careless living! (Vizcarrondo in Commission for the Suppression of Anemia
> in Puerto Rico, 1905: 46)

The campaign realized AMPR's goal of attaining professional status relative to the colonial administration. Although the first anemia commission
was promoted by U.S. colonial administrators like Ashford, King, Hunt
and Post, the second anemia commission was directed by the Puerto
Rican physicians, Gutiérrez Igaravídez, Gonzalez Martinez, and Sein y
Sein. Other Puerto Rican physicians became involved in the first anemia
commission and used the campaign to promote a professional status that
reflected the AMPR's goals. Like Sein who had worked as a municipal
physician and in the campaign, Dr. Rafael Cestero Molina had been
the municipal physician of Juana Diaz in 1901 and the director of the substation in Guayama. In his 1905 station report, he recommended the

commission foster a collective identity when he suggested it meet "at least once every four months in order that there might be unity of opinion in the administration of the work and they should be invested with all the rights and responsibilities of a Commission which directs so large an enterprise" (in Commission for the Suppression of Anemia in Puerto Rico, 1905: 44). His reference to rights indicated his interest in developing professional status for Puerto Rican physicians through the campaign's work.

In many cases, the campaign's medical men reproduced the director's claims about the work's omnipotence and God-like ability to resurrect working men. For instance, Dr. Celso Caballero Balbas, in Adjuntas, related attendance in terms akin to a tent revival when he explained how patients were carried to the station, but rose to their feet a couple of days after treatment (Permanent Commission for the Suppression of Uncinariasis in Porto Rico, 1907). Dr. Pedro J. Palou, in Juncos, substituted his station's lack of clinical history data with his almost religious claim of having effected "cures that were really resurrections because cadavers more than living beings had appeared at the clinic" (in Permanent Commission for the Suppression of Uncinariasis in Porto Rico, 1907: 100). He saw his labor as converting these cadavers and creating "men useful for work and capable of supporting their families" (in Permanent Commission for the Suppression of Uncinariasis in Porto Rico, 1907: 100). The campaign's medical men saw themselves participating in a social regeneration based on scientific principles.

Resurrecting workers was no small matter; it tied a new professional elite to a new colonial administration. Unlike their politicized efforts in the AMPR, the hookworm campaign enabled physicians to secure professional status relative to the U.S. colonial administration. Through the campaign, physicians could also resurrect their status within a problem they participated in defining as the critical issue in the island's social and economic life. The campaign's medical men recognized the work was initiated by the legislative and executive branches of government with the *benepácito,* or with the pleasure and discretion of the U.S. colonial governor (Franco in Permanent Commission for the Suppression of Uncinariasis in Porto Rico, 1907). This *benepácito* distinguished Spanish colonial authority from a new era of good fortune. For instance, Dr. Jose Angel Franco Soto had visited Betances, in France, while he was in exile. Franco Soto (1949) described Betances as old and part of outdated generation. In contrast, through his participation in the campaign, Franco Soto believed the U.S. colonial governor deserved the most prolonged applause from proletarians on the island who could now think, participate in civil society, and build their own wealth and that of the nation (in Permanent Commission for the Suppression of Uncinariasis in Porto Rico, 1907). As the island's proletariat continued to experience significant dislocation, unemployment and hunger in 1907, Franco Soto and the campaign's medical men mimicked the U.S. colonial administration's use of the poor to project their own class-based interests.

CHAPTER FIVE

RACE, PROGRESS AND NATIONAL IDENTITY

Scholars have demonstrated that natural disasters reveal vulnerabilities in social structures. Their analysis extends to how these disasters, like famines and epidemics, are produced through political relationships and social inequality. This perspective informs my analysis of how the 1899 San Ciriaco Hurricane became a disaster. The hurricane was embedded in a process of ongoing land dispossession, reduced agricultural production surrounding the transfer of colonial authority and intensified poverty, hunger and death. This broader context amplified the social meaning of Ashford's discovery of the hookworm, which he inscribed in terms that indicated the epidemic proportions of infection, disease and death. By associating hookworm infection with anemia and death, the hookworm survey following Ashford's discovery obscured hunger as a social fault line of disaster. The hookworm campaign following the survey produced several documents which became public proof of how white rural laborers in coffee-producing regions of Puerto Rico were most likely to be infected as a result of their inadequate personal hygiene. Through its surveys and records, the campaign restored an emphasis on laborers' productivity and reshaped older metaphors that associated anemia with colonialism, hygiene, racial degeneration and death.

Disasters and epidemics are socially stratified in terms of their effects, but the hookworm campaign's interventions tapped into a pre-existing discourse on anemia and medicine critically tied to late-nineteenth century changes involving land and labor. The transformation of agricultural production encouraged the development of professional and intellectual elites. They developed a medicalized discourse blaming Spanish colonialism for the island's anemic social, economic and cultural progress. Led by liberal elite physicians, the emerging discourse used the *jíbaro,* a rural peasant, as a symbol to elaborate the consequences of the colonial relationship. The symbol of the *jíbaro* enabled these physicians to mobilize an association of progress with not only labor, but also land as part of the tropical environment. Their writings elaborated the relationship between these ideas using a variety of metaphors tied to rural isolation, hygiene, climate and racial difference. Above all, the medicalized discourse reflected a larger, and increasingly organized, political community that struggled to renegotiate the terms of Spanish colonial authority and their place in the social hierarchy. This community included professionals, intellectuals, politicians, landowners and laborers, but the groups overlapped in unexpected ways. For instance, some physicians were among the intellectual elite, while others inherited significant landholdings and enjoyed formal political influence. Similarly, organized labor leaders' writings contributed toward intellectual production on the island. The amorphous group referred to as *jíbaros* also overlapped based on landownership and labor and included a landed peasantry, tenant farmers, sharecroppers and rural laborers.

The context of disaster, crisis, and chaos are discursive products that also obscure social stratification and change. In the transition of colonial authority, this complex discourse ultimately involved the changing meanings of national identity, racial difference and socio-economic development. If the *jíbaro's* anemia was a dominant narrative in late-nineteenth century discourse on the island, the Puerto Rican hookworm campaign represented itself as a modern intervention in both an epidemic and a broader economic disaster. It claimed to cure the "pallor of years, of centuries" and restore some mythical state of health before Spain's colonial tyranny (Ashford, 1934: 3). Through its surveys and records, the campaign played a central role in reshaping the discourse on the island's progress and building consensus around a changing social structure, which it explicitly and repeatedly referenced in the terms of race, class and political behavior. It represented an intervention in Puerto Rico's body politic that claimed to ameliorate the disastrous dislocations shared by Puerto Rican planters, physicians and peasants following the hurricane as they migrated toward urban areas in search of housing, work and food. The campaign sought to attack a parasite that became a metaphor for Spanish colonization, colonize a predominantly agricultural population, and recolonize the island's rural areas. The campaign provided a method for colonizing rural areas and accommodating a variety of interests, including the development of scientific medicine, the insular administration, and broader imperial projects.

The discourse on hookworm as a curable epidemic was inextricably tied to agricultural production. This discourse targeted patients, referred to as both *jíbaros* and peons, and suggested interventions that were tied to rural production and planters. Its focus on labor productivity simultaneously incorporated an older discourse on energy, vigor and excess and the U.S. colonial administrators' comparable emphasis on "laziness." At the same time, the campaign's published documents de-emphasized the importance of three groups that were critical to its success: physicians, politicians and planters. These groups shared an interest in labor control, particularly in order to develop a dependable wage-earning labor market. If medicine could make the rural laborer well, then it could also heal social positions compromised by U.S. colonization. The campaign not only reshaped the moral implications of medical practice in terms of patients and a diseased body politic, but also fostered medical consensus and physicians' professional status. More generally, the campaign built local political support through municipal physicians and among municipal governments.

In this chapter, I trace the discursive shift in anemia as a political cause and symbol of a diseased body politic to one of a disease curable through medical treatment. I focus on the changing relationship between land and labor in relation to agricultural production to demonstrate how the meanings of race, progress, and national identity in late-nineteenth century Puerto Rico were redefined through the development of tropical medicine in the early-twentieth century. This shift implied a new role for scientific medicine and professional elites within the U.S. colonial administration. As the leadership of many intellectual and political elites was restored, the discourse on anemia nonetheless reproduced an emphasis on rural workers' productivity and native responsibility for the island's economic development.

Professionals and Intellectuals among Liberal Elites

In his 1904 annual report, Governor Hunt explained the majority of labor in Puerto Rico was a class of agricultural peons. He recognized skilled labor in urban areas, but insisted it was a small population and "any consistent effort to better the condition of the laborer should be directed principally toward the peon class" (Hunt, 1904: 22). His simple binary obscured dynamics among rural labor that included a landed peasantry, sharecroppers and tenant farmers, semi-nomadic squatters and rural workers. This binary constructed peasants in order to underscore the colonial administration's modernity. As Rosa Carrasquillo has argued, the concept of a peasantry emerged "as a category...to prolong the life of a threatened...binary notion of primitive versus civilized...by simply changing the equation to peasant versus modern" (Carrasquillo, 2006: xvii). In Puerto Rico, this peasant was a *jíbaro* who was associated with rural isolation, whiteness and coffee production (Gonzalez, 1980). Although the meanings of the *jíbaro* changed in the twentieth century, he was generally constructed as "an illiterate white male peasant engaged in agricultural subsistence, isolated from the rest of society" (Guerra, 1998: 6).

In the same way Hunt obscured internal differences between social groups, recent scholarship on the discourse of race, hygiene and the *jíbaro* in late-nineteenth century Puerto Rico does not distinguish physicians in their analyses of *letrados,* or the intellectual elite (Guerra, 1998; Rodríguez-Santana, 2005; Rodríguez-Silva 2004, 2012; Scarano, 1996; Trigo, 2009; Wamester Bares, 2008).[1] In contrast to the study of literature, however, medical history demonstrates medical and scientific paradigms are debated and medical practitioners can include both a diverse elite and a similarly diverse group of rank-and-file members. (Starr, 1984; Tesh, 1988; Tomes, 1999). In Puerto Rico, physicians did not share a general consensus among themselves or with the general public on the lack of hygiene as the only cause of anemia and other diseases (Ashford and Gutiérrez Igaravídez, 1911: 23). Nonetheless, physicians demonstrated significant intellectual and political leadership and were critical to the development of liberal ideas and administration in Puerto Rico. Physicians practicing in Puerto Rico were not only distinguished among the intellectual elite through their unique and intimate relationship with patients, but also by virtue of their education. An empirical analysis of where published physicians' obtained their medical degree before 1898 reveals the majority were trained and graduated from Spanish universities. This was generally true for the creole political elite as well (Cubano-Iguina, 1998: 636). As a result, their cosmopolitan ideas were shaped in relation to Spanish liberal politics. Physicians' education also enabled them to gain a greater degree of political influence compared to other intellectual elites.

By the mid-nineteenth century, Puerto Rican physicians' education in the Spanish peninsula became a concern for Spanish colonial authorities because "sons of the island [learned] ideas and habits prejudicial to morals, religion, and the state... [when they return, they find] nothing good in the home of their parents, nor in the government that protects them" (Spanish Governor General in Cortés Zavala, 2006: 175). At the same time, physicians developed new avenues for intellectual development on the island when the Spanish colonial government established the *Real Sub-delegación de Medicina* and the *Real Sub-delegación de Farmacia* in 1841.

---

[1] The concept of *letrados* refers not only to a class, but also a "colonized consciousness... that has interiorized racialized and gendered discourses to [manage] a body differently racialized and gendered from their own" (Trigo, 2000: 9).

Their education and intellectual influences fostered their political involve-ment. Physicians led the development of the first political party (Liberal Reformist) on the island in 1871, as president (Goyco, P.G.) and vice-president (Carbonell, S.) (Guerra, 1975). Another physician (Gómez Brioso) wrote the proposal demanding greater political and administrative auton-omy from Spain and became the president of the party after it reorganized as the Autonomist Party (Guerra, 1975). Dr. Barbosa split a faction of the Autonomists into the Orthodox Autonomist Party (*Partido Autonomista Ortodoxo*). Several physicians were also involved in the brief autonomist government interrupted by the U.S. invasion. Physicians' significant polit-ical involvement made them leaders in a discourse that was adapted by a broader intellectual elite.

As a vanguard within liberal reformist movements that pushed for Puerto Rican autonomy under Spain, physicians organized their politi-cal activity through pharmacies.[2] As one physician described these meetings:

> ... the Doctor was the frequent guest in every pharmacy gathering that formed in late afternoons, in his tired hours of labor, after having exhausted the daily work of visiting his sick. Animated gatherings, to which, regularly, fellow citizens of the most prominent of the locality attended. Among those the Judge, the Mayor, the parish priest and someone else, enthused to par-ticipate in the animated and interesting talks, that, of everything good and edifying, they had. The same was said of politics, that was and has always been, passion or sentimentalism, a longing or anguish of agitated and sour struggle, far at times from being of the supreme ideal national pride. (Quevedo Báez, 1949: 5)

These meetings occurred in other settings as well. Also called *tertulias,* physicians used these gatherings to organize and discuss politics in public settings where community members could meet without fear of being caught because they were "under the nose" of Spanish authorities (Báez, 1949: 5). *Tertulias* complimented the function of newspapers that organized political ideas and activities and drew many future political leaders together. At pharmacies like *Farmacia Guillermety, Farmacia Babel* and *Farmacia del Valle*, prominent figures developed political ties.[3]

---

[2] The "pharmacy" was perhaps best understood as a *botica*, or an apothecary, insofar as its owner-operator functioned as a chemist who prepared and dispensed a variety of medi-cines and offered medical advice to other medical practitioners and patients. The use of "pharmacy" here is perhaps a more literal translation of the Spanish "farmacia."

[3] People who met at *Farmacia Gullermety* included the pharmacist, Fidel Guillermety, the physicians Celso Barbosa, Francisco Del Valle y Atiles, and José Gómez

Physicians fostered their influence by maintaining close relationships with one another across different *tertulias*.[4]

Physicians' contributions to a discourse through pharmacy *tertulias* and published writings may have been influential among the intellectual elite, but they also reflected differences among liberals. For instance, many *tertulias* were led by prominent citizens, but occurred across the island and in different settings, including printing press offices, bookstores, residences, town plazas, the Ateneo Puertorriqueño and boarding houses.[5]

Figure 9. Drug Store.

Brioso, politicians, landowners and poets (Pedreira, 1937: 40). Different pharmacies implied alternate political projects and distinguished older and younger elites and professionals. For instance, during the mid-nineteenth century, *Farmacia Babel* was noted for political discussions on slavery among Dr. Quintero and Acosta y Baldorioty who were accused of having "yankee" ideas against Spanish colonialism and slavery (Brau, 1956; see also Tio, 1987).

   [4] Among Barbosa's intimate personal circles were other influential physicians, including like "Saldaña, Tizol, Fernando Núñez, Hernández, Del Valle, Gómez Brioso, Ferrer, Iguina, Romero Togores." (Pedreira, 1937: 38).

   [5] The Ateneo is a cultural institution and a precursor of the university because it organized educational and cultural activities including art and music performances, lectures, publications and awards (see Rodríguez Otero, 2008).

These multiple settings increased the attendance and participation of men without significant economic or political influence and compensated for the problems of a large illiterate population (Cubano-Iguina, 1998; Valdés, 2011). These social interactions "created ties of mutual sympathy and admiration without blurring social barriers or affecting basic power relations. Although the creole elite's moralizing discourse condemned most of these customs, many well-known politicians participated in this culture" (Cubano-Iguina, 1998: 658). The frequent combination of intellectual and professional activities denoted a radical and democratizing tendency that reflected elites' desire to gain greater control over an increasingly organized rural labor force (Figueroa, 2005).

Associations of the liberal political, intellectual and professional elite could be grouped into two general camps (Arana Soto, 1961; Cubano-Iguina, 1997; Pico, 2004). Reformist liberals were exemplified by Dr. Manuel Zeno Gandia who was a founding member of the Autonomist Party. His social standing stemmed from his father, a sugar planter and slave owner (Rodríguez-Silva, 2012). Zeno Gandia became a port inspector in Ponce from 1883–1897, which reflected his political influence under Spanish colonial authority. He was also owner and director of the popular newspaper, *La Correspondencia*. Zeno Gandía was not only a physician, but also a nationalist, novelist, journalist, poet, and historian. His medical work, including studying the effects of the tropical climate on disease, and his emphasis on the natural environment as a determinative factor in human reality explains his classification as a hispanic naturalist within Spanish literature (Nouzeilles, 1997).

Zeno Gandia published *La Charca* (The Pond) in 1894, which is regarded as the first Puerto Rican novel and has become critical to the study of the elite discourse on illness and racial degeneration. As in his other novels in a series on "Chronicles of a Sick World," (*Crónicas De Un Mundo Enfermo*), Zeno Gandia "criticized and degraded" rural peasants' culture. He expressed "an evolutionary disregard for...ignorant and backward peasants...[who] held Puerto Rico hostage, sickened it, and kept it stuck, literally...in a *charca* (a muddy, polluted quagmire)" (Guerra, 1998: 56). He was also influential among the intellectual elite as owner and director of one of the most important newspapers at that time, *La Correspondencia*. After the change in sovereignty, Zeno Gandia left medicine to dedicate himself to politics and journalism. He was part of the committee with Dr. Henna that met with President McKinley in 1899 to advocate for a civil government (Henna and Zeno Gandia, 1899). He also participated in forming the Unionist Party, served as a member of the House of Representatives and later co-founded the Independence Party. Although he never used the word *jíbaro* in his novels, like many *jíbarista* writers, Zeno Gandia reconstructed peasants' needs based on his class interests and his own political ambitions (Torres-Robles, 1999).

Although scholars have focused on the medical/hygienic discourse produced through the works of Zeno Gandia, his writings were produced in the last decades of the nineteenth century. As a result, important influences on this discourse preceded Zeno Gandia. For instance, although it has received little attention in recent scholarship on *jíbarista* literature and discourse, the *jíbaro* was reintroduced by physicians in the 1849 publication of *El Gibaro* by Dr. Manuel Alonso Pacheco.[6] Like other mid-nineteenth century elites, including physicians, Alonso Pacheco wrote at a time when a liberal vision of progress was associated with the abolition of slavery on the island (Arana-Soto, 1962a). Writing in an earlier period, unlike Zeno Gandia, Alonso Pacheco "merely documented *jíbaro* culture as [he] saw it" (Guerra, 1998: 56). His study of culture and customs bridged literature and anthropology and marked an interest in not only building a national identity, but also fostering modernization by rejecting the colonial past (Wamester Bares, 2008). His text critiqued all social classes, but demonstrated what would become persistent trends in Puerto Rican literature, including the medicalization of deviance, illness as a body out of control, the authority of the author (represented through their characters) over popular classes, and a silencing of blackness on the island (Wamester Bares, 2008: 32; Rodríguez-Silva, 2004). Alonso Pacheco's conceptualization of *jíbaros'* cultural hybridity was of particular significance because it represented a longer struggle over the racial composition of Puerto Rican national identity. Although he notes a Puerto Rican is black, or *moreno,* in color, Alonso Pacheco "proceeds to limit the force and resonance of this image to the status of something no more racially compromising than an enviable suntan, with a decidedly less ambiguous stress on 'the face pale' and the presumably more conventionally European, tellingly non-negroid 'well-wrought nose'" (Márquez, 2007: 72). In this analysis, paleness became a signifier to whiten the *jíbaros'* European ancestry despite his or her color and apparent lack of civilization.

Alonso Pacheco's text is indicative of a much more variegated discourse on the *jíbaro* than the one fostered by Zeno Gandia. Many other nineteenth-century authors of *jíbarista* literature, including

---

[6] The *jíbaro* as a trope in elite discourse was born much earlier in the century (Scarano, 1996).

Drs. Cayetano Coll y Toste and Francisco del Valle de Atiles, were physicians who were active in both politics and medicine. Alonso Pacheco's career, however, remained focused on medical practice as a social responsibility. After publishing *El Gíbaro*, he became the municipal physician of Cangrejo, today called Santurce. His emphasis on education was manifest in his work when he became Director of the Charities Asylum (*Asilo de Beneficencia*) in 1871. There he educated abandoned children and attended to the insane and invalid elderly. Unable to realize the reforms he sought at the asylum, he complemented his work with medical labor in rural areas to "cure, inspire, and 'strengthen' the *jíbaro*" (Rivera Rivera, 1980).

Another group of liberal physicians was more radical in their associations and discourse. For instance, Dr. Jose Celso Barbosa Alcala, an Afro-Puerto Rican *criollo* physician who favored a greater degree of autonomy under Spanish colonialism, led the split of Autonomists as the Orthodox Autonomist Party (*Partido Autonomista Ortodoxo*). Barbosa shared many liberals' interest in capitalizing on workers' new political significance following the abolition of slavery, but his working-class background made him particularly committed to building political alliances with urban artisans. He led the development of the second cooperative savings society in the Americas in 1893, *El Ahorro Colectivo* (Negrón-Portillo, 1990).

In their analyses of the medical/hygienic discourse, scholars have emphasized how intellectual elites asserted their leadership by imagining a nation built on racial difference and degeneration through miscegenation. Their scholarship has paid less attention to how this elite was comprised of distinct groups that interacted and competed with one another based on political ideology and economic interest. They have overwhelmingly focused on a narrative of this elite's discourse that is reflected in Zeno Gandia's writings, as a:

> medical/hygienist discourse...[of] ideas and practices to police the interactions among the diseased bodies of the working classes in the name of maintaining the health of the national body. The purpose...was to redraw old pre-abolition racial and gender hierarchies because the so-called diseased bodies and minds were those of the racially mixed, working classes...They focused on the 'roots' of the peasantry's degeneracy (their sexual, racial, and class inferiority)...the regeneration of the peasantry into 'workers' was crucial for the island's economic and political progress. (Rodríguez-Silva, 2004: 121–122)

Dr. Manuel Quevedo Báez's recollection of *tertulias* that occurred in public space, "under the nose" of Spanish colonial authority, also suggests physicians' participation among more radical liberal elites. In secret meetings held by radical liberals, "especially in the southern and western coastal areas...multi-racial popular classes" allied with white liberals to assert *criollo* influence against Spaniards (Rodríguez-Silva, 2004: 124). Radical liberal autonomists found their political alliances increasingly scrutinized. For instance, after being imprisoned in 1968, Dr. Julio J. Henna went to New York and participated in the founding of the Puerto Rico Section of the Cuban Revolutionary Party. Exiled in the Dominican Republic, Drs. Ramón Emeterio Betances and José Francisco Basora were founding members of the Revolutionary Committee of Puerto Rico to promote a united effort between Puerto Rico and Cuba in support of independence from Spain (Arana-Soto, 1962a). Other prominent physicians were later imprisoned as Spanish repression escalated, particularly in the infamous *componte* arrests and tortures of 1887, such as Dr. Salvador Carbonell Toro who was arrested for a second time (Arana-Soto, 1962a). Dr. Agustín Stahl was stripped of his teaching position and exiled from Puerto Rico in 1898 for his political beliefs, but returned after the change in sovereignty (Carreras, 1974; Gutiérrez del Arroyo, 1976: 17). Although liberal elites asserted their authority over the popular classes, they were also prominent leaders of dissent.

Labor as Progress

Scholars have recently paid close attention to the medical/hygienic discourse in vogue in late-nineteenth century Puerto Rico. They argue this discourse intensified in the late nineteenth century, following the abolition of slavery, as the intellectual elite sought to legitimate their authority relative to Spanish (white) colonial authorities. This scholarship demonstrates the discourse had three major elements: the relationship between hygiene and progress, the meaning of the tropical environment, and the consequences of the colonial relationship. In relation to progress, scholars explain how the medical/hygienic discourse associated hygiene with self-discipline and control of the body. They find elites explained disease as a consequence of the purported absence of hygiene and self-control among popular classes. For instance, elites projected their anxieties about racial mixing onto ostensibly isolated rural populations that could not be controlled and could not control themselves. Elites believed rural populations lacked self-control and engaged in sexual practices that encouraged miscegenation, which they [elites] associated with racial degeneration as a physical and cultural disease that compromised the nation's progress. Scholars argue intellectual elites focused on rural peasants' racial identity in order to foster their leadership over a nation they envisioned as essentially white and threatened by blackness and miscegenation. Elites produced a medical/hygienic discourse to position themselves as leaders (intellectuals) and managers (professionals) of a mixed-race population and racially-stratified nation.

Although the scholarship on the medical/hygienic discourse underscores the relationship of hygiene and race, it underemphasizes the relationship between race and labor on the one hand, and tropical environments and land on the other. Land and labor informed elites' "moral and material interests" and sense of leading the modernization and progress of the island. The medical/hygienic discourse was conflated with a language of labor and relied on a variety of legal efforts to control labor. For instance, Ileana M. Rodríguez-Silva's analysis of Zeno Gandía and Atiles's writings demonstrates labor "was a main category for social organization" for elites (2004: 159). She describes how these writings reflected a broader effort to not only "shape the peasantry" as "political entities [and] potential allies," but also to build "reliable, healthy, moral and disciplined workers" that would meet "the island's need for a reliable and steady labor force that could secure the profitability of the agricultural industries" (Rodríguez-Silva, 2004: 139, 159, 205). To promote their tenuous ability to control free labor, elites resorted to a variety of measures. Discursively, elites constructed the antithesis of workers as vagrants who were marked by their clothing, sickness, shoes and teeth. Elites used physical appearance to police social boundaries and mark poor urban residents as a sick, threatening and a potentially contaminating presence (Rodríguez-Silva, 2004: 216).

As elites policed boundaries with a diverse society, they also promoted the persecution and segregation of vagrants more generally in practice and in order to develop a "compliant working class" (Rodríguez-Silva, 2004: 214). In urban areas, new hospitals and asylums developed to complement the efforts of prisons in segregating vagrants and controlling labor: "Asylums and charity institutions were like jails, where prisoners were sentenced to labor in public works. They sometimes channeled 'unproductive' people to employers in need of laborers and/or trained their residents in high-demand occupations" (Rodríguez-Silva, 2004: 219; see also Findlay, 1999). These institutional developments were also fundamentally tied to promoting wage labor "in order to mitigate the labor crisis in Puerto Rico" and complemented police efforts to promote labor discipline and impose a "capitalist labor ethic...of working enthusiastically for long hours, day after day, week after week, for employers with private property. Docility and contentment were also expected, but because workers did not readily adopt this ethic, the police were called upon to enforce it" (Carrasquillo, 2006: 69). In rural areas, taxes and fines functioned to create debt among the poor and occasion their imprisonment, which "was just another form to enforce compulsory work...rural laborers, sharecroppers, and the landed peasantry worked side by side with prisoners, who were assigned to public work in the 1880s, 1890s, and early twentieth century" (Carrasquillo, 2006: 80). Anti-vagrancy laws, selective enforcement of prohibitions on cock-fights and card games that "destroyed the individual's capacity to work...a lack of legal documentation...[and] an endless list of misconduct, such as disrespect for authorities, missing a day or arriving late to work, drinking, cursing, and so on" also occasioned fines and forced the poor to work for municipal governments (Carrasquillo, 2006: 80, 82).

The development of compulsory labor in public works following the abolition of slavery, ultimately sought to create a work ethic and discipline that elites associated with progress. As one government func-tionary explained:

> in this country is felt the overwhelming need for something to change the customs and habits of the free worker who puts little of his part to be cared for and considered, given his almost nomadic way of life. The frugality of his existence, the vehemence of his passions, the ease of an inconvenient social freedom, the climate in its destructive effects, the influence of its [island's] natural wealth, the centralization of wealth in few hands, the common idea of birds of flight, has founded a way of being in this society where it is almost completely unknown the relationships that every cultured society has [between] work, the economy, capital and public virtue. (Sicher in García, 1989: 864; translation mine)

This quote is significant for several reasons, not the least of which is its contribution to the language of labor that dominated elite discourse in the late-nineteenth and twentieth centuries. Although it is not expressed in medical terms and was not authored by a physician, the description of the "customs and habits" of free labor contrasts sharply with Quevedo Baez's quote that values physicians' work in moral terms. It is rare to find a refer-ence in any political or medical discourse that did *not* explicitly address the energy or vigor of labor. Although the medical/hygienic discourse certainly involved debates about national identity and race, it also represented an explicit attempt to foster the island's economic progress through labor. The functionary's quote also underscores the fundamental distinction between free labor and physicians' work. The medical/hygienic discourse ignored the seasonal cycles of agricultural labor, which were dissimilar from the discipline encouraged by modern, industrial production. Despite this distinction, elites viewed rural workers' attitudes and habits as threatening their ability to control labor. Their concern was intensified by workers' mobility, which became a dominant form of evading multiple and developing forms of labor control, including municipal taxes and forced labor. This mobility was also critical to improving rural populations' ability to secure land for subsistence farming. Access to land outside the employer-wage worker relationship implied not only access to food, but also greater autonomy. This autonomy was increasingly delimited in the twentieth century by the expansion of the sugarcane industry (Valdés, 2011).

Land as Tropical Environment

The medical/hygienic discourse was fundamentally embedded in an attempt to promote the development of wage labor, labor supply and work discipline. By associating "the value and purpose of labor [with]... the development of private property," the discourse also complemented legislative efforts to separate "former slaves and...the racially mixed population from the land" (Carrasquillo, 2006: 66, 69). Elites included municipal government officials and large-holding landowners (*hacendados*) who shaped the fortunes of Puerto Rican peasants.

Aside from large landowners who expanded their landholdings in the last decades of the nineteenth century, however, other rural groups' access to land and subsistence production became increasingly precarious in the late-nineteenth century as land tenure was transformed by the "formalization and legalization of land titles" (Carrasquillo, 2006: 41). This transformation was encouraged by legislation, including the Mortgage Law of 1880 that promoted individualized property rights. As informal access to land eroded, a second regulation in 1884 enabled "people with money" to formalize land titles and further displace "peasant squatters who practiced semi-nomadic agriculture" (Carrasquillo, 2006: 42). Even small- and medium- farmers could find themselves quickly *desclasados,* literally declassed, after losing land and its associated benefits.

In addition to laws affecting land tenure, sharecroppers and the landed peasantry were also dispossessed through municipal taxes based on productivity. The same rate applied to subsistence farmers and large landowners who derived significant profits from their crops. The latter group also enjoyed political influence, which enabled them to successfully obtain tax reductions. To pay for these reductions, municipal governments increased taxes on smaller and less-influential landowners. Landed peasants were forced to maintain production on their land to pay the taxes or sell their land. Municipal governments also collected peasants' debt by confiscating "anything of value on their farms-the harvest, domestic animals, furniture, tools, and so-on," which had the effect of forcing peasant farmers to sell their land (Carrasquillo, 2006: 46).

Amidst this context, the medical/hygienic discourse involved a vision shared more generally by elites who saw agricultural production as a means to promote economic development in relation to the fertility and productivity of land. Influenced by naturalist ideas, *jíbarista* authors also constructed the environment as fundamentally productive, but emphasized the island's economic progress (Brau, 1956: 15). The medical/hygienic discourse not only shared *hacendados'* interest to expand their control over rural areas, but also to promote their authority over a civilizing process in relation to the development of private property and agricultural production (Méndez, 1983). The medical/hygienic discourse associated a productive natural environment with *jíbaros'* limited incentive for labor and their indolence (Ames, 1901; Schwartz, 1992). This indolence was also referred to as indifference and marked a persistent form of evasive resistance.

The medical/hygienic discourse also associated rural environments with illness, which projected elite physicians' anxieties about their national leadership. More specifically, although elite physicians could police urban populations, their ability to intervene in the lives of rural *jíbaros* was compromised by an inadequate road infrastructure. As elite physicians did not have direct access, their discursive constructions of "tropical" difference emphasized rural isolation. Despite peasants' integration in urban markets, elites discursively isolated the *jíbaro* in rural areas, far away from modern civilization. For instance, Dr. Cayetano Coll y Toste claimed the "unhappy creature's" birth in the "rural hut" distanced him/her from religion and civilization, which led to a profound "cachexia of body and soul" (1892: 178–179).[7] Viewed through the lens of the upper class, the *jíbaro* had become the Other, whose moral decay and resistance to progress threatened to infect the Puerto Rican body politic. As Coll y

---

[7] Cachexia refers to general ill health typically associated with emaciation. Coll y Toste's description influenced the U.S. colonial administration and the hookworm campaign (see, for instance, Ashford and Gutierrez Igaravídez, 1911).

Toste wrote, "the proletariat, invaded by a terrible leprosy," i.e. *jíbaro* culture, threatens to infect "our social body" (Coll Y Toste, 1899: 179). The *jíbaro* had become not only sick but also sickening.

The medical/hygienic discourse surrounding the natural environment idealized nationalist depictions of suffering and provided fertile ground for physicians' ideology of healing interventions. On the one hand, elite physicians represented rural areas as inaccessible and threatening places. On the other hand, these threats became targets for interventions on the tropical environment. For instance, in 1883, del Valle y Atiles saw climate as the island's "principal scourge," but explained it was "in part modifiable: and...the enervating tropical heat...would be more bearable if there were no swamps...let us rid ourselves of the swamps, and...we will make disappear the profound anemia that turns peasants into literal skins of water, inert and useless to the land that feeds us" (Atiles in Trigo, 2000: 80–81). The swamp was a metaphor that not only reconciled the miasmatic ("gaseous secretions") and parasitic ("fly like vampires") theories of disease, but also implicated the contamination of the "'white' *jíbaro*" with the "bad blood" of the "African race" (Trigo, 2000: 81).

The swamp informed the meaning of tropical difference not only in terms of race, but also in terms of labor. The swamp became a symbol of a climate that threatened whiteness and white labor. The association of swamps with decay was evident in Zeno Gandía's novel, *La Charca* [The Swamp], where he depicted the *jíbaro's* environment as a stagnant pond. The veritable swamp was part of a "chaotic" tropical environment that included "exhausting heat, dirt, [and] insects" (Rodríguez-Silva, 2004: 135). The swamp also became a powerful symbol of how rural isolation could encourage backwardness and cause moral decay and physical (anemic) weakness. Land without elite intervention became dangerous, which served to bolster physicians' authority and significance to agricultural production.

Elite physicians used swamps to represent a discursive intervention in rural areas in the late-nineteenth century, but they became a very practical and critical aspect of how physicians colonized rural space in the twentieth century. Although the association of tropical difference with climate persisted, the hookworm campaign focused on contaminated soil to renegotiate the terms of racial difference and labor under the U.S. colonial administration. Despite the discursive shift, the tropics continued to inform the implications of climate and racial difference on the relationships between land and labor. For instance, Ashford and the Puerto Rican hookworm campaign referenced del Valle y Atiles in their analyses of the *jíbaro*. Quevedo Báez also referenced del Valle y Atiles in 1946 as he explained, "the White man was naturally directed to the mountains, in search of shade and low temperatures that they offer; whereas the black, finding himself at home in the heat of the coast, works happily under the hot sun in the sugar cane plantations" (1946: 374). These references reflect the enduring allure of medical interventions in the tropics and physicians' interest in promoting a white racial order to colonize land, labor and production.

Social Conditions and the Colonial Relationship

Like many elite physicians, Dr. Coll y Toste authored influential publications and held political positions in addition to his medical career. He was director of the Catholic Hospital of Arecibo, and under the autonomous government established in February 1898, the Sub-Secretary of Agriculture and Commerce. After the change in the island's sovereignty, he was involved in insular politics as Civil Secretary under the military governor and, under the civil government, as Commissioner of the Interior and delegate to the House of Representatives. Aside from his political influence, he maintained his position as a dominant member of the intellectual elite, which was indicated by his leadership in the Puerto Rican Historical Academy, the Ateneo Puertorriqueño, and when he was named "Official Historian of Puerto Rico" in 1913. Like Alonso, however, Coll y Toste has received far less attention from scholars who have analyzed the medical/hygienic discourse on *jíbaros*, probably because, like Zeno Gandia, Coll y Toste did not use the word *jíbaro*. Like both Alonso and Zeno Gandia, Coll y Toste received his medical training at the University of Barcelona. These associations were indicative of his liberal politics and support of Luis Muñoz Rivera both before and after the change of Puerto Rico's sovereignty.

Coll y Toste was a dominant figure who informed the meanings of race and of rural labor for U.S. colonial administrators. Like del Valle y Atiles, he was referenced in the Puerto Rican hookworm campaign's documents. Of greater significance, he authored an influential study of the social, economic and industrial conditions of the island under the U.S. military occupation and influenced early conceptions of Puerto Rican labor in the 1901 study, "Labor Conditions in Porto Rico" (Coll y Toste, 1899; Ames, 1901). Perhaps for these reasons, Coll y Toste is most commonly remembered as a historian and his tone of neutrality contributed to the authority of his writings. Nonetheless, his social position as a physician was clearly reflected in his medical practice in Arecibo, where he and his children were born, and in his later membership in the *Asociación Medica de Puerto Rico* and his contributions to its journal, the *Boletín de la Asociación Medica de Puerto Rico.*

Coll y Toste's medical associations reflected his unique contributions to the discourse on progress and national identity. For instance, in his response to Dr. Stahl's study on the tradition of medicine among the island's native inhabitants, Coll y Toste (1904) emphasized medicine as a social development that occurred only with settlement and civilization. By promoting elite leadership and negotiating a national identity before Spanish colonization, he reflected ideas shared by many other elite physicians and *jíbarista* authors. Unlike del Valle y Atiles, however, Coll y Toste viewed Puerto Ricans as essentially white and derivative of the "Spanish race." This alternate meaning of whiteness had colonial implications relative to Puerto Ricans' ambivalence about the increasing dominance of Anglo-Saxon whiteness, represented by the threat of U.S. colonization (Cubano-Iguina, 2005). Coll y Toste's writings also negotiated a reformist critique of Spanish colonization, and specifically its centralization of authority, as promoting a heavy and asphyxiating atmosphere and as a "defective system" that had a negative influence on the island's progress (1892: 167, 170).

Coll y Toste shared *jíbaristas'* concerns about the island's progress, which was compromised by the "moral and physical vices" of laborers, "the son of our fields, one of the most unfortunate of the world" (1892: 178). He similarly represented the laborers in terms of their pale face, bare feet, emaciated body, ragged clothing and indifferent gait. Like Zeno Gandia who associated Spanish abandonment with peasants who had been left to stagnate in the countryside, Coll y Toste reproduced the construction of rural isolation as a pre-modern legacy of Spanish neglect that compromised the island's progress. Like del Valle y Atiles who privileged the rural countryside and claimed the health and vitality of rural populations was superior to urban groups, Coll y Toste reasoned it was not possible that the tropical zone, otherwise exuberant and vigorous, could produce such disgrace, an "organic anemia" (1899: 178). After all, he reasoned, other humans "with the same organs fight to exist and overcome" (1899: 179).

More than other *jíbarista* authors, including del Valle y Atiles who blamed the lack of modernization for overworking peasants, Coll y Toste paid close attention to the relationship between modernization and the availability of food to rural laborers. He blamed the lack of modernization for a Malthusian disparity between population growth and the availability of food. He explained that stores only carried rotten sausages and cod fish. Like del Valle y Atiles, Coll y Toste also blamed municipal taxes for doubling the price of meat compared to the price of rotten codfish and making the former inaccessible to the poor (see del Valle Atiles in Rodríguez-Silva, 2004). His references implicated the colonial relationship in the lack of modern production and the reliance on inadequate imported food. For Coll y Toste, the lack of meat and other nutritious food for the muscles made it impossible to demand *mens sana in corpora sano,* or healthy mind in healthy body. He prioritized modernization over other hygienic reforms that centered on regenerating *jíbaros,* for instance, when he suggested cockfights should be suppressed *after* agriculture had been modernized. Coll y Toste's analysis of food reflected a nationalist interest in reducing the laborers' reliance on imported food stuffs (rice) and promoting more nutritious and self-sufficient production: "Come therefore the model farms, the Spanish hamlets, the meats accessible to the poor, the inexpensive bread, suppressing the municipal shackles that monopolize it...corn, grain more nutritious than wheat and that is in abundance in this land, substitute rice..." (1892: 179). Despite his attention to how colonialism impeded modern progress, he did not refer to Spanish control over land, municipal tax structures, or the unequal distribution of wealth through production.

An understated, but significant theme among *jíbarista* authors and scholars of this literature is the metaphor of death. The threat of continued miscegenation among peasants implied the impossibility of racial regeneration among Puerto Rican elites as whites. For Zeno Gandia, the genetic mixture of white Spaniards and indigenous Tainos had not only made peasants anemic, weak and inferior, but their "deprivation of blood" also implied their eventual death: "The *jíbaro* was portrayed without fail as the living death" (Rodríguez-Santana, 2005: 177). For del Valle y Atiles, both Spaniards and Tainos had been racially mixed, the isolated rural peasant was predominantly white and had not experienced significant miscegenation, and the latter's evolutionary progress and whiteness could be regenerated with the support of selective immigration and breeding (Rodríguez-Silva, 2004). As a result, death was a metaphor used sparingly to indicate a threatening possibility where elites explored the limits and potential of their own whiteness.

The meanings of death shifted in the early twentieth century. The medical/hygienic discourse, and its related symbols of bare feet, tropical swamps and pale faces, shifted through the Puerto Rican hookworm campaign. These symbols retained much of their intended purpose of bolstering elite authority, but physicians' social position as intellectual leaders shifted. Their place in the social structure was radically disrupted, first by the hurricane and then by a new civil government. Although some elite physicians became involved in the insular government, a new generation of physicians became professional intermediaries under the U.S. colonial administration. Through the campaign, physicians continued to contrast bare feet with productive labor but the symbol became generalized beyond vagrants to include rural workers. A new generation of physicians labored in coffee-producing rural areas to overcome *jíbaros'* isolation and conquer the problems of humid and contaminated soil. Physicians participated in a new colonial project of colonizing the parasite, which implied a disruption in medical/hygienic discourse. Although the medical discourse developed through the Puerto Rican hookworm campaign retained many dominant symbols associated with labor, production, and the legacy of Spanish colonialism, the parasite was represented in relation to the persistent, impending and alarming specter of death.

Death and Resuscitation in Tropical Medicine

There are multiple ways of interpreting the Puerto Rican hookworm campaign. The dominant narrative undoubtedly involves a medical discourse of conquering death. For instance, in the foreword to Ashford's autobiography, the President of the University of Puerto Rico implies the campaign was responsible for reducing the death rate from anemia "from 16,000 to 1,000 persons per year in just a few years" (Maldonado in Ashford, 1998: xv). Another author asserts that "by 1905, just one year after their creation, the fatalities attributed to uncinariasis were reduced from 17,009 to 414" (Feliú, 2002: 156). These claims do not discuss concerns about reliability in measuring cause of death and the latter does not explain how such dramatic results could be obtained in less than one year with only $5,000 dollars. Nonetheless, the general narrative about the campaign and death ignores an observation even Ashford later recognized: hookworm was not fatal in other parts of the world, including the U.S. South (Ashford, 1928; Crosby, 1987).

Other factors provide a more concrete explanation of how death emerged as a dominant metaphor under the U.S. colonial administration and how it (death) became associated with hookworm infection. First, as exemplified by the images of skulls and bones in urban areas, U.S. colonial administrators were concerned death was a disincentive for tourism and the entry of new capital. Second, the campaign strategically referenced death in their reports. Ashford and Gutiérrez Igaravídez shaped the ways death was associated with the campaign's work in order to construct the hookworm as a symbol of a pre-modern Spanish colonial legacy. The campaign claimed it could cure the "pallor of years, of centuries" and restore the *jíbaro* to some mythical state of health that existed before Spain's colonial tyranny (Ashford, 1934: 3–5). They described the hookworm as a destructive force that slowly decimated whole populations (Ashford and King, 1904: 653). The resulting current narrative about the hookworm campaign is embedded in this medico-scientific discourse and "the history of science that has centered, classically, in the formal stories...to exalt the heroism...or the valor of great men of science...[but] hides competition, the errors, the failures and the change of direction" that tropical medicine has taken (Caponi, 2003: 136–137).

Tropical medicine was distinct from bacteriology: it demanded association with "other knowledges (that cannot be reduced to military medicine) and other methods of constructing knowledge" (Caponi, 2003: 128). Rather than pessimism about tropical climates, tropical medicine implied understanding how "radical otherness," indicated by the parasite's existence amidst precarious social and sanitation conditions, could be altered through civilization and hygiene (Caponi, 2003: 128). Tropical medicine emphasized the parasite as a "third animal...a tropical species" that competed for survival in relation to humans and their environment (Caponi, 2003: 123). If the microscope helped bacteriologists become microbe hunters, it also helped tropical medicine to conduct a war that was expressed in moral and military terms (De Kruif, 1996). This war was discursively framed as a struggle for modernizing production. In Puerto Rico, this struggle was carried out in relation to *jíbaros'* radical otherness and complimented modern forms of colonization.

Knowledge of precarious social conditions in Puerto Rico was plainly evident to most elites. By the 1880's, Puerto Rican physicians had already associated bare feet with parasitic infection. They had also attributed anemia indirectly to parasites by association with mosquitoes and malaria (Ashford and Gutiérrez Igaravídez, 1911; Trigo, 2000). What exalts the discovery of the hookworm on the island is the parasite's implied struggle against rural labor and agricultural production. Through the campaign's use of the microscope, Puerto Rican physicians could re-invent medical interventions on labor, agricultural production and the island's progress. These interventions were detailed in Ashford and Gutiérrez Igaravídez's report on the first decade of the campaign's work. The "medical and economic problem" detailed in the 335-page report centered on Puerto Rican labor. Its first section suggested a new medical discourse on the *jíbaro* as it embedded labor in a social context. The report began with the claim that in order to understand the uncinariasis "pandemic...it is necessary to make a brief summary of social and economic conditions in the island since its discovery to the present day" (Ashford and Gutiérrez Igaravídez, 1911: 3). By beginning its narrative in this way, the report situated the campaign in relation to a colonial past that promoted disease and as an intervention that distinguished the social and economic present.

The second paragraph of the hookworm campaign's report indicates the association of tropical medicine with a knowledge of radical otherness. Specifically, it resuscitated elites' medical/hygienic discourse when it explained "our knowledge of the life of the jíbaro" relied on del Valle y Atiles (Ashford and Gutiérrez Igaravídez, 1911: 3). The report racialized social and economic conditions on the island by inscribing a history of colonization, disease and reduced population size. The report located the hookworm within this history and in relation to "the extinction of the unhappy 'Borinqueño,' or Indian, and the introduction of the negro" (Ashford and Gutiérrez Igaravídez, 1911: 6). The narrative associating "the negro" with the hookworm reflected a discursive ambivalence around race. On the one hand, this narrative suggested hookworm was introduced by slaves and the founding of sugar plantations. On the other hand, other campaign documents insisted the parasite could not survive in the dry and sunlit areas of the coast (Ashford and Gutiérrez Igaravídez, 1911). In either case, the narrative tied hookworm to this history of colonization and anxieties about racial mixture.

The hookworm had a complex relation to *jíbaros'* blood, and therefore, his racial identity. The references to *jíbaros'* whiteness is frequent in the 1911 report and reflected the role of tropical medicine in negotiating the meanings of race in a U.S. colony. In the report, the *jíbaro* is conditionally white. The report cites two other reports: one conducted in 1765 by a Spaniard who observed a generalized "laziness" encouraged by climate and another from 1834 by an Englishman who repeats symbolic associations between "common white people...(called jibaros)" and colonists (in Ashford and Gutiérrez Igaravídez, 1911: 6). The report questions whether "these people [natives] were merely innocent victims of disease, modern only in name?" (Ashford and Gutiérrez Igaravídez, 1911: 6) In this analysis, "natives" indicated a shared ancestry between white Spanish colonists and the "sick workingman, without only half the blood he should have in his body" (Ashford and Gutiérrez Igaravídez, 1911: 6). The hookworm allowed the campaign to medicalize "native" difference and construct the ways whiteness was compromised by tropical climate. Although the report recognized "a reasonable doubt of pure blood raised by Dr. Weyl for at least a portion of those called 'white,'" and referred to "traces of the negro, and, not rarely, hints of the Indian," Ashford and Gutiérrez Igaravídez ultimately insisted "the vast majority of the mountain people should be considered white" (1911: 8).[8] The campaign represented another method of constructing knowledge about not only hookworm infection, but also *jíbaros'* whiteness.

The campaign's multiple reports as a public health effort, i.e., before its work was more narrowly delimited to research as the Institute for the Study of Tropical Medicine in 1912, relied on numerical data to whiten patients. Their frequent inclusion of numerical tables underscored that "whites" were more numerous than the reports' narrative references to census data, which also confirmed the majority of the island's population was "white." Although these data implied sick patients were more likely to be "white," it was embedded in a narrative that framed disease in terms of the island's general population, e.g., percent of island infected, number treated, etc. By asserting blacks were less likely to be sick from hookworm, race determined immunity as much as immunity defined race (Feliú, 2001: 161). In essence, the campaign was a method to whiten the Puerto Rican population, which could be used to justify expanding the benefits Puerto Rico derived under U.S. colonial authority.

In other campaign documents, the hookworm threatened *jíbaros'* whiteness and required not only treatment, but also an effort akin to a "crusade" (Commission for the Study and Treatment of Anemia, 1904: 88). This threat implied racial degeneration and was recognized by other physicians. For instance, Dr. Jane Howell Harris quoted the campaign's 1904 report that, without treatment, the hookworm would "continue to reduce the white and mixed inhabitants forming the country class of the island, to a lower and lower grade, mentally, morally, and physically, until the very existence of the class will be threatened" (1906: 305–306).

If tropical climate compromised the *jíbaros'* whiteness, then tropical parasites located in contaminated soil became the target of intervention. According to Ashford and Gutiérrez Igaravídez, the *jíbaro* was a patient who, "in times past...and in time to come," would be "the pale man of Porto Rico" and shared a home with the *necator americanus* (1911: 11). Their

---

[8] In a report he wrote in 1900, King asserted "these lower classes are a mixture of Spanish, Indian, and Negro blood, the latter predominant" (2006: 39).

narrative had two important implications. First, it discursively established the timelessness of the *jíbaro's* home, which contrasted his actual displacement from rural areas by Hurricane San Ciriaco and colonial policies that fostered the misfortunes of the coffee industry. Second, by squarely locating the *jíbaro* in a space threatened by parasites, the campaign displaced attention for social and economic conditions away from the U.S. colonial relationship and onto rural labor. As the report explained, the *jíbaro* was "a type to be well studied before we essay to interest him in bettering his own condition" (Ashford and Gutiérrez Igaravídez, 1911: 11).

Although the hookworm was born in soil, it took on new life through the eye of Ashford's microscope at a moment when rural labor faced daunting odds of survival. The hurricane had washed away important means of self-subsistence and livelihood. If coffee-planting elites hoped to control workers' mobility and labor in the late-nineteenth century, this desire seemed to wash away along with their coffee bushes as workers migrated to coastal and urban areas in search of jobs. Amidst this context, Ashford's microscope delivered proof he had solved the persistent problems of rural labor and the lack of progress under the previous colonial regime. Rather than a question of limited labor supply, the hookworm campaign that followed Ashford's discovery underscored the significance of efficient production to promote the island's progress. The hookworm became a potent symbol that became associated with threats to this progress, including labor demands, coffee production and the new colonial relationship.

Recapitalizing Elites

The hookworm campaign that developed in Puerto Rico after 1904 emerged through a longer struggle between humans and their environment. On the one hand, elite physicians on the island had constructed this struggle in terms of labor and agricultural production. They sought to facilitate labor control and a dependable wage-earning labor market that would support agricultural production. They also complemented state efforts to undermine workers' mobility and resistance to labor in the employer-wage worker relationship. On the other hand, five years after the military occupation, political opposition to the U.S. colonial administration had escalated in its nationalist tone. Puerto Rican politicians opposed the lack of "territorial" or political autonomy. The new Unionist Party was a backlash against U.S. domination, evidenced by the "the offensive regime of the Foraker Law" (Scarano, 1996: 630). It was also a popular coalition that united many formerly oppositional classes, parties, and social groups, including the mountain peasantry and professionals. The Unionist Party found particularly strong support among coffee plantation owners who protested government support of a sugar industry that was dominated by U.S. interests (Carrion, 1983).

The decline of the coffee industry after 1898 represented a major transformation in the island's social hierarchy. The coffee economy was a "Puerto Rican creation...product of the old society that desperately fought for survival after 1900 in the face of the onslaught of investment capital on other areas of the economy" (Bergad, 1978: 85). The coffee industry's persistent problems with securing and controlling labor were compounded by Hurricane San Ciriaco, which displaced many rural peasants and forced migration to urban areas in search of work. Coffee producers were further disadvantaged by the Foraker Act that prohibited the island from making commercial agreements with other countries, "a prohibition from which coffee especially suffered" because it ensured the loss of export markets in Spain and Cuba (Dietz, 1986: 90). The disadvantaged market conditions for coffee further reduced the value of rural property. In their hopes of an economic recovery, and embedded in a struggle with natural hazards and the political environment, their control over labor was further eroded through changes in the municipal government structure. When the municipal tax structure was centralized under the U.S. colonial administration in 1901, large landowners lost not only land to U.S. corporations, but also the ability to control a municipal police force that had facilitated labor control.

The hookworm campaign that began in 1904 represented the first Puerto Rico Anemia Commission. It marked the initial stage of a longer trajectory and was characterized by its effort to develop elite, professional and popular support for the campaign's work. Although Ashford's discovery of hookworm in Puerto Rico occurred in 1899, it would be another three years before he returned to Puerto Rico where he had been reassigned to care for troops. In Ponce, he met Walter W. King, the port's Public Health Officer and assistant surgeon of the U.S. Public Health and Marine Hospital Service. They began a survey of 100 hookworm cases at the Tricoche Hospital in 1902. Despite the location of their survey in a coastal city they would later claim was not conducive to infection, they nonetheless concluded hookworm was "the great scourge of fully 90% of the agricultural laboring classes in Porto Rico, and what has come to be a most prominent economic question in the betterment of the island" (Ashford and King, 1903: 391). The conclusions Ashford and King drew in

1903 contrasted with Ashford's more cautious initial speculation that the hookworm "killed its hundreds" (1901: 123).

The campaign's reports emphasized its work as an intervention in a "curable and preventable" problem that shifted over time (Ashford, 1934: 88). The hookworm narrative demonstrated the change of direction in tropical medicine in many ways, including four indicative ones that distinguished not only Ashford's reports from 1900 to 1904, but also this early narrative with later campaign reports. First, the early narrative used the word anemia loosely in their discussion of hookworm infection, or uncinariasis, and by association with references to death and mortality rates. These constructions participated in locating hookworm within a medical discourse on conquering death. Second, Ashford's early narrative about uncinariasis discussed infection among a variety of groups, including U.S. soldiers, children and persons who were "always accustomed to live well" (Commission for the Study and Treatment of Anemia, 1904: 38; Ashford, 1901; Ashford and King, 1903). This narrative shifted by 1911 to one that overwhelmingly emphasized agricultural labor, *jíbaros* and peons. Third, Ashford recognized the temporary and limited benefits of medical treatment in 1899. He subsequently defended the importance of medical treatment even as the medication used by the campaign changed over time and underscored the significance of iron deficiency (Ashford, King and Gutiérrez Igaravídez, 1905).

The significance of the campaign's intervention was especially indicated by how it crafted the method of curing and preventing what it considered a medical and economic problem. Ashford insisted on the importance of medical treatment despite recognizing the persistent problem of reinfection, even after a 1919 Rockefeller Foundation found over 80% of the rural population infected at various test points (International Health Board, 1919). In his early narrative following his relief work, Ashford paid closer attention to social conditions that were generalized in Puerto Rico, particularly sanitation, and identified diet as "a powerful factor" in uncinariasis (Ashford, 1901: 121). By 1911, however, Ashford largely abandoned what had been, at best, an inconsistent effort at hygiene education and sanitation reform. He did not believe sanitation campaigns could eradicate hookworm and Gutiérrez Igaravídez concurred with this assessment (Ashford in Farley, 1991: 40).[9]

---

9 As Director of the Tropical and Transmissible Diseases Service, Gutiérrez Igaravídez wrote, "there are only two feasible means of controlling uncinariasis in Porto [sic] Rico: 1.

The campaign also represented the first major medical effort on the island. Its reports suggest the 1899 compulsory smallpox vaccination campaign influenced its interest in mass treatment. Its references to the Charity Board's work, tying food relief to work, also contributed to the campaign's emphasis on labor. Despite the influences of the U.S. colonial administration, the campaign also corresponded with the native elites' pre-existing interest in broader modernizing reforms, which included expanding control over rural labor and regenerating the *jíbaro* to promote the island's progress. U.S. colonial authority displaced the native elite, but offered new opportunities for professionals in the administration (Bergad, 1978). The campaign became an attractive endeavor for medical professionals who sought to establish their social position. The campaign became embedded in a new purpose and its directors claimed, once the problem of anemia was solved, that Puerto Rico "will enter upon an era of prosperity which to-day [sic] our most extravagant dreams can not [sic] foreshadow" (Ashford and Gutiérrez Igaravídez, 1911: 22). The campaign's effort to simultaneously colonize and modernize the island ultimately required a form of medical intervention that was supported by the colonial administration and facilitated by the native elite.

Ashford explained the significance of the campaign, and, specifically, its emphasis on medical treatment, in a 1910 report to Governor George Colton. He explained that, at the Bayamon Municipal Hospital in 1903, Puerto Rican physicians had "an opportunity to observe the practical work and the results of treatment" (Ashford, 1910). This reflected his fundamental vision of the campaign as "an important demonstration of the innate power of our medical fraternity in the Island to successfully meet the present situation" (Ashford, 1910). Framing the campaign in this way is analytically useful to us now because it reflected the ways Ashford shared

---

By treating the infected. 2. By educating the people to avoid infection" (Ashford and Gutierrez Igaravídez, 1911: 241). Ashford grew increasingly frustrated with the limits of educating individual patients, which included searching for ways to build latrines that would force rural peasants to sit rather than squat. By 1909, Ashford wrote a letter to Major Charles Lynch of the Army Medical Corps expressing his exasperation: "after trying every known means of combating the disease from a sanitarian's standpoint, the Commission hit upon the only true way to exterminate *uncinariasis* from among a whole people", i.e. medicine (Ashford, 1909). As a result, the campaign's attention to soil pollution was inconsistent through 1920, when the Rockefeller Foundation's International Health Board (IHB) began advancing sanitation control measures following a hookworm survey on the island (International Health Board, 1920; see also International Health Board, 1919; Farley, 2004; Hewa, 1995: 97).

the U.S. colonial administration's understanding of the campaign as a demonstration to promote favorable public opinion. The campaign demonstrated the significance of medical professionals to the U.S. colonial administration. It also demonstrated the ability of physicians to intervene more broadly in a "situation" that was not only medical, but also economic (Ashford, 1910). Finally, the report granted native physicians' authority and agency. Like Alonso, Ashford, and the Puerto Rican hookworm campaign, physicians' authority over *jíbaros* was represented through *jíbaros* as caricatures, albeit as patients in a new story that framed a modern Americanized medical discourse.

Ashford titled his autobiography *A Soldier in Science* (1934), alluding to the multiple struggles he confronted as an American medical scientist in the U.S. Army working among rural laborers and Puerto Rican physicians. His battle to convince these groups that he had discovered an explanation for the inefficient production of the Puerto Rican peasant, a significant obstacle to economic progress, ultimately rested on convincing them that the hookworm, a microscopic parasite, could explain Puerto Rico's most significant health problem.

The campaign's success developed through a series of local efforts and in relation to the financial and logistical support of municipal governments. The first Commission extended its efforts beyond Bayamon to Utuado in 1904 and Aibonito in 1905 and eventually included substations in many surrounding towns (see Figure 10). The first anemia commission was of particular significance for three reasons. First, it involved municipal governments and physicians and contrasted the centralization of health, charities and corrections within the insular government in 1904. Second, Utuado and Aibonito were critically tied to national interests. Utuado was a town at the center of coffee-production, *criollo* (island-born creoles) influence and native resistance (Picó, 1993, 1981). Aibonito was "symbolically and deeply linked with *jíbaro* society and culture" (Scarano, 2012). The campaign's work in Aibonito contributed to Dr. Walter E. Weyl's impressions of "Labor Conditions in Porto Rico," which he published in his 1905 report in the *Bulletin of the Bureau of Labor.* Third, the first campaign consolidated and expanded public and professional support and international visibility for the Commission's work. Beginning in Bayamon, Dr. Gutiérrez Igaravídez, the director of the Bayamón Hospital and health officer of the town, joined the Commission as one of its directors. The Bayamon station was directed by Dr. Agustín Stahl. Native physicians' collaboration "creolized the [first] campaign" (Scarano, 2012).

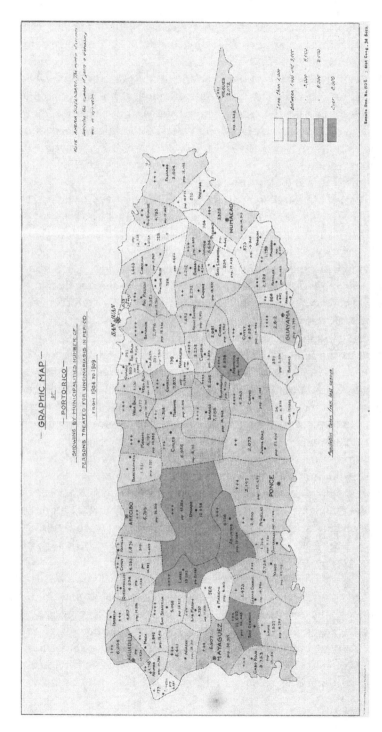

Figure 10.   Anemia Map (Ashford and Gutierrez Igaravidez, 1911).

The War Waged in the Utuado Clinic

Perhaps no municipality was more affected by the changes at the turn of the twentieth century than Utuado, the principal coffee producer in Puerto Rico before the U.S. invasion. In the last decades of the nineteenth century, it had the second-largest population growth on the island. Its wealth meant many local elites sought to modernize agriculture and sought autonomy from Spain, but in 1898, the Utuado elite had been divided in its support for U.S. protection (Píco, 2004). Increased agricultural production was exacted through multiple forms of labor control, which resulted in rural violence that exploded during the change in sovereignty, particularly in Utuado (Picó, 1993). For coffee producers, the violence was another blow in an onslaught that included a "reduction in prices, shrinking of credit, political uncertainty...[and] Hurricane San Ciriaco" (Píco, 2004: 65). By 1904, Utuado's elite found its legal, social, and political interests compromised by the U.S. colonial authorities (Marín 2006). The municipality was known as a stronghold for the *criollo* bourgeoisie and was overwhelmingly supportive of the Unionist Party (Grant, 1920; Picó, 1993). Amidst the disillusionment with the new colonial administration, a U.S.-initiated hookworm campaign engaged in a "war." This war was a demonstration, a popularity contest designed to promote public opinion and appeal to the *criollo* elite.

The campaign's 1904 report begins with a section titled, "History of Uncinariasis in Porto Rico." Ironically, this nine-page history is not focused on a parasite, but on the U.S. colonial administration and its efforts to invent a demonstration. More specifically, the U.S. colonial administration dominates this narrative as prominent actors who organized the campaign. For instance, it explains:

> The Governor, in his message to the Legislative Assembly, January, 1904, specifically called attention to the necessity of beginning an active campaign against the disease. A bill, providing for the formation of a commission for the study and treatment of anemia, and carrying with it an appropriation of $5000, was introduced by Mr. Post [at that time auditor], passed by the Assembly, and approved, February 16, 1904, by the Governor. (Commission for the Study and Treatment of Anemia, 1904: 8)

This quote is particularly noteworthy because it contrasts the campaign discourse that ensued. The campaign would come to enjoy significant local and insular support in the years that followed and the narrative about this popularity indicates this support was cultivated. In this early narrative, however, the report indicated that initial impetus for the campaign came from the colonial administration. For instance, in this narrative, U.S. colonial administrations "introduce" and "approve." Governor Hunt also requested the Army grant military leave to both Ashford and King in order to expand the campaign.

Brimming with popular support and backed by the financial and partisan assistance of the U.S. Governor, Ashford consolidated the campaign's influence in Utuado, "one of the most 'anemic' districts of the Island" and also "the most hungry of all of the Porto [sic] Rican municipalities" (Ashford and Gutiérrez Igaravídez, 1911: 1759; Commission for the Study and Treatment of Anemia, 1904). Ashford suggested his initial decision to move the camp to Utuado was part of his political strategy. He meant to counter anti-American sentiment in that area:

> When I discussed the matter of a move with Governor Hunt, I advocated Utuado, but he felt that, as this was the center of a party said to be anti-American and very hostile to the idea that the anemia was caused by anything but hard times and bad treatment of the natives, it would be unwise to risk failure at such a crucial period. I pointed out that if we succeeded, as we proposed to do, the effect on the rest of the country would be correspondingly strong. And so we went, armed with a letter to the only man in the town in whom the Governor felt sufficient confidence to ask the favor- because he had appointed him mayor-requesting that the Porto Rico Anemia Commission be assisted in its demonstration that the anemia of the Island was really a curable and preventable disease. (Ashford, 1934: 56)

The role of diet and hunger in Ashford's original 1899 narrative about uncinariasis contrasted this later one and positioned the Utuado clinic in relation to U.S. colonial interests. Ashford countered the colonial governor's concern about native resistance in the area by explaining the campaign would demonstrate anemia, rather than a product of colonization, "hard times and bad treatment," was really a curable and preventable disease (1934: 56). In this way, Ashford promoted the campaign as a colonial intervention where medicine could redefine hunger as a medical problem. The campaign worked through the administration to gain authority over the social context of suffering.

Ashford's early research could be seen as part of a mission to redirect Puerto Rican physicians toward developing scientific cures, rather than focusing on the politicized context and implications of diet and nutrition. Although many groups originally resisted Ashford's theories, he relentlessly defended them on the merits of his scientific training and the explanatory power of scientifically-derived facts. When Puerto Rican physicians and politicians challenged Ashford, he attributed their resistance to ignorance as well as political biases. Using a scientific-laden rhetoric, he engaged in an all-out war of words in the public arena to prevail over his detractors and win support for a new medical discourse on the anemia problem.

The campaign reproduced a medical discourse on rural environments. It claimed to counter the *jíbaro's* isolation and bring medical treatment to remote and isolated rural areas, but reproduced medicine's location in municipal centres like Utuado and Aibonito. From the town's centre, the campaign prioritized winning greater local support for the campaign's work. Ashford explained this approach to the Governor in 1910:

> From the very first the work against hook-worm disease was planned for the towns and their vicinity, leaving to a more favorable time the extension of this campaign to the, as yet, inaccessible mountain districts, approachable only by steep and rude paths. This was done, first, because we desired to prove to all town dwellers, and to as many country laborers who would be attracted to the dispensaries for treatment, that anemia was not 'starvation,' but a preventable parasitic disease; second, because we felt that thus public opinion and hence legislative action would be more rapid and efficacious; third, because this was the cheapest and quickest way of accrediting a work which was as yet unpopularized, the towns being the centers for the formation of public opinion. (Ashford, 1910)

The anemia campaign was hardly apolitical, which was evident from its inception. Ashford and King began the survey with the support of the "pro-American Director" of the Tricoche Hospital, Dr. Luis Aguerrevere. Ashford describes Aguerrevere as a politically-active physician who loved "furious denunciation and wild applause from the contending factions" and his contemporaries concurred in this assessment (Ashford, 1934: 53). Similarly, Ashford explained that Gutiérrez Igaravídez joined the first Commission in Bayamon and participated in the "unpopular work at the expense of his private interests" (Ashford and Gutiérrez Igaravídez, 1910: 1760). Although Aguerrevere may not have obtained any significant rewards for his support, the Commission offset Gutiérrez Igaravídez's expenses with a stipend that was more than double the $600 annual salary Dr. Stahl earned as a city physician (Parke, 1901).[10] Gutiérrez Igaravídez

---

[10] Stahl had alternate proposals for explaining anemia. He was lauded in the campaign's documents, but criticized as one among many self-interested physicians in Ashford's biography (1934). The issue of physicians' "collective orientation" was fundamental to the development of professional identity and medical ethics in the United States (Parsons, 1991). In Puerto Rico, the alternate meaning of a "collective orientation" was reflected by Stahl's political and social beliefs as president of the Puerto Rican Medical Association from 1905–1908, i.e., before it incorporated with the American Medical Association.

used his influence and "host of friends" to support the campaign's work and win the support of local elites (Ashford and Gutiérrez Igaravídez, 1910: 1760).

The campaign was not only about curing hookworm infection. It also took on moral tones as the campaign used its support to influence politics. In one example of how Ashford tied the campaign to formal, electoral politics, he undermines a local political figure through the campaign's work. Informed of a hired assassin among a line of patients, Ashford immediately determined the man had anemia and gave him water and thymol to treat it. As if relating a dehumanizing baptism, Ashford wrote he "drenched him just as we used to do to mules when they were sick at Fort Washington," jumped on the man's chest and told him to come back only if he wanted to "get well" (1934: 60). In this dramatic and physical conflict, Ashford claimed the man returned, explaining he was "a well man, and you [Ashford] have cured me, and now I want to know what you would like to have done to the man that sent me here." Ashford believed the erstwhile assassin was sent by someone who was involved in formal politics and his response was telling: Ashford ordered the "cured" man to "see to it that that man [who sent him] has no more to do with politics in Utuado" (Ashford, 1934: 59–62).

The campaign offered new status for a declining elite and its offspring. Many elite physicians were particularly interested in political, administrative, and professional autonomy. In contrast, many non-elite physicians, particularly those employed by municipal governments, were embedded in local politics. They found a new source of income and prestige through the hookworm campaign. Eventually, elite physicians also gained new political influence in relation to the U.S. colonial administration. For instance, Dr. Francisco Maria Susoni Abreu first became involved with the campaign and then went on to gain formal political positions within the insular government. Octavio Jordan was involved with the campaign in Utuado in 1904 while a freshman student at the Jefferson Medical College of Philadelphia and almost twenty years later became a senator (Commission for the Study and Treatment of Anemia 1904; Jefferson Medical College 1904).[11] For the most part, however, elite physicians

---

[11] Jordan was also part of a special commission sent by the Legislative Assembly to meet with Columbia University in 1924 regarding the establishment of a School of Tropical Medicine in Puerto Rico. The assembly also met with the Committee on Territories and Insular Possessions regarding Senate bill 2448 and Jordan referred to sanitation, the decreasing death rate and the school as justification for "American citizens...to be granted the power to elect their own governor" (Jordan in Senate, 1924: 32).

advocating political autonomy remained distinct from the physicians carrying out the research and treatments in the hookworm campaign.

The disparate participation of Utuado physicians also suggests the conflicts between political influence and new professional status.[12] A native of Utuado, Dr. Isaac Gonzalez Martinez was born on a coffee plantation (Hernandez Paralitici, 1983; Blanes, 1954).[13] In the tradition of Alonso, Zeno Gandia and Coll y Toste, he received his medical degree at the University of Barcelona. Unlike these physicians who were already in the 40s, however, Gonzalez Martinez represented a new generation of young, elite physicians on the island. Gonzalez Martinez began cultivating his scientific prestige through the campaign when he spent "ten days working with the Commission" in 1904 and discovered bilharzia (another parasitic disease) on the island (Commission for the Study and Treatment of Anemia, 1904: 14). Like Ashford, he was oriented toward an international medical community. Gonzalez Martinez joined the second, Permanent Commission as co-director in 1906, but fought to distinguish his unique medical contributions to medical science from those of the Commission (González Martinez, 1928). He had been a member of the Autonomist Party and joined the Unionist Party (Blanes, 1954). He later joined the Republican Party and "adapted to U.S. citizenship with great enthusiasm and advocated the development of ties between Puerto Rico and the United States" (Blanes, 1954).

González Martinez's career trajectory as a medical scientist contrasted Utuado's two municipal physicians in terms of their political and professional trajectory. González Martinez was a municipal physician of Mayaguez in 1899, which integrated him in a much larger and politically-connected medical community where he met other influential practitioners (Pacheco Padró, 1954). Utuado's two municipal physicians in 1901, Drs. Adrian Cueto and Julio R. Audinot, were not referenced in the

---

[12] These physicians included Dr. Manuel Quevedo Báez, a co-founder of the *Asociacion Medica de Puerto Rico,* who was in private practice (Hernandez Paralitici, 1983).

[13] Hernandez Paralitici (1983) asserts Isaac Gonzalez Martinez was born in Caguana, on the northwestern side of the municipality. This would have placed Gonzalez Martinez's associations close to (about six miles away from) his contemporary, Dr. Adrian Cueto, who resided in Salto Arriba, according to the 1910 Census. In 1919, however, both Gonzalez Martinez's passport application and a ship passenger list indicated he was born in San Sebastian, about 26 miles west of Caguana. This discrepancy may refer to changing municipal boundaries, but they nonetheless indicate the regional framework of shared conditions and associations. For instance, the distance between Caguana and San Sebastian includes Lares, which was the residence of Dr. Francisco Sein, another co-director of the second Anemia Commission.

campaign's multiple reports (Parke, 1901). All three physicians were Unionists, but in Utuado, where Republicans "could be counted with the fingers of one hand," the Party was deeply divided between moderates and radicals (Hernandez Paralitici, 1983). Moderates were represented by the pharmacist, Antonio de Jesús López, and radicals by Cueto. By 1906, Audinot was elected to the House of Delegates. In 1912, as a candidate of the newly-formed Independence party, Cueto became a popular mayor in Utuado. After his election, many local residents feared he would be killed (Hernandez Paralitici, 1983). When Cueto died in a car accident, the other driver was called to detail the events and mediate public doubt about his participation in a conspiracy to have the former assassinated (Hernandez Paralitici, 1983).[14]

Soiling Land and the Right to Rebel

If the spoil of tropical medicine's "war" was public opinion, the battles were waged by reconstructing *jíbaros'* "radical otherness" and the hookworm campaign's intervention on land and labor (Caponi, 2003: 128). This intervention was shaped through a nationalist discourse that found its origins in coffee production and that included the leadership of an urbanized and educated elite. Ashford called on the leadership of the "well-to-do, refined, educated class" to aid the campaign's development (Amador, 2008: 131). Similarly, Gutiérrez Igaravídez secured the support of political bosses and local elites in Bayamón (Amador, 2008: 131). This support facilitated the development of the hookworm campaign.

This discourse obscured class inequality. The campaign appealed to native elites by promising to regenerate the *jíbaro* as an efficient and productive worker (better health means more work). Ashford and Gutiérrez Igaravídez appealed to planters' "innate patriotism" to promote the campaign's intervention:

> to change the jibaro we must convince him that he will be bettered by the change... these changes must be begun by the men to whom the jibaro has always looked for light...From our acquaintance with the men...we should say that they are not only sufficiently good business men to realize the benefit they would get out of a healthy laboring class, but that the innate patriotism of the Porto Rican agriculturalist and the deeper underlying

---

[14] Cueto might be the brother of, or the same person, referred to as "José María" in multiple references within the AMPR's history (Arana-Soto, 1966: 121; see also Quevedo Báez, 1946, 1949).

sympathy for his jíbaro will some day bring about reforms that they alone can make possible. (Ashford and Gutiérrez Igaravídez, 1911: 15)

The campaign's appeal to elites and planters occluded the increased inequality and class conflict characterizing the coffee industry in the early twentieth century. In contrast, labor leaders focused on class relations. For instance, elected as House Delegate of the Socialist Party in 1904, Ramón Romero Rosa challenged the idea of nationalism and patriotism as ideological tools of the dominant class, writing "where there are slaves there can be no nation" (Rosa in Quintero Rivera, 1981: 30). According to Rosa, anemia was embedded in unequal labor relations that produced "slaves" and that implied a relationship where "our people are degraded; and because of this [exploitation], degenerates [the nation] because of anaemia of the blood and of the brain" (Rosa in Quintero Rivera, 1981: 30). His analysis challenged Ashford and King's narrative of uncinariasis as "the most important factors in the inferior mental, physical and financial condition of the poorer classes" (Ashford and King, 1904: 658). According to Rosa, capitalism was the blood-sucking parasite that had to be eliminated on the island. While Rosa understood the root causes of Puerto Rican suffering as a problem whose cure could be found in the social structure, the anemia campaign followed a path that maintained the status quo.

The war against death, featuring medical men as its soldiers, became particularly pressing in 1904 for two reasons. First, the campaign's directors asserted "the most heavily infested sections on the island" were coffee plantations (Ashford and Gutiérrez Igaravídez, 1910a: 22). Ashford and Gutiérrez Igaravídez were aware coffee represented a small and diminishing part of Puerto Rico's exports, particularly because the industry had been devastated by the 1899 San Ciriaco hurricane and it was not favored by U.S. markets (Dietz, 1986). Nonetheless, they repeatedly defined hookworm infection as an economic problem that jeopardized the island's prosperity.

Second, the economic disruptions to the coffee industry were only intensified by persistent problems with labor control. Elites had shared a concern about evasive forms of resistance, particularly as it was reflected in workers' mobility and a weak labor market for agricultural production. These markets were further disrupted after the hurricane as workers migrated to urban areas in search of work. Rural violence had also suggested labor could undermine the coffee industry's recovery. Still fresh in many Utuadenses' memory, rural violence against landowners and traders escalated in the latter decades of the twentieth century and during the transition of power between Spanish and U.S. colonialism. Laborers participated or were complicit in more militant and covert forms of protest, such as torching plantation property, which "attacked directly the most tangible symbol of planter economic, social, and political domination" (Figueroa, 2005: 189). These protests intensified during the change of sovereignty and "almost every case of burning a plantation...[was] traced to the hired men on the plantation" (in Go, 2008: 122). The *tiznados* burned ledgers that recorded their debts and re-appropriated stored food, which suggested the oppressive weight of hunger, debt, and dispossession on subsistence farmers and rural laborers. The hurricane and the Foraker Act increased the cost of, and need for, imported foods, which amplified hunger and immiseration. For instance, King explained that "many thousands during the past year have been living on a very meager diet and many have starved outright" (2006: 40).

The potential for violence in rural areas threatened economic recovery. Violent protests reflected the disruption of paternalistic planter-labor relations and the increasing proletarianization of workers on the island, which had only increased after 1898. For U.S. colonial administrators, for instance, the seditious bands of *tiznados* distinguished the rural interior as "poor, rebellious...dangerous, treacherous, cunning and backward" (Picó, 2004: 125). If the *tiznados* had altered their appearance for the purpose of violent resistance, the colonial administration and native physicians sought to compliment the colonial state's efforts to control rural violence through interventions on peasants' bodies. The campaign drew *jíbaros* to towns where they came into contact with campaign staff and both colonial and native elites. The clinic's cards recorded not only clinical histories, but also patients' social standing, trade and location, both in terms of rural district and farm.[15] The campaign prescribed and monitored multiple visits for medical treatment. As a result, the effort to eradicate the hookworm was also an effort at total colonization that included the island's mountainous interior.

Ashford and the physicians participating in the campaign attempted to popularize their war and generalize elites' interest in colonizing rural peasants and the rural interior. In the proposed intervention, Ashford's narrative about anemia privileged science. His singular focus on

---

[15] Campaign inspectors used more detailed cards and collected information about farm owners, kind of farm, the owner of the house, the house inhabitants and whether these inhabitants attended a particular anemia commission's station (Permanent Commission for the Suppression of Uncinariasis in Porto Rico, 1907).

hookworm as the "one definite cause" of anemia minimized other medical explanations dominant in Puerto Rico, including nutrition and living standards (Ashford and Gutiérrez Igaravídez, 1910a: 25). Ashford's (undated) emphasis on the hookworm facilitated medical intervention, but minimized the role of "an insufficient or improper diet" when he wrote: "we as medical men may deplore but cannot help such conditions wherever they may exist" (Ashford, undated). In other contexts, the doctrine of specific aetiology has been conservative and obscured the importance of other social causes in causing disease (Dubos, 1959; Tesh, 1988). Ashford's theory of how anemia was caused, which he located singularly in the hookworm, focused on medical treatment and detracted from programs of broader social change that implicated a disease ultimately "embedded in the socioeconomic and cultural circumstances of the population" (Ramírez de Arellano and Seipp, 1983: 10). By focusing on the parasite, the campaign's new medical men could offer the *jíbaro* a solution to an anemia that medical practitioners had previously declared "beyond their power to cope with" (Ashford, undated).

Ashford and Gutiérrez Igaravídez wrote that the *jíbaro* had been neglected and criticized the way "all the Porto Rican people...treat them as though they were children," yet themselves reconstructed the *jíbaro* in terms that reinscribed his subservience to an "educated and controlling class" that undoubtedly included Ashford's "medical men" (1911: 13). They reported that:

> the jibaro loyally follows his educated, emancipated fellow citizen, perfectly satisfied to be guided as the latter sees fit. Much of this guidance is excellent, and it is not our mission to seek to break down barriers which to-day may be needful...had he been ill treated by the educated and controlling class in the island he would be sullen and savage, but this has not been the case. (Ashford and Gutiérrez Igaravídez, 1911: 13)

Despite how they understood their own motivations, Ashford and Gutiérrez Igaravídez replicated the same infantilization of the *jíbaro.* Just as they struggled to reform the *jíbaro,* they ignored the exploitation s/he endured and ultimately shared the elite's interest in bolstering the coffee industry and maintaining the *criollo* bourgeoisie.

Ashford and Gutiérrez Igaravídez began their 1911 report by drawing attention to the patient, the "real man," behind the hookworm pandemic. They constructed the *jíbaro* as "a peasant, a tiller of soil...a separate and distinct class, a class of country laborers [who] live now as they 'live 100 or 200 years ago, close to the soil'" (Ashford and Gutiérrez Igaravídez, 1911: 12). This construction is particularly puzzling because economic, colonial, and

industrial changes had uprooted much of the island's peasantry. The overwhelming majority of coffee-producing farms were in the hands of peasant owners before 1900, although they represented a small percentage of
the total cultivated acreage (Bergad, 1978: 85). This meant most producers
were small landowners and were particularly vulnerable to the declining
fortunes of the coffee industry. In contrast, the majority of workers were
landless. The latter group had been displaced by debt and the expansion
of the coffee industry over the last quarter of the nineteenth century.
Peasants were further dispossessed after the hurricane and amidst the
declining fortunes of the coffee industry. These campaigns' references to
land and soil were nonetheless ubiquitous. They served to emphasize the
close relationship between laborers' bodies and production. In a narrative
that blamed labor for the coffee industry's problems, the campaign's
reports demonstrated how the laborer's bodily practices threatened modern, efficient production, his livelihood and, ultimately, his life. The *jíbaro*
became both source of and solution to the island's greatest problems.

By emphasizing the relationship between *jíbaros* and coffee planters in
a dynamic class formation, the campaign redirected the latter's attention
to their responsibility for the former's development: "The planter is the
man of all men in Porto Rico who must begin to help the *jíbaro* upward in
order to emerge from his own present industrial depression" (Ashford and
Gutiérrez Igaravídez, 1911: 15). They saw the *jíbaro's* development as inter-
dependent with coffee planters' financial fortunes. The authors discussed
the low price of Puerto Rican coffee, but argued it nonetheless "permits a
fair margin of profit" (Ashford and Gutiérrez Igaravídez, 1911: 16). The planter's problem was that this profit was eroded by a variety of factors: "The
heaviest load he [the planter] has to carry is the infirmity of his laborers,
their almost universal anemia, and the ignorance of the class of labor
upon which he has to depend" (Ashford and Gutiérrez Igaravídez, 1911: 16).
Although planters paid peons "for a full day's work...their degree of anemia is such as to prevent their doing but about 50 per cent of what they are
paid for doing" (Ashford and Gutiérrez Igaravídez, 1911: 16). Ashford and
Gutiérrez Igaravídez implied the most significant problem facing the coffee industry was caused by the *jíbaro* who would not, could not, work
harder. This medicalization of the coffee industry's misfortunes detracted
from planters' concerns about U.S. colonization.

Although Puerto Rican physicians may have seen their work with the
hookworm campaign as an aspect of broader modernization on the island,
they ultimately reproduced their authority through the language of labor
that defined health by repeated contrasts with perceived laziness. Reports

emphasized work over the subjective experiences of dis-ease caused by hunger, work strain, or medical treatment (thymol). Through this narrative, the campaign ennobled patients who came to the clinic, "not because they felt sick, but because they could no longer work" (Ashford and Gutiérrez Igaravídez, 1911: 7). Their narrow focus on productive labour ignored many important aspects of the social context and helped to maintain the sources of distress and suffering (Waitzkin, 1991).

Ashford and Gutiérrez Igaravídez noted several problems faced the island's coffee workers. Wages were low, work was difficult and "an immense number of mountain people" were unemployed or underemployed for a better part of the year (Ashford and Gutiérrez Igaravídez, 1911: 10).[16] These problems only intensified amidst adverse market conditions encouraged by U.S. policy and the colonial administration. The *jíbaro* also had a restricted diet and "only a few cents difference in wages will cut out the small proportion of animal proteins he obtains" (Ashford and Gutiérrez Igaravídez, 1911: 12). Despite their observations, the authors were unsure wage increases would improve the *jíbaros'* diet: "If wages were better, it is said he would leave his ration as it is now and spend his surplus otherwise...he takes also more rum than he is given credit for" (Ashford and Gutiérrez Igaravídez, 1911: 13). The authors did not propose increasing wages or the price paid per unit of coffee picked to solve the *jíbaro's* problems. Instead, Ashford and Gutiérrez Igaravídez believed the solution lay in his own "bodily, mental, and moral development" (1911: 15).

Ashford's emphasis on *jíbaros'* feces was not simply a cultural distinction based on standards of hygiene or a new scientific reordering of medicine's approach to the *jíbaro*. Through the human act of defecation, the *jíbaro* is symbolically reduced and positioned as a subject in the campaign's scientific truth about disease. The campaign constructed the physical spaces where *jíbaros* deposited their feces as seemingly arbitrary and as a marker of not only their lack of discipline, but also their ignorance. Through a reduction of the *jíbaros'* problems to his dirty "otherizing"

---

16 Walter E. Weyl, a progressive reformer, visited the field hospital in Aibonito in 1905 and studied these labor conditions. The campaign was an effort to intervene in these conditions as an antidote to the effect of weak coffee markets on labor. Coffee laborers "were the lowest paid...hours were long and work was seasonal...coffee producers...struggled to survive in the face of adverse market conditions in the face of the calculated policy and benign neglect of the United States" (Dietz, 1986: 102). Despite these limitations, "coffee provided cash or collateral with which to buy food, clothes, and other items that could not be produced, or were difficult to produce, within the peasant household, and to pay taxes and repay loans" (Dietz, 1986: 65).

behavior, the campaign not only stigmatized and humiliated the patient, but also endeavored to resurrect the *jíbaros'* faith in a modern intervention on their behavior. On the one hand, rural peasants were tortured by high prices on imported food, low wages or profits on harvests and, ultimately, hunger. On the other hand, like a victim of torture, they were presented with an explanation for their problems that centered on their filthy behavior and unhygienic habits. As in the late-nineteenth century, peasants were restigmatized as isolated and backward. In the twentieth century, however, the campaign stigmatized peasants in relation to patients' feces. Like a victim of torture, *jíbaros* were stigmatized by their feces, which became the locus of a socio-cultural breakdown that enabled the development of faith in reforms initiated by the United States. The campaign intervened in the relationship between the development of capitalism and the worker and became a part of his torture. He was "faced not with the value or horror of the system – a ground upon which he would stand strong - but with a rift and intimate rottenness – a ground of weakness for him. The revelation of his own filth, which is what torture tries to produce by degrading him, should be enough to deprive him…of his right to rebel" (de Certeau, 1986: 42).

The Medical Men who Shaped a New Medical Discourse

The medical men of the campaign included station, substation and dispensary directors. They were critical functionaries mediating the brutal conditions of hunger in the early twentieth century. Through the campaign, an "important demonstration of the innate power of our medical fraternity in the Island to successfully meet the present situation," they engaged in a war for elite support and developed a new medical discourse that medicalized the coffee industry's misfortunes (Ashford, 1910). The weapon in this war was medical treatment to regenerate the symbol of a barefoot population as a productive wage earner. Like late-nineteenth century *jíbarista* authors, the campaign also used the *jíbaro* as a discursive weapon. Unlike its predecessors, however, this modern medical war was fashioned in opposition to the Spanish colonial legacy and relied on local engagement and penetration. In contrast to the earlier authors' interventions on isolated swamps, the hookworm campaign's intervention focused on recruiting patients to cleanse contaminated soil and its implied relationship to production and progress. By 1904, this soil was also metaphorically contaminated by increased political resistance to U.S. colonial authority.

The hookworm campaign that followed the first anemia commission expanded into new municipalities, reflecting its growing popularity among elites and its political influence. The campaign also developed support among municipal governments such that, "in four of our ten stations the town offered to bear all the expenses if we would administer the work and furnish the medicines" (Ashford and Gutiérrez Igaravídez, 1910: 1760). As the campaign's standing and operations grew, its appropriations increased. Ashford emphasized his victory in the war for public opinion in political terms when he described how "gentlemen in frock coats who took no interest whatsoever in such things nervously consented to any proposition that would keep their constituents quiet and satisfied" (1934: 68).

Ashford may have won a war using Puerto Rican physicians as soldiers and *jíbaros* as weapons, but it is not readily apparent that the victory extended beyond promoting surveillance in rural municipalities and consolidating elite and U.S. colonial authority. For instance, the dominant narrative about the campaign includes references to the number of patients that were treated. Although the campaign maintained case histories, there was no record in its numerous documents of any attempt to reconcile patients treated at different stations, sub-stations, dispensaries and field hospitals. We know workers migrated in an attempt to navigate adverse social conditions. Ashford also recognized patients were reinfected by the hookworm and they visited the dispensaries at different times during the campaign. By 1911, the campaign claimed to have treated 30% of the island's population, but the number of patients treated in any given year was a small proportion of the overall population within a given district. The 1919 Rockefeller Foundation's survey that found 80% infection rates in some districts suggested the limits of the campaign's success.

The campaign's records also indicate many patients did not return to the dispensary after an initial treatment to complete the prescribed medical regimen of three to four treatments, in order to be cured. The campaign's evidence consistently demonstrates the "practically cured" patients were a larger population than reports of those who were "cured" (Permanent Commission for the Suppression of Uncinariasis in Porto Rico, 1907). Campaign physicians also pursued different medical treatment regimens and different dosages of thymol. Research in and beyond the campaign indicated thymol was a toxic and unpleasant medication, which may have increased the likelihood patients avoided taking the medication they obtained from campaign stations once they got home.[17] Despite treatment, patients continued to carry the hookworm and some probably avoided taking the medication. Even where patients completed the campaign's medical treatment regimen, iron deficiency is caused by a variety of factors and may have remained a persistent medical problem (Crosby, 1986).

The campaign's records indicate the number of patients treated fell far short of Ashford's (1907) goal of mass treatment. They also cast doubt on his exaggerated claims about the campaign's work; for instance, of having treated, in the period from 1905 to 1909, "8,598 out of a registered total of 8,596 inhabitants" in Aibonito (Ashford, 1934: 69). Following the campaign, the Rockefeller Foundation focused on "worm burden" and displaced the campaign's previous attention to curing individual patients as part of its demonstration. Instead, the International Health Board's interventions in Puerto Rico and other countries focused on removing "the largest possible number of worms from the largest possible number of persons" (1922: xxv). These later efforts demonstrated the significance of mass treatment.

The dominant narrative about the campaign's popularity depended on assertions involving rural patients. For instance, referencing individual

---

[17] Ashford and Gutierrez Igaravídez noted their "experience in Bayamon proved to us that it was reasonably safe to allow thymol to be taken at home, even in severe cases" (1911: 107). In contrast, the British medical association's committee to study hookworm in the colonies recommended "thymol and other toxic anthelmintics should only be used under medical supervision" (Palmer, 2010: 44). Many physicians recognized thymol as an unpleasant medication (International Health Board, 1922). Several campaign physicians avoided using thymol. For instance, Dr. Bou la Torre described the unpleasant effects of thymol treatment at a dosage demonstrated by Dr. Sein and used at other stations, which included dizziness, chills, ringing in the ears and vertigo. He resorted to half the dosage used by Dr. Izquierdo who observed patients continued to demonstrate hookworm after four or five doses of thymol. Their findings indicated medical treatment may have been limited in its success, particularly among the majority of the campaign's patients who were classified as "partially cured." Dr. Dueño also explained many patients were cured by the fourth dose, but the average was 6.4 doses. He noted some patients required 15–25 doses and implied that they, because of "bad faith or fraud," may not have taken the medication (in Permanent Commission for the Suppression of Uncinariasis in Porto Rico, 1907: 105). Dr. Gatell expressed similar concerns and doubts about dispensing thymol and naphthol 8–10 times. Similarly, Drs. Franco Soto and Igaravídez y Landron preferred napthol. Dr. Ferran explained he began using napthol exclusively in order to accelerate cures. In 1905, Dr. Cestero acknowledged thymol's "poisonous effects…[and] toxic properties…in which case even death may follow" (in Commission for the Suppression of Anemia in Puerto Rico, 1905: 43). By 1907, Dr. Cestero suggested the Commission use an alternate anthelmintic medication because he frequently observed patients infected with other parasites that were immune to thymol. Other physicians used iron in treating patients, including Drs. Vidal, Vizcarrondo and Gaztambide (Commission for the Suppression of Anemia in Puerto Rico, 1905; Permanent Commission for the Suppression of Uncinariasis in Porto Rico, 1907).

patient's testimonies, historians who have studied the campaign reproduce its broader narrative that most patients loved Ashford and stations
developed in response to popular demand (Amador, 2008; Rigau-Pérez,
2000). Although many individual's feelings were undoubtedly positive
about the campaign, the demand for stations did not come from patients
in early-twentieth century Puerto Rico. The distinction between government support and patient demand becomes evident when the number of
patients treated by the Permanent Commission for the Suppression of
Uncinariasis in Porto Rico is compared to the overall number of residents
from any particular municipality (See Table 8: Percentage of Municipal
Population Treated, 1906–1907). This comparison demonstrates an average of 8% of the municipal population was seen and treated, but not necessarily "cured" or "partly cured." Municipalities where 20% or more of the
population visited the station were clustered in areas west of the Utuado
clinic, particularly Añasco, Camuy, Las Marias, Lares and San German.
The first four of these municipalities roughly corresponded with the
regional influence and networks of physicians in the Mayaguez area,
which centered on the northwestern corner of the island. In contrast,
many municipalities that fell under the average were clustered on the
eastern half of the island and on the southern coast. In almost a quarter of
all 66 municipalities, about 1% of municipal residents were treated by the
Permanent Commission.

These percentages did not correspond neatly with the amount of time
a particular station had been in operation. For instance, approximately
10% of Utuado's residents attended the station annually from 1904–1907,
despite the fact the campaign based its narrative about its own popularity
from its operations in this municipality and was probably most known
there. In Lares, Dr. Benet Valdes perhaps referenced the municipal physician's earlier work with the campaign when he explained that almost 50%
of the municipality had attended the station between 1904 and 1907,
"obtained the cure and very few of these have contracted the disease
again" (in Permanent Commission for the Suppression of Uncinariasis in
Porto Rico, 1907: 101).[18] Dr. Benet Valdes did not explain how he knew or

---

[18] Dr. Francisco Sein, the Lares municipal physician, had worked with the campaign at
the station that began in 1905, but Valdes suggested 13,000 patients were treated in the
years from 1905–1907 (in Permanent Commission for the Suppression of Uncinariasis in
Porto Rico, 1907: 101). In 1905, Dr. Sein explained he had 12,273 visits to the Lares clinic, but
this did not mean each visit was a new patient. He also explained that he was not able to
diagnose patients and obtain systematic verification of hookworm infection (Sein in
Commission for the Suppression of Anemia in Puerto Rico, 1905).

Table 8. Campaign Popularity.[1]

Municipality	Total Population of Municipality in 1910	Patients Treated in 1906–1907	Percentage of Population Treated
Adjuntas	16,954	2,184	12.9%
Aguada	11,587	1,142	9.9%
Aguadilla	21,419	1,246	5.8%
Aguas Buenas	8,292	89	1.1%
Aibonito	10,815	2,338	21.6%
Anasco	14,407	3,511	24.4%
Arecibo	42,429	2,555	6.0%
Arroyo	6,940	291	4.2%
Barceloneta	11,644	1,531	13.1%
Barranquitas	10,503	1,129	10.7%
Bayamon	29,986	956	3.2%
Cabo Rojo	19,562	2,542	13.0%
Caguas	27,160	139	0.5%
Camuy	11,342	2,294	20.2%
Carolina	15,327	522	3.4%
Cayey	17,711	1,669	9.4%
Ciales	18,398	1,639	8.9%
Cidra	10,595	803	7.6%
Coamo	17,129	1,336	7.8%
Comerio	11,170	1,242	11.1%
Corozal	12,978	2,364	18.2%
Dorado	4,885	156	3.2%
Fajardo	21,135	191	0.9%
Guarabo	11,139	253	2.3%
Guayama	17,379	1,106	6.4%
Guayanilla	10,354	408	3.9%
Hatillo	10,630	722	6.8%
Humacao	26,678	2,641	9.9%
Isabela	16,852	2,218	13.2%
Juana Diaz	29,157	139	0.5%
Juncos	11,692	1,554	13.3%
Lajas	11,071	1,637	14.8%
Lares	22,650	4,464	19.7%
Las Marias	10,046	2,154	21.4%
Loiza	13,317	21	0.2%
Manati	17,240	2,157	12.5%

Table 8. (*Cont.*)

Municipality	Total Population of Municipality in 1910	Patients Treated in 1906–1907	Percentage of Population Treated
Maricao	7,158	79	1.1%
Maunabo	7,106	2	0.0%
Mayaguez	42,429	3,901	9.2%
Moca	13,640	2,163	15.9%
Morovis	12,446	3,325	26.7%
Naguabo	14,365	49	0.3%
Naranjito	8,876	517	5.8%
Patillas	14,448	145	1.0%
Penuelas	11,991	9	0.1%
Ponce	63,444	1,454	2.3%
Quebradillas	8,152	1,223	15.0%
Rincon	7,275	7	0.1%
Rio Grande	13,948	14	0.1%
Rio Piedras	18,880	2,310	12.2%
Sabana Grande	11,523	1,060	9.2%
Salinas	11,403	21	0.2%
San German	22,143	6,103	27.6%
San Juan	48,716	315	0.6%
San Lorenzo	14,278	183	1.3%
San Sebastian	18,904	2,331	12.3%
Santa Isabel	6,959	16	0.2%
Toa Alta	9,127	458	5.0%
Toa Baja	6,254	8	0.1%
Trujillo Alto	6,345	320	5.0%
Utuado	41,054	4,444	10.8%
Vega Alta	8,134	498	6.1%
Vega Baja	12,831	2,197	17.1%
Vieques	10,425	801	7.7%
Yabucoa	17,338	123	0.7%
Yauco	31,504	1,558	4.9%
Average percentage of population treated	8.2%		

[1] (Data abstracted from Permanent Commission for the Suppression of Uncinariasis in Porto Rico, 1907).

verified that few had been reinfected, and did not claim, for instance, that cured patients stopped by at the station. He also recognized that at least 30% of the rural population hadn't yet appreciated the benefits of the campaign's work (Valdes in Permanent Commission for the Suppression of Uncinariasis in Porto Rico, 1907).

The campaign treated the *jíbaro* as a patient and, beyond clinical histories, didn't give much voice to their individual narratives.[19] Several of the campaign's medical men did provide some limited indications of how patients understood their symptoms and the intervention. Many station directors noted how patients had reported experiencing mazamorra, which the campaign's directors explained was "a Spanish word whose use is corrupted by the jíbaro. It usually means to them a separate and distinct disease of the feet...they declare it to be the penetration of the skin by 'culebras,' or little serpents, to be found in certain pools of stagnant water, decomposing vegetable matter, and mud" (Ashford and Gutiérrez Igaravídez, 1911: 48).[20] Some physicians noted the *campesino* (peasant, farmer) referred to the edema that accompanied uncinariasis as the "*hermosura,*" "*linda,*" "*bonita,*" or "*niña bonita,*" which implied beauty (Commission for the Suppression of Anemia in Puerto Rico, 1905: 40; Permanent Commission for the Suppression of Uncinariasis in Porto Rico, 1907: 79, 92). Although one physician considered these names for the disease were developed out of a sense of irony, they also indicated those infected were less alarmed than physicians by hookworm infection. The infected may have been more concerned about the forms of intervention promoted by the campaign. For instance, several physicians noted patients abandoned the treatment regimen after their [patients'] curiosity about the stations wore off. Dr. Luis Gonzalez Garmendia, in Isabela, noted his request for patients to bring a feces sample were not followed because they didn't think it was necessary and considered it dirty and denigrating (Permanent Commission for the Suppression of Uncinariasis in Porto Rico, 1907: 98). Dr. Acisclo Bou la Torre, the station director at Corozal, noted "the public" had come to believe the campaign's medical

---

[19] Campaign physicians were most likely to use the term *campesino* rather than *jíbaro.* Their attention to *campesino's* customs and "special language" were comparable to the intellectual elite's denigrating references to the *jíbaro* (Gonzalez Garmendia in Permanent Commission for the Suppression of Uncinariasis in Porto Rico, 1907: 98).

[20] The recognition of mazamorra preceded the campaign's intervention and indicates a broader awareness of the problem. As a result, the campaign's claim to educate patients, and its popularity, was conditioned by not only physicians' pre-existing discourse about progress, but also rural populations' understandings of health and infection.

treatment caused edema and, subsequently, death (in Permanent Commission for the Suppression of Uncinariasis in Porto Rico, 1907: 93). Physicians may not have enjoyed the professional legitimacy they hoped to cultivate through their own participation in the campaign and other medical associations.

The medical men provided an alternate narrative about the campaign's popularity. In individual stations, they resorted to a variety of measures in order to promote the campaign's work. For instance, Dr. Cestero Molina considered "the unwillingness of the country people in this region to attend the dispensary clinic" a serious obstacle that cost him hard work (in Commission for the Suppression of Anemia in Puerto Rico, 1905: 43). Dr. Cordero y Escalona used his own money to have 2,000 flyers printed that announced his work, the cause of uncinariasis and methods for preventing hookworm infection (in Permanent Commission for the Suppression of Uncinariasis in Porto Rico, 1907). Dr. Gatell felt all his efforts in a coffee-producing municipality had been "sterile" because less than 10% of the local population had visited the station (in Permanent Commission for the Suppression of Uncinariasis in Porto Rico, 1907). Dr. Gonzalez Garmendia explained he had to "drag 2,595 jibaros out of the error of believing that anemia is due to poor food and to convince them that it is due to an intestinal parasite" (in Ashford and Gutiérrez Igaravídez, 1911: 219).

Despite their efforts, many campaign physicians compared themselves to other stations, felt they had not been successful in attracting large numbers of patients to visit their stations, and resorted to alternate measures.[21] Dr. Garriga contrasted the support of local authorities with the *campesinos'* apathy (in Permanent Commission for the Suppression of Uncinariasis in Porto Rico, 1907: 74). Before recognizing patient's unwillingness to attend his clinic, Dr. Cestero Molina had thanked the municipal mayor in 1905 for providing two employees to support his (Cestero Molina's) efforts at "arousing the interest of the people in the country districts and for admonishment concerning the construction of latrines" (Commission for the Suppression of Anemia in Puerto Rico, 1905: 45). He also thanked the president of the municipal council and the pastor of the Methodist Episcopal Church, which indicated the broader support among elites for

---

[21] Although many campaign physicians presented comparisons about attendance at their station in general terms, several comments about Aibonito suggested they felt they should match or surpass the attendance at an early and popular station where many had observed the campaign's methods. This narrative was not explicitly tied to any specific reward, but physicians may have associated higher attendance rates with greater professional prestige.

the campaign. Several physicians echoed reliance on municipal authorities to compel visits to the campaign's stations. Dr. Dueño recognized the lack of attendance at his station, which puzzled him because an inspector had gone through the countryside *"hacienda propaganda,"* or propagandizing, among *campesinos* (in Permanent Commission for the Suppression of Uncinariasis in Porto Rico, 1907: 106). Dr. Igaravídez y Landron thanked the mayor for sending the *comisarios de barrios* to "stimulate attendance at the dispensary" (in Permanent Commission for the Suppression of Uncinariasis in Porto Rico, 1907: 89).[22] Dr. Cestero Molina confirmed the critical role of police in efforts to compel patients' attendance. He referred to patients' resistance and explained their visits only increased when a lieutenant assigned a police officer to the station's service (Permanent Commission for the Suppression of Uncinariasis in Porto Rico, 1907).[23]

The campaign's medical men reverted to the medical/hygienic discourse of the late-nineteenth century and revived their efforts at labor control in two ways. First, distinct from their earlier contrast of workers and vagrants, some believed they converted beggars into working men through medical treatment. For instance, Dr. Palou claimed he converted cadavers that appeared at the clinic into "men useful for work and capable of supporting their families, some of them abandoning beggary, the sad extreme they had to resort to because they had found it impossible to earn their sustenance" (in Permanent Commission for the Suppression of Uncinariasis in Porto Rico, 1907: 100). He ignored the contingent and seasonal nature of agricultural work by focusing on the power of medicine to produce productive labor.

Second, by expressing their support for coercive sanitation measures, campaign physicians sought to use the campaign to effect more efficient forms of surveillance and discipline. Dr. Guillermo Carreras y Iglesias, in Vieques, recommended severe laws that would obligate the "delinquent and apathetic" to visit an anemia station until they obtained a health certificate akin to business licenses that would be required for employment (in Permanent Commission for the Suppression of Uncinariasis in Porto

---

[22] *Comisarios de barrios* policed rural populations and extended state power throughout the countryside under Spanish colonial rule. They "policed the countryside and represented the municipality in administration...maintained order and pursued fugitives" (Carrasquillo, 2006: 29). They were often landed peasants themselves who were familiar to other residents in a particular barrio and represented "the authorities closest to the laboring population" of rural barrios (Carrasquillo, 2006: 82). They also protected the interests of large landowners and some used the position to advance their own interests.

[23] Cestero noted patients' visits declined when the officer changed because other officers didn't have the same interest in the campaign.

Rico, 1907: 116). Physicians also sought to compel compliance with sanitation measures, including building and using latrines. For instance, Dr. Atilio Gaztambide argued that controlling sources of infection might require coercive measures, if necessary, to complement the efforts of urban police and obligate *campesinos* (peasants, small farmers) to defecate in stable places (in Permanent Commission for the Suppression of Uncinariasis in Porto Rico, 1907: 85). His associations tied labor mobility to decreased working capacity and production vis à vis the hookworm. Similarly, the Cayey and Juncos station directors suggested insular guards should complement the campaign's propaganda and supervise latrine construction (in Permanent Commission for the Suppression of Uncinariasis in Porto Rico, 1907). Dr. Igaravídez y Landron echoed the desire for a rural hygiene police force attached to each station for "their own good and for [public] health in general" (in Permanent Commission for the Suppression of Uncinariasis in Porto Rico, 1907: 89). Although the campaign physicians' calls for police support indicated their interest in exerting control at the local level, some physicians sought to share control with local elites or the colonial administration. For instance, Dr. Caballero cast his support in favour of employers and argued "owners of these plantations...can enforce these rules [sanitation] better than the police" (in Ashford and Gutiérrez Igaravídez 1911: 217). Dr. Palou appealed to the colonial administration to "excite" judges to take violations of sanitation regulation more seriously (in Permanent Commission for the Suppression of Uncinariasis in Porto Rico, 1907: 100).

Few of the campaign's medical men referred to diet and/or shoes or expressed their support for alternate preventive measures that did not involve developing sanitation regulations, policing and/or legal enforcement. The notable exception was the otherwise prominent and influential scientist and physician, Dr. Stahl. From the Bayamon station, he persistently reminded the Commission of the need for prophylactic measures and the importance of diet. Unlike Ashford and allopathic medicine's emphasis on medical intervention and treatment, Stahl also insisted prevention was the objective to which all men of science had directed their efforts "in all times and places" (in Permanent Commission for the Suppression of Uncinariasis in Porto Rico, 1907: 81). Stahl insisted prevention should precede, or at least accompany, medical intervention, but lamented the campaign's lack of executive power to enforce sanitation regulations that existed on the island. He also criticized the colonial administration for inconsistent support for prophylactic measures: the Governor had not followed through with a recommendation to the

Commissioner of the Interior to provide portable latrines to prisoners working on road construction (Stahl in Permanent Commission for the Suppression of Uncinariasis in Porto Rico, 1907). This criticism implied the campaign hoped employers would lead sanitation reforms the colonial administration could not, or would not, employ. Stahl's criticism also implied the colonial administration was irresponsible in compromising workers' health. Stahl's emphasis on diet was also suggestive of the terms upon which Ashford said they disagreed about causes. Stahl represented an older generation of physicians who had done research on anemia before 1898 and he emphasized diet and nutrition as "the reason" for anemia.[24] Stahl continued to emphasize diet in 1907 in his report that opened with the claim, "undoubtedly the most serious cases of Anemia by Uncinariasis are observed in malnourished individuals...by a diet deficient in quality and quantity" (in Permanent Commission for the Suppression of Uncinariasis in Porto Rico, 1907: 80).

Other directors underscored the political and economic effects of the campaign. Dr. Felipe B. Vizcarrondo, in Barranquitas, related how "the commission has made mighty little echo in some few municipalities...which have accepted the installation in their towns of a dispensary more as pretext to lower the salary of the 'Medico Titular' [municipal doctor]" (in Ashford and Gutiérrez Igaravídez, 1911: 217). Dr. Susoni in Arecibo praised "the most beautiful work, the most meritorious, the most trascendental [sic] and humanitarian that has been effected under the American flag" (in Ashford and Gutiérrez Igaravídez, 1911: 217). Dr. Franco Soto celebrated the Governor as the benefactor of the campaign who deserved the "most prolonged applause and warmest congratulations from the proletarian class who had glimpsed amidst their tribulations a new era of luck and fortune (*dichas y bienandanzas*) (in Permanent Commission for the Suppression of Uncinariasis in Porto Rico, 1907: 112). Dr. Canino at the Aibonito station commented the "Porto Rico Leaf Tobacco Co. has contributed much to the progress of this station" (in Ashford and Gutiérrez Igaravídez, 1911: 217). In Comerto, Dr. de la Rosa noted that "tobacco culture is increasing progressively every year...and that which has chiefly contributed to this new industry is the station for the treatment of anemia" (in Ashford and Gutiérrez Igaravídez, 1911: 218). The campaign labored to cure the ailments of the coffee industry.

---

[24] In his autobiography, Ashford criticized Stahl for coming to the camp in Bayamon "seemingly, in order to make impromptu speeches filled with complicated eloquence in the Spanish language to the wall-eyed populace seeking a sign, not a reason" (Ashford, 1934: 55).

The dominant narrative about the early Puerto Rican hookworm's "success" ultimately relied on reproducing a narrative on death. The mortality rates provided by the insular Director of Sanitation indicate the campaign did not conquer death on the island (see table 9). In fact, the enormous rate suggested death remained a common reality for many Puerto Ricans. It also symbolized the distinction between their experience and their U.S. counterparts where mortality had declined from 17.2% in 1900 to 14.7% in 1910. In contrast, death rates in Puerto Rico were not so different in 1911 from what they had been in 1893. In fact, mortality increased some years during this period, including in 1906, during the first year of the Second Anemia Commission.

The campaign may have succeeded in fostering support for its intervention on rural labor, but it also changed the meaning of anemia on the island and compromised the ability to document the actual incidence of death by uncinariasis. Statistical reports on death from "anemia" may have indicated a change in cause of death, but it is probable that the campaign's popularity influenced the way these statistics were reported.

Table 9. Mortality Rates in Puerto Rico, 1888 to 1912.[1]

under Spanish colonial administration		under U.S. colonial administration	
1888	31.50	1898	35.70
1889	31.80	1899	36.90
1890	32.10		*(41 in Davis 1900)*
1891	28.30	1900	40.81
1892	28.30	1901	36.63
	(27.6 in Davis 1900)	1902	24.63
1893	**24.60**	1903	25.35
1894	28.00		*Hookworm Campaign Began*
1895	29.10	1904	22.16
1896	27.80	1905	22.17
1897	34.40	1906	22.56
		1907	25.25
		1908	21.65
		1909	20.00
		1910	22.14
		1911	23.44
		1912	**24.02**

[1] (Yager, 1914: 75).

The campaign worked at the local level and in urban institutions to foster support within the medical community. As a result, many physicians who might have attributed death to anemia before the campaign may have become convinced they should reclassify the cause of death to some other cause. Alternately, some physicians who wanted to promote the development of a station in their own municipality may have been more likely to attribute the cause of death to anemia.

The evidence suggests Ashford's claim that Puerto Ricans normalized death from anemia, the so-called *"muerte natural,"* was a discursive strategy embedded in the campaign's work. Death was a metaphor that promoted physicians' interventions on *jíbaros'* bodies. For Ashford, death also gave meaning to U.S. authority over a problem Puerto Ricans physicians had declared "beyond their power to cope with" (Ashford undated). Death served a vital purpose in a war against soil pollution and to compel public support for the U.S. colonial administration. By associating workers' production with contaminated soil, the campaign displaced attention from the social context of suffering, hunger and U.S. colonial policies that strangled Puerto Rico's coffee industry. In fact, the campaign contributed to the re-construction of the *jíbaros'* "radical otherness" in relation to labor. After visiting the Aibonito station in 1905, Walter E. Weyl began his introduction to "Labor Conditions in Porto Rico" by framing the "inherently different...labor conditions...[on] a tropical island...[where the] equitable climate reduce the necessities of the population" (1905:723).

CHAPTER SIX

DECOLONIZING DOMINANT NARRATIVES

The medicalization perspective sees medicine as a dominant institution in which physicians gained social influence by categorizing and labeling abnormal behavior as disease and by expanding these categories. According to this perspective, medical judgments redefine and depoliticize other social, economic and political factors that cause disease and promote social control. This perspective sees physicians as dominant social actors, but leaves medicine's structural, discursive and symbolic relationship to the state under-theorized.

In contrast, scholars who study colonial medicine see it as an institution subsumed to state-sponsored activities that justify imperial ventures. For these scholars, medical ideology reproduces colonial dominance, but scientific medicine becomes one of several agents that legitimate colonialism by producing ideas of colonial supremacy and benevolence. For instance, historians argue medicalized constructions of natives' bodies invite external intervention in order to reform not only bodies, but also politics. They find sanitation was not only a development in the administration of public health, but also a profoundly political endeavor in legitimizing colonial dominance.

Despite these contributions, medical historians have paid less attention to the ways native physicians negotiated the contradictions of medicine and colonial modernity. Where they consider Western medicine in non-Western societies, for instance, they conclude the latter accepted scientific modernity despite its implications of colonial authority and native inferiority (Arnold, 2000). To address the theoretical limitations of this determinism and the assumption colonization was a coherent process, scholars of U.S. colonization insist colonial subjects "negotiated" the terms of their subordination (Go, 2008: 9). Although they concede greater agency, most frequently, they conceptualize colonization narrowly in terms of the relationship between colonialists and natives and reproduce a homogenized understanding of how this agency was/is exercised. For instance, some scholars find nationalist discourse "replicated" colonial discourse (Quiroga, 1997: 116). This tendency limits the epistemic potential of their analyses.

This book contributes to the scholarships on medicalization/professional dominance, colonial medicine/tropical medicine and U.S. colonization by analyzing Puerto Rican physicians' involvement in the "protracted and more or less concealed civil war" that characterizes the development of capitalism as a modern world system (Marx in De Genova, 2002: 424; Mignolo, 2002). As a new body of subaltern studies indicates, modernity and colonial expansion were complementary. This assertion implicates colonial politics in both global inequality and the ongoing, "undetermined struggle" between labor and capital (Holloway in De Genova, 2002: 424). By analyzing Puerto Rican physicians' ideas, professional associations and work in the late-nineteenth and early-twentieth century, I found they were less managers who "aspired to replace" Spanish colonialists than they were locked into this war in which they sought to wrest collective benefits from a colonial modernity and promote national progress (Trigo, 2000: 82). Puerto Rican physicians were distinguished in this struggle because they dealt directly and concretely in matters and metaphors of life and death. Nonetheless, they were also part of a larger, unique status group that proffered its own modernizing project. As Francisco Scarano suggests, this intermediate elite of professionals both "abhorred the institutions and practices that gave [large landowners] their power and prestige...[and was] tormented by the contradictions of colonial life" (Scarano, 1998: 598). Physicians were also distinguished by their intimate clinical interactions with patients, their associations with a variety of medical practitioners on the island and their influence within the local and insular (island-wide) administrations. Puerto Rican physicians used these interactions, associations and influence to translate colonial interventions related to medicine and public health.

By paying close attention to variations within the native elite, the analysis in this book identified unique features of U.S. colonization that have important and broader implications for understanding the nature of U.S. global influence, particularly in terms of the political and social consequences of its [United States] claims about representation. Although my analysis did not ask whether U.S. Empire was distinct from other forms of colonization, Puerto Rican physicians saw the former distinct from a coercive colonial administration that limited the island's modernization. The analysis of medicine and public health in Puerto Rico also revealed how U.S. colonial administrators mobilized unique cultural repertoires about democracy and modernity to define the public interest. As a former colony itself, the United States led economic expansion, but its mission was grounded in an ideology that "was not, and could not have been, European"

(Mignolo, 2002: 80). I found U.S. colonial authority established new boundaries of knowledge to bolster its administrators' claims to represent the public interest, undermine political challenges and support the expansion of U.S. capital.

The colonial relationship was part and parcel of developing U.S. capital interests on the island. In the late nineteenth century, economic interests shaped political demands for greater autonomy. The coffee industry enjoyed favorable market conditions under Spanish colonial authority, but its expansion was compromised by the lack of credit. Coffee was imbued with national significance because credit was controlled by Spanish *peninsulares* while the industry was numerically dominated by both small- and medium-*criollo* landowners. Production also required little capital and technical investment and its cultivation complimented subsistence farming. This context informed an inauspicious fissure between elites and coffee farmers and workers on the island. After the change in sovereignty, U.S. colonial policies and the 1899 hurricane dramatically undermined coffee production and set the stage for a sugar monoculture dominated by U.S. capitalists. Many workers migrated to urban areas and frustrated coffee farmers began turning to other industries. These changes were powerfully reflected in the restricted access and availability of food, particularly meat that had already been inaccessible for many Puerto Ricans in the late-nineteenth century because of high taxes imposed by Spanish authorities. The cost of meat increased further in the early twentieth century as pasture lands were converted for sugar production and as the importation of meat increased.

Although many social groups, including the coffee elite, farmers and rural laborers, faced radically altered economic changes following the Spanish-American War, U.S. colonial administrators blamed Puerto Ricans for their problems. For instance, at the same time the U.S. colonial administration promoted sanitation regulations and food inspections that condemned hundreds of thousands of pounds of food (including meat), they blamed Puerto Rican men and municipal governments for controlling the availability and price of meat and "the necessities of life [...] to the detriment of the people, and especially so that of the peasantry of the island" (Post, 1907: 57). Colonial administrators' narrative indicated the ways they distrusted free markets and maligned local elites. Their narrative about meat also reflected the political dimensions of a patterned strategy: they claimed to protect the people, particularly landless peasants, from native elites through local interventions on municipal governments.

The economic context amplified the political contradictions implied by U.S. colonization. Following the 1898 war, U.S. colonial administrators attempted to reconcile their national identity by claiming they served the interests of the people. Colonial administrators developed policies to conform to what they purported were American customs even as they noted these regulations were more "advanced" than those in force in the United States (Hoff, 1900: 798). They also directed reforms to public institutions, such as municipal governments and the public health administration, in order to teach colonial subjects about democratic self-governance. These policies and reforms claimed to fight sickness and conquer high death rates even as the colonial relationship itself created sickening and deadly conditions. Although the economic contradictions of colonial capitalism were never resolved, they were reconciled through administrative and medical interventions. The U.S. colonial administration supported these interventions through forms of surveillance that complemented its efforts to develop self-regulating colonial subjects, discipline their choices and increase their labor productivity.

In part to reconcile its own national identity and partly out of expedience, U.S. colonization in Puerto Rico depended heavily on native elites and administrators to legitimize U.S. colonial authority. These relationships were developed through administrative and medical interventions that U.S. colonial authorities used as object lessons in modern governance. The U.S. colonial administration attempted to reconcile the contradictions of colonial governance and liberal democracy by negotiating the meaning of modernization and progress in relation to the island's elite and its landless workers. On the one hand, U.S. colonial administrators frequently referred to the reputations and prominence of men within the insular administration. On the other hand, the same administrators cast the elite as self-interested politicians who sacrificed the public interest to patronage politics.

In Puerto Rico, the U.S. colonial administration managed the contradictions of colonial capitalism by claiming to represent the public interest and selectively rejecting what colonial officers insisted was a self-serving Puerto Rican elite. It defined the public through the symbol of a peon whose interests were served by an ostensibly benevolent colonial administration. This claim to represent the people was a rhetorical strategy to support U.S. colonial administrators' efforts at consolidating their legitimate authority. To support its claims, the U.S. colonial administration selectively recruited some physicians and developed other rank-and-file physicians as part of a new professional elite positioned within the colonial administration and removed from formal electoral politics.

The case of municipal autonomy was especially significant for elucidating the changing meanings of modern colonialism. It reflected the ways native elites struggled at not only local, but also insular levels for a greater degree of political autonomy under U.S. colonial authority. For example, the issue that drove the Federal Party to conclude the U.S. governor was partial to the Republican Party and ultimately withdraw participation in the civil government in 1900 was about drawing municipal boundaries and defining local governments' relative autonomy. Under Spanish colonial authority, struggles for local influence had enabled elites to organize their efforts at the regional level and exercise greater control over taxes, labor control, public works and the implementation of colonial policies. This control was critical to basic bread and butter issues, including the availability of food, which was compromised by colonial authority. Although the meaning of local autonomy was therefore not surprising in 1900, U.S. colonial administrators defined the issue as one that reflected Puerto Ricans' inability to govern themselves. The distinction between elites' desire for local autonomy and colonial administrators' paternalistic discourse about Puerto Ricans was particularly ironic because many of the same issues about local control and centralization, for instance over sanitation, were being debated in the mainland United States.

These discursive maneuvers found a potent expression among physicians who struggled to develop medicine and public health on the island. The work of physicians reflected the ways the U.S. colonial administration attempted to set the terms of the debate about what defined public and self-interest. On the one hand, these definitions were profoundly implicated within broader colonial claims that the United States could export democracy. On the other hand, physicians' work demonstrated the limits of U.S.-initiated scientific and intellectual expansion.

The U.S. colonial administration's effort to develop legitimate authority in Puerto Rico has significant implications for U.S. Empire and bolsters the concept of Americanity as a unique geopolitical formation. In order to elucidate this finding, this concluding chapter first reviews the data-specific findings of the book which are more closely related to the historical record of medicine and public health in Puerto Rico. In this way, the chapter makes an initial effort at decolonizing dominant narratives about medicine and public health. I review the changing meanings and competition to define the people through the peon, the landless peasant, the *jíbaro.* I summarize the major obstacles Puerto Rican physicians confronted as an intermediate elite in their attempt to reconcile the meanings of national progress under U.S. colonial authority, and specifically, in relation to the development of medicine and the public health administration. I suggest these empirical findings had subsequent implications for global health and for the expansion of capital more generally. I conclude the chapter by exploring the relationship between these findings and identify the underlying dynamic of competition that centered on defining politics and the public interest with critical political implications not only in the early twentieth century, but also well beyond into the twenty first century as well.

The Public Interest(s)

Individuals and groups did not craft meaning independent of one another but rather influenced one another. Through their work, a variety of social groups negotiated the multiple meanings of disease in relation to a colonial modernity and in an attempt to wrest benefits within constraints imposed not only by the colonial relationship, but also by the development of capitalism on the island. Under U.S. colonialism, anemia became the subject of both medical and political debate as U.S. colonial administrators, Puerto Rican physicians, municipal governments and labor competed to privilege their claims about how these multiple groups should respond to the problem. As groups outside of medicine competed to define the truth about disease, they negotiated the terms of medical colonization.

In the late-nineteenth century, liberal elites viewed the *jíbaro* as weak and lazy. He embodied their preoccupation with labor productivity. An increasingly restive labor force posed real–and material–challenges to the power of elites and threatened elites' bourgeois culture. The liberal elite could not control the *jíbaro's* drinking, gambling and sexuality, which was dissonant with their visions of modernity. Constructing the *jíbaro* in terms of his difference from bourgeois culture allowed the Puerto Rican elite not only to legitimate its claims to authority, but also to undermine his demands for social reform. Their discourse on the *jíbaro* shifted in the twentieth century. Whereas physicians were encouraged by the terms of U.S colonization to depoliticize medical practice, nationalists increasingly made the *jíbaro* a product of the political economy and economic dislocations caused by U.S. colonialization. For nationalists, the *jíbaro's* anemia was produced not by his pre-modern cultural backwardness but by poverty and hunger that resulted from a capitalist modernization gone awry. Their writings and political mobilization reconstructed a "Puertorrican personality" that required protection from U.S. colonialism.

Municipal governments, losing administrative control relative to the U.S. colonial administration, blamed the political economy for malnutrition, starvation and disease. For instance, Dr. Vizcarrondo indicated municipal governments supported the campaign to alleviate their beleaguered budgets while simultaneously meeting demands for public health. These budgets were closely monitored by U.S. colonial authorities. Other campaign physicians similarly indicated local mayors and/or municipal physicians did not support the campaign, which reflected broader opposition the campaign faced in undermining not only claims that anemia was a consequence of political forces, but also broader attempts to deal with disease in explicitly political terms.

Samuel Gompers, president of the American Federation of Labor (AFL), insisted anemic weakness was a symptom of long work hours in difficult conditions such as the tropical heat. For many laborers associated with the AFL, anemia was the product of capitalist modes of production. While laborers found in the anemia campaign an attention to public needs they lacked in local municipal administrations, they resisted many of the individual changes the anemia campaign advocated.

The debates surrounding anemia not only produced disease as a political problem, but also defined a new role for Puerto Rican physicians within the U.S. colonial administration. In the late-nineteenth century, liberal elite physicians in Puerto Rico had portrayed anemic *jíbaros* as complicit in their victimization and emphasized the problems of a degenerate rural culture. They saw the *jíbaro* as a threat to economic progress, but sought to lead the island's modernization. Liberal elite physicians' efforts to gain political autonomy from Spain were undermined by the U.S. colonial administrators' control over the public health administration. Puerto Rican physicians confronted the possibility of becoming expert professionals and intermediaries between labor and government. They also faced the reality of medical and administrative interventions that policed individual behavior and that promoted new forms of surveillance. Puerto Rican physicians continued to see the *jíbaro* as an obstacle to modernity, but under the U.S. colonial administration, he seemed to compound the threats to political autonomy posed by colonization. Physicians were drilled with object lessons in sanitation through the insular and municipal administrations and in scientific medicine through the hookworm campaign. These interventions presented modernity as truth and depoliticized competing narratives about disease, decay and death. Campaign physicians blamed the hookworm for a variety of diseases that were subsequently tied to social conditions and nutritional deficiencies, including pellagra (Gutiérrez Igaravídez, 1912).

Ashford began the hookworm campaign's demonstrations in Utuado, a town in the rural interior of the island and a heartland for coffee and political mobilization. During and after the Spanish-American War, many peasants in the region had demonstrated their capacity for violence and for destabilizing an oppressive social order. From the Utuado station, the hookworm campaign's work was poised to influence rural peasants, local elites and the island's physicians by radically changing the boundaries of scientific knowledge. The campaign's laboratory, tent hospital, dispensary clinic and microscope were all symbols of modern progress, but intervened in workers' fortunes only indirectly. Ashford claimed the problem facing coffee production and its workers was not one of hunger, diet, or wages, but rather one where a parasite compromised labor productivity. The broad and widely publicized claims about the U.S. administration's successes were premised on the idea that the hookworm campaign could promote self-governance by producing self-regulating individual workers and by ostensibly depoliticizing the administration of public health.

Ashford's concerns about anti-Americanism in Utuado reflected a need to use science to manage not only the *jíbaros,* but also their municipal government. He hoped to prove the benefits of U.S. governance and co-opt Puerto Rican resistance. Ashford claimed his truths about medicine were scientific and therefore apolitical. He defined his work by contrasting it from many Puerto Rican physicians' practices. He also explicitly worked to co-opt anti-American sentiment and influenced local government policies. Ashford used the hookworm campaign to align a stratified society within U.S. colonial interests.

Colonial Modernity

For U.S. colonial administrators, the Puerto Rican people were easily defined. Governor General George W. Davis and Dr. Bailey K. Ashford both repeatedly characterized the people through the symbol of a peon wielded to consolidate their legitimate authority. For the colonial administrators, the peon's significance was greater than that of a landless peasant; he was a man whose whiteness was compromised by tropical environments and whose primitive nature was a consequence of the Spanish colonial legacy. Crafting his difference in this way was critical to establishing the boundaries of colonial difference under U.S. colonial authority. These characterizations underscored the historic burden of dispossession and subordination to an authoritarian administration that ostensibly existed in the past and that, like premature death, had to be conquered in order to allow for the newness of the U.S. colonial administration's interventions. Colonial administrators shared a consensus on their self-image as a modernizing influence conquering a degenerative past. Their "deification and reification of [the] newness" of U.S. colonial authority was ideologically fundamental to shaping U.S. hegemony in the world system (Quijano and Wallerstein, 1992: 551).

U.S. colonial administrators used the threatening specter of the death of peons as a metaphor to reject the Spanish colonial legacy and bolster their own authority. They claimed to conquer death in order to establish their legitimacy as exceptionally benevolent rulers. They enrolled native elites in reproducing this metaphor by professing to share a common goal: the island's progress. U.S. colonial authorities argued high death rates compromised the island's modernization and economic development. Their metaphor of death also presented the colonial narrative in terms of dire needs, which mediated competing ideas about modernization and progress.

The metaphor of health, and its association with vitality and vigor, served a more strategic and divisive effort to position U.S. colonial administrators as representatives of the public interest. For instance, Ashford portrayed some native physicians as a threat to public health. He considered Puerto Rican physicians who advanced alternate explanations for anemia and those who did not support the hookworm campaign in ways that were similar to how U.S. colonial officers denigrated native politicians as self-interested and unable to promote democratic self-governance. Colonial officers, like Ashford, considered physicians who were formally involved in politics as part of a colonial past associated with the Spanish colonial legacy on the island. In this way, U.S. colonial administrators were like many reformers who expanded their political influence by creating a false dichotomy between politics and public administration. Although their medical and administrative interventions were undoubtedly political, U.S. colonial administrators defined politics narrowly in relation to formal, electoral politics and argued native elites who were involved in politics compromised health. U.S. colonial administrators conflated the metaphor of death with the Spanish colonial past and used the metaphor of health to legitimize the illusion of a modern, albeit still colonial, present.

U.S. colonial administrators focused their interventions on local governance. They claimed efficient self-government served the interest of landless peasants, the so-called peon, and displaced blame onto municipal governments for the structural dislocations occasioned by U.S. colonization. On the one hand, U.S. colonial administrators like Secretary Charles Hartzell blamed municipal physicians for the failures of local sanitation. As Dr. Luis Aguerrevere observed, these failures reflected the limited authority and arbitrary enforcement of the Superior Board of Health, an insular body controlled by the U.S. colonial administration. A variety of groups also experienced the tensions of enforcing the numerous sanitation regulations, including those on food inspection, on an island that depended heavily on imported food. On the other hand, U.S. colonial administrators like Governor Davis made peasants' pallor a measure of how municipal administrations could promote labor productivity by supporting U.S. intervention. Ashford designed the campaign as a non-coercive intervention on local governance. For Ashford, anemia was a problem that could be solved by medical science, which he claimed stood outside of politics, but while he set out to convince Puerto Ricans of the truth about anemia, he also attempted to influence local politics and make them more amenable to U.S. intervention. As a result, Ashford could chastise mayors who had never in their "placid life done anything whatsoever to merit the high-sounding title" they held (1934: 71). According to Ashford, supporting the campaign's work was "a chance to become famous" while resistance was akin to political suicide. As he later observed, the doctor of public health became beholden to "but one client-the government" (Ashford, 1934: 86). Despite administrative claims to represent the public interest, U.S. colonial administrators' more narrow emphasis on the peon had reduced him to a patient and created his utility within the new ideological apparatus of U.S. colonial politics.

The native elite, members of the liberal political parties that included intellectuals and political activists who had advanced formal education, degrees and certifications, saw the peon as not only a rural peasant, but also a *jíbaro*. In the late nineteenth century, liberal elites had imbued the symbol of the *jíbaro* with significant symbolic meaning. They used the *jíbaro* to refract their own interest in modernizing the island to correspond with their vision of reform and national progress. In the early-twentieth century, the *jíbaro* gained new symbolic significance amidst the coffee industry's decline. For physicians, the *jíbaro* went from being a symbol of sickness, decay and Spanish colonial repression to a potent symbol of their newly-found powers.

Under the terms of a colonial modernity that preceded U.S. colonization, physicians came to believe the *jíbaro* embodied the salvation of medicine. He became a symbol of the "inexhaustible wealth of clinical material"
that could usher in scientific modernization on the island (Ashford, 1931: 10).
What appeared to be physicians' narrow desire for scientific advancement
and professional dominance, however, was more broadly tied to their
national interest in mediating the island's economic (mis)fortunes.
Through medical treatment, Puerto Rican physicians sought to cure the
negative consequences of the development of capitalism on the island.
They sought to wrest benefits from a colonial modernity that posed constraints that were both geopolitical (capitalism) and epistemic (coloniality) (Mignolo, 2002). On the one hand, colonial modernity preceded U.S.
colonization and provided an ideological justification for the expansion of
capitalism on the island. On the other hand, the U.S. colonization of
Puerto Rico marked the beginning of a form of dominance that did not
depend on territorial annexation, but instead on subordinate integration
in the modern world system. This emerging form of "coloniality" implied a
new structure of dependency that was not only economic or political, but
also "above all, it is epistemic" (Mignolo, 2008: 250). In other words, "of the
many doors through which one could have entered the room [...] only one
was open. The rest were closed. One understands what it means to have
only one door open and the entrance heavily regulated (Mignolo, 2008:
233). In what appears a phenomenon generalizable to Latin America, the
epistemic violence of dependency confronted a variety of Puerto Rican
social actors' alternate claims about disease and implicated Puerto Rican
physicians' position relative to colonial modernity. Puerto Rican physicians confronted this colonial condition with a highly-delimited option of
either maintaining their colonial difference, insisting on the social and
political causes of disease and undermining their credentials (marginal-
ization) or subsuming their truth about disease to Western modernity and
dismissing their distinctive contributions to medical science (invisibility).
Puerto Rican physicians attempted to resolve this "double bind" by translating medical science on the island and developing tropical medicine
(Bernasconi in Mignolo, 2002: 70).

Physicians abandoned their views of the *jíbaro* as a mask to disguise
their political opposition to a colonial regime. For them, the *jíbaro* was
more than a curable patient who could restore their own social status.
Instead, the *jíbaro* had broader import as a symbol within the "protracted
and more or less concealed civil war" (Marx in De Genova, 2002: 424).
The *jíbaro* had simultaneously become an abstraction of the people and

the peon, the poor man, a *campesino,* the peasant, the rural laborer, the *prole,* and the rural proletariat. Physicians responded to a symbol that had been seized upon and refashioned by the U.S. colonial administration as a thing, like a tricycle, a crude symbol of technical machinery reduced to his colonial difference and primitive functions in order to reconcile the conflicting demands of colonial modernity. On the one hand, the *jíbaro* was expropriated by U.S. colonial administrators who used the symbol of the peon to stabilize their authority and justify subordinating the island to political tutelage. On the other hand, physicians' ability to mobilize claims to universal modernity was delimited by the U.S. colonial administration. The appeal of non-motorized transportation for tourists in exotic, tropical destinations, represents the ways the belief in the universal (pedal-powered transportation and "the ideological arch of historical capitalism") ultimately depended on racial difference ("the cultural pillar of historical capitalism") (Wallerstein in Mignolo, 2002: 78). Like the weight of colonial modernity on the *jíbaros'* back, however, non-mechanized transport can neither represent the suffering of colonization nor convey the rider's "double bind" in which Puerto Rican physicians were uncomfortably trapped (Bernasconi in Mignolo, 2002: 70).

Incorporated under the terms of U.S. expansion, Puerto Rican physicians wrestled with the implications of modern medical science under U.S. colonial authority and its purported universality. Through the hookworm campaign, they were positioned to use science in whitening the nation and curing the legacy of Spanish colonialism on the island. Campaign physicians were tasked with eradicating a parasite Ashford had associated with this legacy, by reference to slavery and the introduction of the hookworm on the island. They set out to convince *jíbaros* to adopt modern hygienic practices and overcome their primitive nature. They used medical science to draw blood, monitor hemoglobin levels, and record the regeneration of both the *jíbaro* and the nation's blood. They were regimented through a centralized organization (the central station) that reported directly to the U.S. colonial governor. They produced multiple reports in order to document the progress and development of tropical medicine. Although the campaign's work appealed to physicians' interest in promoting modernization, they shared the conditions of colonial modernity with the so-called *jíbaro.* Through their interactions with patients, campaign physicians struggled to overcome the limits of colonial modernity, but doctor and patient were ultimately caught up in the wheels of their colonial difference and repetitively blamed for their inability to govern themselves.

As inheritors of the "Spanish race" and its legacy on the island, Puerto Rican physicians played a singular role in simultaneously navigating the colonial and the municipal administrations and promoting the public interest vis-à-vis the so-called peon. They were profoundly implicated in a colonial struggle to transform the island's native elite. Many liberal elite physicians led the island's political changes at the end of the nineteenth century. Some were central to the mobilization and developments of the Autonomist Party on the island, while others were involved in separatist activities on and off the island. Physicians like Julio J. Henna had actively pursued Puerto Rico's independence from New York through a segment of the Cuban Revolutionary Party. Others, like Dr. Ramón Emeterio Betances, worried about U.S. intentions to annex Puerto Rico (in Scarano, 1998). On the island, physicians were also the first to mount protests against the military occupation and U.S. colonial government (Henna and Zeno Gandia, 1899). Because Puerto Rican physicians were often trained abroad, they became important members of both the elite and the intelligentsia. Their scientific training seemed to offer a modern approach to defining and directing the island's "moral and material" progress. They saw their work as an important catalyst in Puerto Rico's modernization.

The physicians involved in the hookworm campaign competed with an established elite in their claim to represent rural laborers, which they more broadly conflated with the public interest. The campaign associated the hookworm with the legacy of servitude under Spanish colonization because it caused a "pallor of years, of centuries" (Ashford, 1934: 3). Through many published documents and photos and ideas that were publicized among a variety of Puerto Rican and U.S. audiences, the campaign's medical men claimed to represent the poor man, the peon and the *jíbaro,* which referred to the same category of rural agricultural working men. The campaign's new medical men distinguished themselves from a variety of social groups because, as the campaign's directors insisted by referring to both established elites and competing practitioners, "this lack of mental contact, of a common ground of interest between the jibaro and the better class of Porto Ricans drives the former to charlatans for his medical advice" (Ashford and Gutiérrez Igaravídez, 1911: 15).

According to Ashford and many other U.S. audiences concerned with preserving the illusion of liberation and "the physical emancipation of Porto [sic] Rico," the hookworm also distinguished the people from the Spanish colonial legacy. It distinguished "the poor man [from] the well-informed and better class of Porto [sic] Ricans, who were well fed and well shod, and therefore protected from infection, being skeptical and having centuries of prejudice behind them" (Grinnell, 1914: 719, 721). Campaign physicians shared the U.S. colonial administrators' conflation of the poor man with the public whose interests they promoted by distinguishing themselves from the so-called "better class" (Grinnell, 1914: 721). For physicians who participated in the campaign, their own interests were not simply about negotiating colonial authority or the change in political sovereignty. Instead, many municipal physicians participated in the campaign in order to realize a goal of greater professional autonomy from municipal governments' influence and authority. Other campaign physicians hoped to use the campaign to improve a social position that had been compromised by U.S. colonial authority, which included increased difficulties obtaining compensation and competition for markets of patients. Ashford (undated) asserted "we as medical men may deplore but cannot help such conditions wherever they may exist." The campaign's medical men supported demonstrations that not only cultivated public favor for the U.S. colonial administration, but also fostered medical authority for physicians on the island.

The Colonial Narrative and The Great Man of Puerto Rican Medical Science

Many Puerto Rican physicians, even those employed in the hookworm campaign, questioned U.S. medicine and U.S. political interests and authority on the island, which demonstrates how many claims about politics, medicine and the people were tied to the ongoing battles involved in colonization. Decolonizing the narrative about Puerto Rico's modernization, and the critical role played by medical science in the process, requires careful consideration of how Puerto Rican physicians endeavoured to wrest the benefits of modernity from the colonial relationship. Physicians believed these benefits served not only their interests as professionals, but also those of the nation and its people. Physicians translated modernization to fit within their claims about national progress.

Like the smallpox campaign, physicians who participated in the early hookworm campaign received little credit for their work. Unlike the campaign developed under the U.S. military occupation, however, their work did not involve coercion and did not cultivate public distain. Ashford's careful attention to cultivating favourable public opinion, by the strategic location of stations, the selective employment of physicians in the campaign, and the careful avoidance of thorny political issues like rural sanitation regulations meant campaign physicians paid more attention to patients as cases than to the social conditions of the peon, the *jíbaro,* or even the physicians carrying out the work. The narrative that emphasizes the campaign's popularity is a product of this facework and a part of the U.S. colonial legacy that serves to reproduce U. S. authority over the island. This narrative about the campaign's popularity is embedded within Puerto Rican historiography that reproduces a colonial interpretation of the past. Like U.S. colonial administrators, the narrative about the campaign's popularity assumes the past was one of political patronage before democracy and medicine before science. This categorical rejection of the past assumes political contests were solely about political patronage rather than reasoned concerns about U.S. colonization. It also assumes there was no modern medical science on the island before Ashford set foot on the island. In fact, neither claim about politics or medicine were entirely true.

Part of the colonial narrative was that the majority of Puerto Ricans loved and demanded the campaign. The campaign's clear distinctions between the number of patients that had been treated and those that had been cured challenge this narrative. Many patients were treated, but between 1904 and 1907, when the campaign had consolidated a significant degree of political and professional status, the majority of stations reported treating a minority of the overall municipality population. The average across municipalities was less than 10% of the local population and we don't know much this percentage may be inflated by migrants who were treated at different dispensaries. We now know that patients are rapidly reinfected after deworming, which makes hookworm control interventions that center on individual treatment unsustainable. The campaign's reports indicated that, of the minority of the local population that actually visited the station, the number of patients treated was calculated based on presumed compliance with physicians' instructions. In addition to the dispensaries, Ashford, Gutiérrez Igaravídez and other campaign physicians also dispensed medication. In their individual narratives, however, campaign physicians noted their frustration that patients probably refused to take the medications they had been given because of unpleasant side effects. Many more patients refused to return for treatment in order to be cured. For many observers, rural peasants' apparent non-compliance excluded them from the alleged benefits of modern and colonial medicine. Many other rural peasants probably made conscious choices that resisted physicians' advice. After all, the battle depended on peasant obedience. Rural populations' resistance to modern scientific medicine also represented a critical resistance to a colonial discourse that burdened peasants with national progress through seemingly universal scientific and natural laws about personal hygiene and new standards of behavior. The so-called peons inverted dominant narratives about medical truth and U.S. tutelage through their physical practices. At times, this inversion simply meant individuals made themselves invisible to medicine and colonialism. Resistance to modern medicine meant individuals were also agents who resisted and negotiated colonialism.

The campaign and the dominant narrative about the campaign conflate patients who were treated for hookworm with those who were cured, which indicates the ways medical claims were conflated with political ones. For instant, the "sign" of medication with thymol was only one of several treatment options and not even the best one for hookworm infection. Medical treatment with *naptol* was also used by campaign physicians and prominent Spanish newspapers had discussed the benefits of this medication by the early 1890s. Ashford claimed discovery of the hookworm, but in fact relied on established medical research that indicated much of what he proposed as a discovery was already known within the scientific community (Rockefeller Foundation, 1922). In the development of the campaign, Ashford was directly involved in interpreting his findings on the hookworm in the public health work of the campaign (treating patients), from 1904 to 1906 when he returned to Army duty. In fact, Puerto Rican physicians were the ones who translated medicine in their work in the clinics, hospitals, stations and substations. Although Ashford was a useful ally who traded on the political influence of his father-in-law, it was Puerto Rican physicians who ultimately conducted research, treated patients and developed a public health and medical infrastructure on the island. They would continue to struggle in the battle to develop rural and urban sanitation under, and in relation to, U.S. colonial authority.

Jíbaros were largely illiterate and could not avail themselves of written forms of communication. Their clandestine revolts in the rural countryside proved they were as concerned about delimiting the control multiple groups tried to exert over their lives in order to increase their productive capacity. Scholars have demonstrated that prostitution and gambling were part of a politic of survival that allowed individuals to negotiate the constraints of a new economic structure. Surely these also seemed to be "irrational choices" for many, while for others they represented a lack of consciousness. As colonial governance attempted to map itself increasingly onto the lives of those previously invisible to it, including *jíbaros*, many attempts to reform Puerto Rican bodies failed. The reasons for their failure, however, were not ignorance, irrational choices, or a lack of consciousness but rather, an alternate and competing knowledge. Puerto Rican women continued to rely on *parteras,* alternately known as *comadronas* or midwives, rather than scientific medicine. Women protected their honor by resisting physical examinations by male physicians. Puerto Ricans resisted compulsory vaccination and the imposition of sanitation measures.

Puerto Rican Physicians: Double Binds and Messy Realities

Medicine experienced radical changes in the late-nineteenth and early-twentieth centuries. Puerto Rican physicians studied and worked in a variety of settings that placed them at the cutting edge of scientific and medical development. Physicians who completed their medical degrees in Spain and Europe had already accepted and experimented with germ theory and many of the technologies on the island that spread under the U.S. colonialization. Their experience of U.S. medicine was a different matter altogether because it was introduced under the terms of colonial tutelage. Liberal elite physicians found their claims for political and professional autonomy undermined and were derided for their political involvements. Municipal physicians wrangled between insular and municipal governments for authority. Both liberal elite and municipal physicians joined other rank and file members of the profession in haggling for compensation and wages that were negatively compared to those of dock workers, but at least workers could resort to a strike and other forms of collective bargaining. For Puerto Rican physicians, however, developing a collective identity involved them in complex struggles over the medical profession's relationship to labor, public health and the island's progress.

As scientific experts, physicians were professionals who faced insurmountable odds in overcoming the intractable problems of colonial modernity. Despite their vision and desires for modernizing the island, Puerto Rican medicine in the early-twentieth century faced limited options for development. Their ability to develop a collective identity depended on negotiating their direct and indirect relationship to the U.S. colonial state because many of the few Puerto Rican physicians on the island worked directly or indirectly within the U.S. colonial administration. Physicians could not control the island's treasury or initiatives supported by the U.S. colonial administration, including the compulsory smallpox vaccination campaign and sanitation regulations modelled on those in force within the United States. Many Puerto Rican physicians participated in these efforts, some with more or less enthusiasm than others. Other physicians maintained private practices and enjoyed some degree of immunity from negotiating the U.S. colonial administration, but even they were forced to obtain a license to practice from a U.S.-controlled state structure rather than an autonomous medical profession.

One issue that compromised Puerto Rican physicians' ability to control their work involved doubts about their competence. For instance, colonial administrators interpreted physicians' resistance to mandatory reporting as evidence of their inability to render accurate diagnoses. They devalued Puerto Rican physicians' knowledge and expertise despite the fact that many Puerto Rican doctors had been educated in Europe or the United States. Puerto Rican physicians had been unfavorably compared with "the bedrabbled old *curandera,* or medicine-woman of the town, with her stringy hair and one remaining tooth" (1934: 67). Although many of the same physicians who were living and practicing on the island in 1898 worked with the second Anemia Commission in 1906, the perception of their competence had shifted through a campaign that distinguished a new generation of professionals neutered of their former interest in becoming political leaders. Campaign physicians had emerged victorious in their competition with other physicians and with local administrations on the relative significance of diet on death and disease. This new generation of campaign-affiliated physicians indicated the ways the U.S. colonial administration controlled the evaluation of competence.

In contrast to campaign physicians who were complicit in obscuring workers' immiseration, municipal physicians shared much in common with other rank-and-file members of the profession who struggled for compensation. They went to court in a variety of cases against former patients and even municipal and insular governments. Municipal physicians were poorly paid, but heavily criticized. They navigated the impossible demands of insular and municipal governments, businesses, employers and local residents. They were required to implement sanitation regulations, conduct autopsies, testify in court cases, conduct food inspections, carry out chemical analysis, craft reports and attend to the medical needs of indigent residents. It seemed a thankless position that drove many to seek representation through the *Asociación Médica de Puerto Rico* (AMPR). This strategy seemed to work when municipal physicians' salaries increased, but their pay increase was accompanied by greater public scrutiny and criticism. Although physicians' struggles for compensation were somewhat endemic to the profession, municipal physicians' salaries were particularly compromised by U.S. colonial administrators' efforts to increase scrutiny and control over municipal budgets.

Although municipal physicians were affected in unique ways by colonial policies, all physicians suffered the setbacks of U.S administrators' control over the profession. In the late-nineteenth century, physicians formed cooperative relationships with a variety of medical practitioners that included pharmacists, *practicantes* (assistants) and *curiosos*. On an island where the ratio of academically-trained physicians was approximately 1 for every 7,500 persons, alternate practitioners were critical to expanding access to medical attention (Guerra, 1998). The island also lacked a medical school, which made these informal apprenticeships critical to transmitting knowledge and information about medicine and public health on the island. This alternate economy of medical development and attention was radically disrupted by the terms of U.S. colonization. Physicians' practice was highly regulated by the Superior Board of Health (SBOH) and persons who practiced without a license from the U.S.-controlled body faced stiff fines and possible imprisonment. The institutionalization of medicine and public health similarly undermined these informal associations and apprenticeships.

Physicians' professional opportunities shifted from ones that included protesting Spanish colonial legislation and its negative consequences for the nutrition of the poor to ones that promoted concrete interventions that undermined the significance of diet on disease and that were designed to develop labor productivity on the island. Through their work within a radically restructured colonial government under U.S. colonial authority, campaign physicians provided critical information on the political institutions and rural populations of the island to U.S. colonial administrators. This data not only served the colonial administration's interest in expanding surveillance over remote and inaccessible areas, but also modeled how medical interventions could justify limitless authority to police rural populations. In what appeared to be a co-operative effort to develop public health, U.S. colonial administrators colonized Puerto Rican society. They appropriated the work of campaign physicians to consolidate their authority over municipal governments and the island's residents.

Puerto Rican physicians working with the hookworm campaign claimed to have a unique authority over what they defined as the *jíbaro's* problem, but the microscope and the laboratory encouraged their distance from the *jíbaro*. Physicians' interventions on individual patient's bodies as discreet entities abstracted patients' behaviors from their broader context. On the one hand, medicalizing the *jíbaro* meant redefining him as an innocent victim of disease. On the other hand, campaign physicians emphasized science and ultimately shifted the blame for anemia onto *jíbaros* for their personal hygiene. To the extent campaign physicians constructed the *jíbaro* as irresponsible, they also facilitated U.S. colonial governance, intervention and their own privileged status in regenerating Puerto Rico. Physicians' medicalized characterizations of the *jíbaro* privileged their role in defining problems and spoke to their difficulties in managing their authority in the period preceding U.S. colonization.

As many Puerto Rican physicians sought to expand their control over the island's modernization, their attempts to control anemia moved beyond efforts to attain professional status. Although sociologists most frequently understand professionalization as a struggle for market control and social mobility, the case of Puerto Rican physicians demonstrates that the process can include developing a politicized identity that challenges the structure of the colonial state and the discriminatory institutions it established. In the early-twentieth century, Puerto Rican physicians used professionalization as a political strategy to gain a status that the U.S. colonial state threatened. The terms of this professionalism largely resulted from physicians' unsuccessful competition with the U.S. colonial state. Puerto Rican physicians struggled to define the terms of professionalism and promote their political-professional status, but they had a minimal role in decisions affecting the growth of medicine and could neither compete nor gain autonomy from U.S. colonial interests in public health or medical work. Neither the AMPR nor native physicians controlled the centralized insular administration of public health they had lobbied to create, which became the Sanitation Service. In essence, Puerto Rican physicians were critical to U.S. colonial state formation, but the U.S. colonial state regulated both the medical profession and the development of public health on the island.

Elite physicians' more narrow pursuit of professionalism included reviving the status they enjoyed under the Spanish colonial state, advancing their position within a shifting economic order, and challenging the U.S. colonial state's threat to their social location. The ideological meanings supporting elite physicians' professional project also shifted as Puerto Rican physicians articulated their cultural difference under early U.S. colonial rule. Elite physicians opposed U.S. colonial state control as a "conqueror of race, language, laws, customs, and banner" (Quevedo Báez, 1949: 2). They insisted colonial policies invaded and constrained the profession and imposed a new "culture, language, and standard of work"

(Quevedo Báez, 1949: 2). Early efforts at gaining professional status under U.S. colonial authority implied developing a collective identity around national difference that negotiated colonial state control.

The desires of Puerto Rican physicians to modernize Puerto Rico were inextricably tied to their desires to expand their professional status. Academically trained physicians attempted to gain greater autonomy over their work by seeking independence from local governments. Their version of a "Puertorrican personality" was not universally shared and their visions of national progress competed with those of municipal mayors and those of the *jíbaros* themselves. They established the AMPR to minimize the appearance of political alliances within medicine. Physicians sought to co-opt those elements of colonial power that would give them a strategic advantage in undermining the constraints of U.S. colonialism. Yet, despite gaining some measure of increased political independence from municipal governments through the Office of Health, Charities and Corrections, the AMPR doubted the "morality" of the *Consolidado's* appointments and reconciled itself to incorporation with the American Medical Association in order to develop physicians' professional status.

The fate of the Puerto Rican Medical Association (AMPR) demonstrated how many elite physicians tried to reconcile their political commitments and their hopes for a greater degree of political and professional autonomy than they were ultimately able to achieve. Their ability to organize the medical profession was undermined by the U.S. colonial administration's influence on the trajectory of public health and medicine in Puerto Rico. By the beginning of end of U.S. colonial rule's first decade, native physicians faced few options beyond accommodating U.S. medicine and expanding their professional authority. U.S. policies undermined the working of the relationship between physicians and the state, limited professional autonomy, and subsumed physicians' work to colonial interests. Thus, in the "messy reality of the interactions between the...state and the professions", the U.S. colonial state transformed elite physicians' political strategies and professional identities (Macdonald, 1995: 100). The relationship between physicians and the state, and the professional role it produced, continues to undermine Puerto Rican physicians' ability to take an active role in the state.

The incorporation of the AMPR into the AMA represented more than a simple shift in a medical association's affiliations. It indicated a more profound transformation of Puerto Rican medicine that involved intraprofessional competition, struggle, and the implications of U.S. colonization on physicians' collective identity. The incorporation of the AMPR in the AMA signaled the disruption of an alternate economy of medicine where academically-trained physicians took on a variety of medical practitioners as apprentices because the AMPR's institutional affiliation with the AMA helped academically-trained physicians collaborate with other allopathic doctors in joint efforts to undermine alternate medical practitioners. It also undermined many Puerto Rican physicians' involvement in preventative over curative medicine. By relying on laboratory research and emphasizing infectious disease, the AMPR encouraged the absorption of its associates in the projects of global health at the expense of a public health centered on preventing disease.

Neither colonialist nor native physicians affiliated with the AMPR and/or the hookworm campaign could simply or comprehensively impose their ideas about disease onto patients or even their peers, including the native elite and their professional colleagues. In fact, the overwhelming majority of Puerto Rican physicians living and/or practicing on the island in 1898 were not included in the AMPR's 1913 membership rolls or involved in the hookworm campaign. The number of physicians employed by the campaign in 1907 (38) were a small minority of all physicians living on the island in 1898 (approximately 250–280). Of the physicians recognized in campaign reports for offering any form of support prior to 1907, the overwhelming majority were eventually employed and paid by the campaign. A minority of all municipal physicians in 1901 (16/81) eventually obtained employment with the hookworm campaign. Campaign physicians criticized their unsupportive colleagues, but even they did not offer their unequivocal or unqualified support. Instead, several campaign physicians used alternate forms of treatment, some favored prevention (sanitation) over, or in addition to, treatment. Many other physicians resorted to a variety of measures to compel patient visits to their stations in what appeared to be more of a public relations campaign than an island-wide, universal public health effort. The hookworm campaign was fundamentally tied to promoting the image of universality despite the tensions it encountered and the debates about modernity it engendered. For instance, physicians who promoted modern medical science on the island competed with a variety of social actors and alternate medical practitioners, including *curanderos* who had greater access to rural populations.

The fact that most Puerto Rican physicians had no direct involvement with the hookworm campaign's work indicated the limits of colonial control. For instance, although U.S. federal and colonial administrators used the menace of disease and the metaphor of death to defend their political interventions in Puerto Rico from the moment of their arrival in 1898, the military occupation allowed local autonomy on matters related to public health and sanitation. When U.S. colonial officers restructured local governments to increase the centralization and their control over medicine and public health, Puerto Rican physicians organized a medical association to promote their status and material interests. U.S. colonial policies mandated that physicians should report vital statistics and contagious diseases to expand surveillance over the Puerto Rican population, but many refused to comply with these regulations. Although U.S. colonial administrators instituted coercive measures related to quarantine, sanitary legislation and medicine, these measures were often ineffective. The Superior Board of Health found their regulations could not efficiently organize Puerto Rican physicians' practice or municipal governments' administration of health and sanitation. Puerto Rican physicians negotiated U.S. colonial interventions related to health and sanitation and undermined colonial efforts at social control. These unaffiliated physicians and medical practitioners were part of subaltern knowledges on the island who marked the limits of medical colonization and who merit further consideration (see notes 46–49 in Rigau-Pérez, 2000b).

Puerto Rican physicians' work did not simply accommodate U.S. medicine or even collaborate in promoting U.S. colonial authority. Instead, they were political actors who challenged colonial dominance even as they negotiated the terms of colonization in order to modernize the island. The tensions of this project, their colonial difference, meant physicians participated in colonial governance in a strategic attempt to appropriate aspects of colonial rule and use them to further their professional and national ambitions. In contrast to Ashford's work that interpreting scientific research on the hookworm, physicians' labor consisted of translating colonial modernity.

Puerto Rican physicians suffered the uncomfortable struggle to translate modern medicine under the U.S. colonial administration. Their persistent attention to sanitation both within and beyond the hookworm campaign reflected some of their battles with the U.S. colonial administration and local authorities on the island. For instance, despite the U.S. colonial administration's early indifference to hookworm, Dr. Luis Aguerrevere provided the critical resources it needed to develop medical science on the island. Although the SBOH was inconsistent in its enforcement of sanitation regulations, Dr. Aguerrevere persisted in his attempts to improve food inspection in Ponce. The hookworm campaign emphasized medical treatment, but many campaign physicians worked directly with municipal administrations to promote latrine construction. Even when the campaign's directors

vigorously promoted treatment with thymol, many of its physicians preferred naphtha, which reflected their immersion in Spanish and European
medical circles. The hookworm campaign focused on the *necatur americanus*, but Drs. Isaac Gonzalez Martinez and Miguel Roses Artau used the stations for their own research on bilharzia. These instances indicated native
physicians had an alternate vision of medical progress that was not neatly
tied to the U.S. colonial administration's idea of the white man's burden or
their plans to control the island's modernization.

The hookworm campaign involved a distinct set of concerns for the U.S.
colonial administration and Puerto Rican physicians. For the former
group, the campaign's work was a way of bolstering its domestic legitimacy and justified colonial intervention for U.S. audiences. In contrast,
Puerto Rican physicians saw themselves embedded in medical communities that spanned Europe and Central and South America. For the latter
group, the development of medical science on the island represented a
way for them to escape the limitations of presumed inferiority and participate in the international development of modern tropical medicine.
Puerto Ricans' efforts to develop tropical medicine drew them into a specialty that had significant implications beyond the medical community.
Their work had important implications for their counterparts in other
tropical settings where climate was associated with a pessimism about
degeneration and racial inferiority. As Dr. Antonio Fernós-Isern, then
assistant commissioner of Health explained, society and economy were
more important in health because "civilized man may live in almost climate; he makes his own 'climate' to suit himself" (1926b: 7). Puerto Rican
physicians used tropical medicine to reject claims about their difference
and inferiority. In other contexts, tropical medicine became a way for
whites to colonize the "other."

For a select group of medical practitioners in Puerto Rico, tropical medicine became a profound endeavour that shaped their relationship to the
U.S. colonial state, the idea of Puerto Rico as a nation and the sick patient.
Through their patients, Puerto Rican physicians not only developed tropical medicine on island, but also fostered their relationships with both U.S.
and Latin American medicine and engaged in international debates for
scientific and professional recognition. Through a campaign that began
with national debates on economic dislocations and the hookworm,
Puerto Rican physicians recreated their leadership in a radically-altered
social hierarchy. They worked toward shaping this hierarchy to their
advantage in not only professional terms, but also national ones that
accounted for their productive relationship with a variety of social groups,
including political elites and laborers.

Tropical Medicine and Global Health

By the end of the twentieth century's first decade, the hookworm campaign's public health and medical efforts bifurcated when the Tropical and Transmissible Diseases Service was taken over by the newly established Sanitation Service in 1911. Under the direction of Dr. William F. Lippitt, an American, the campaign's work appeared suspended until the Institute for the Study of Tropical Medicine was established the following year. Puerto Rican physicians' subordinate relationship to the state became a persistent problem. For instance, the Institute reported directly to the U.S. Governor. Even as the Institute struggled to become a medical school, it was again subordinated to U.S. medicine. Columbia University "co-sponsored" Puerto Rico's School for Tropical Medicine and made many of the key decisions about its direction and operations from New York (Ramirez de Arellano, 1989: 265).

Puerto Rican physicians continued to struggle for professional autonomy in the formation of the School for Tropical Medicine. As Ashford explained, Drs. Gutiérrez Igaravídez and Gonzalez Martinez "wanted a helpful cooperation from the great northern University. They could not accept a master...They wanted the outside world to realize, however, that it was essentially Puerto Rican, and directed by Puerto Ricans [...they wanted] to control the destinies of their own school, which they had taken so great a part in developing" (1934: 359). Ashford, an interpreter of U.S. medicine on the island, felt he "could not accept the attitude of the idealist" and ultimately "went with Columbia University" (1934: 359, 360). Although he implied Puerto Rican concerns had become invisible, he also explained he felt alone in representing "the demands made in the name of the Island" (1934: 360). For their part, Drs. Gutiérrez Igaravídez and Gonzalez Martinez's decision to resign hardly reflected their own limited self-interest in aspiring to replace colonialists, but instead a collective identity rooted in colonial difference. They were persistently "unable to accept certain features of our organization, which they think is so constituted as to leave the country in a place of secondary importance" (1934: 360). This "medical nationalism" also influenced a subsequent generation of physicians who "regarded medicine primarily as an art, shaped and molded by its context" and who worked to establish the island's first independent School of Medicine of the University of Puerto Rico (Ramirez de Arellano, 1989: 266; 1990).

The school's administrative independence in 1949 followed the post-WWII global wave of decolonization. Only the year before, the island's residents had finally been allowed to elect their governor, Luiz Muñoz

Marín. Meanwhile, the island's political status remained unresolved, which had significant consequences for the development of medicine and public health on the island. Although related developments have been summarized elsewhere, the consequences of physicians' subordination to U.S. colonization were perhaps clearest in another ongoing public health campaign. Both North American officials and Puerto Rican "social workers, health professionals, and nurses" shared the idea that "Puerto Rico's problems originated from overpopulation" (López, 2008: 10). Both groups relied on physicians' work and associations in order to carry out a mass compulsory sterilization campaign. Although this campaign changed in form over the twentieth century, it nonetheless created new cultural patterns resulting in Puerto Rican women being among the most frequently sterilized on earth.

Puerto Rican physicians' efforts to navigate and translate colonial modernity also involved making rural populations visible to U.S. colonial authorities and producing "clinical material" for scientific research (Ashford, 1931: 10). This role drew medical research to the island, including the Rockefeller Foundation who became involved in the island's hookworm campaign in 1920. One RF physician mutated native physicians' project of regeneration. Working from the Presbyterian Hospital in San Juan, Cornelius Packard Rhoads wrote a letter in which he presented an alternate medical solution for the "degenerate" race of men (Lederer, 2002: 722). In the letter, he claimed to have used his clinical interventions in order to kill eight patients and, like the hookworm, infect others ("transplanting cancer into several more"). The charges were not proven but many commentators remain skeptical about Rhoads' quick exit from the island and his lack of appearance for the subsequent investigation. Other commentators were critical of his subsequent professional success, which included secret experiments he conducted on soldiers without obtaining informed consent (Rigau-Pérez, 2000).

Post- and Neo-Coloniality

As of this writing, Puerto Rico's political status remains a controversial and unresolved problem at an international level. For instance, the island's "colonial situation" continues to generate debate within the United Nations despite its removal from the United Nations's list of Non-Self-Governing Territories in 2010. In the debates that ensued, the critical issue remains unstated. The genuine will of the people is not necessarily equivalent with a universally-shared position, particularly when the meanings of sovereignty and autonomy are compromised by U.S. global hegemony. Many former colonies navigate neo-colonial relationships to U.S. Empire as Puerto Rico remains "the oldest colony of the modern world" (Trías Monge, 1997: 4). The past informs the current realities shaping neo-colonial relationships in the world system.

This book's general insights about medicine and public health are useful in a seemingly post-colonial world where the imposition of tutelage through a U.S.-dominated political administration is assumed to be part of a deplorable past. For instance, physicians were a heterogeneous group with differing ideas about the colonial relationship. Many sought to selectively appropriate the modernization that U.S. authority offered. Physicians competed amongst themselves and with other nationalists, politicians and laborers to realize their modernization projects and advanced alternate ideas of national progress that included a more equitable distribution of resources, i.e. food, medical attention, latrines and sanitation, etc. Some challenged colonial dominance. As they negotiated U.S. colonial authority, they also reshaped social hierarchies as colonial subjects.

Puerto Rican physicians both enabled and delimited the efficacy of U.S. colonial interventions and the ability of these interventions to consolidate legitimate authority, but their work and influence was also hemmed in by colonial capitalism and scientific modernity. They were not a homogenous group in terms of political party affiliations, but their attempt to gain greater political autonomy also occurred within the global and regional constraints of the an already developed world system where Puerto Rico stood in a clearly compromised colonial position. They were not a homogenous group and medicine itself was subject to internal debates, but even these were heavily influenced by U.S. medicine and the ways medical colonization complemented the expansion of U.S. capital in Latin America. Some Puerto Rican physicians appropriated colonial authority to improve their status relative to local constraints and municipal governments. Others, like Drs. Octavio Jordán y Miranda and Francisco Maria Susoni Abreu used their status, which was partly a product of their involvement with the hookworm campaign, to challenge the terms of U.S. colonial authority.

While many Americans today continue to see medicine as positive aspect of government responsibility, current events demonstrate that medicine promotes the industrialized state's interests in promoting a seemingly universal democracy. In this way, Americans continue to use medicine as a complement to U.S. foreign policy as they did in Puerto Rico during the early twentieth century. Medicine continues to be complicit in U.S. political interventions within the world system, including its experiments in building ostensibly democratic states. For instance, *Médecins Sans Frontières* (Doctors Without Borders) share a privileged educational role with policy experts, diplomats, former UN officials and human rights activists. As Hardt and Negri argue, non-governmental organizations like Doctors Without Borders represent a new form of global governance that transcends the nation-state and paves the way for military intervention. In a similar way, the United States continue to use medicine in state-building and political intervention that claims to promote multilateral alliances around humanitarian issues. Medicine continues to play a dominant role in defining crises in ways that stir international outrage. Physicians continue to define disease and death in far away places for public consumption and portray their medical interventions as beyond the political and in selfless service to the people at the expense of recognizing their complicity in the underlying dynamics of the world system.

I suggest that because medical NGO's play such an important role in defining crisis, they also have the potential to redefine crisis in democratic ways. There is no doubt that NGO such as Doctors Without Borders have access to populations that governments find inaccessible. Physicians' practice is political, but at least in early-twentieth century Puerto Rico, it was not coerced. The challenge for physicians is to define the goals, emphasis and purpose of medical practice less through professional aspirations or political affiliations with governments than through the desires of the patients they claim to serve. As many scholars agree, these NGO's represent new potential for building democracy. Physicians also share in the possibility of having their practice democratically defined by those they hope to serve.

BIBLIOGRAPHY

Primary

(1910) *Business Directory of Porto Rico.* New York, NY: F. E. Platt.

Aguerrevere L (1908) *Los Asuntos Higiénicos en la Ciudad de Ponce.* Ponce, PR: Baldorioty.

Allen CH (1901) *First Annual Report of the Governor of Porto Rico.* Washington, DC: Government Printing Office.

Amadeo J (1904) La Anemia Y La Uncinariasis En Puerto Rico. *La Correspondencia De Puerto Rico,* Jan. 29.

American Medical Association (1905) Proceedings of the American Medical Association Meeting in Portland, OR, July 10–14, 1905. *Journal of the American Medical Association,* 45 (4): 255–258.

Ames A (1903) The Vaccination of Porto Rico-A Lesson to the World. *Journal of the Association of Military Surgeons of the United States,* 12 (5): 293–313.

Ames A (1901) Labor Conditions in Porto Rico. *Bulletin of the Department of Labor* 34 (May): 377–439.

Ashford BK (1934) *A Soldier in Science.* New York, NY: Grosset & Dunlap.

Ashford BK (1931) *Porto Rico: The Seat of the Future Pan-American University.* San Juan, PR: Larroca & Hijos.

Ashford BK (1928) *The War on the Hookworm.* New York, NY: Chemical Foundation.

Ashford BK (1913a) The Economic Aspects of Hookworm Disease in Porto Rico. *The American Journal of the Medical Sciences,* 145: 358–372.

Ashford BK (1913b) The Control and Eradication of Hookworm Disease. *Papers by Officers of the Medical Corps, U.S. Army,* Bulletin No. 2. Washington, DC: Government Printing Office.

Ashford BK and Gutiérrez Igaravídez P (1911) *Uncinariasis (Hookworm Disease) in Porto Rico: A Medical and Economic Problem.* Washington, DC: Government Printing Office.

Ashford BK and Gutiérrez Igaravídez P (1910) *Summary of a Ten Years' Campaign Against Hookworm Disease in Porto Rico.* Chicago, IL: American Medical Association.

Ashford BK (1910) Report to Governor George R. Colton, Jan. 18.In University of Puerto Rico, Recinto Ciencias Medicas, Ashford's Personal Papers, Doc. # 99C.

Ashford BK (1909) Letter to Major Charles Lynch of the Medical Corps, November 16. National Archives, Record Group 112, File #106177, Box 714.

Ashford BK (1907) Where Treatment of All Infected is the Surest Prophylactic Measure: The Problem of Epidemic Uncinariasis in Porto Rico. *The Military Surgeon,* 20 (1): 40–55.

Ashford BK, King WW and Gutiérrez Igaravídez (1905) Pharmacology. *California State Journal of Medicine,* 3 (11): 342–343.

Ashford BK (1905) Letter to Surgeon General, August 31. National Archives, Record Group 112, File #106127, Box 714.

Ashford BK and King WW (1904) Notes and Observations on Uncinariasis in Porto Rico. *New Orleans Medical and Surgical Journal,* 56 (9): 651–674.

Ashford BK and King WW (1903) A Study of Uncinariasis in Porto Rico. *American Medicine,* 6 (Sep. 5): 391–396.

Ashford BK (1901) Ankylostomiasis in Porto Rico. In *Military Government of Porto Rico from October 18, 1898, to April 30, 1900.* Washington, DC: Government Printing Office, 121–123.

Ashford BK (1899) Letter to the US Army Surgeon General, Nov. 25. In University of Puerto Rico, Recinto Ciencias Medicas, Ashford's Personal Papers.

Ashford BK (undated) The Control and Eradication of Hookworm Disease, Document #4740, University of Puerto Rico, Recinto Ciencias Medicas, Ashford's Personal Papers.

Asociación Médica de Puerto Rico (1908) Décima Tercera Sesión Científica de la Asociación Médica de Puerto Rico. *Boletin de la Asociación Médica de Puerto Rico*, 6 (61): 1–4.

Barbosa De Rosario P (1937) *Post Umbra: Juicios Sobre José Celso Barbosa.* San Juan, PR: Imprenta Venezuela.

Blasingame FJL (1959) *Digest of Official Actions, 1846–1958,* v. 1. Chicago, IL: American Medical Association.

Brau S (1956) *Disquisiciones Sociológicas Y Otros Ensayos.* Guatemala: Editorial Cultura.

Brigadier General (1898) Letter to Mayor of San Juan, Nov. 14. In Archivo General de Puerto Rico, *Documentos Municipales,* San Juan, Leg. 125½, Exp. 147.

Bryan WS (1899) *Our Islands and Their People.* St. Louis, MO: N.D. Thompson Publishing Company.

Carbonell JN (1998) El Boletín y su Historia: Medicina Tropical. *Boletín de la Asociación Médica de Puerto Rico,* 90: 56–57.

Carroll H (1899) *Report on the Island of Porto Rico: Its Population, Civil Government, Commerce, Industries, Productions, Roads, Tariff, and Currency, With Recommendations.* Washington, DC: Government Printing Office.

Coll Y Toste C (1904) El Boletín y su Historia: Nuestra Opinión Acerca de 'La Medicina Entre los Indios'. *Boletín Asociación Médica de Puerto Rico,* 2 (22): 6–7.

Coll Y Toste C (1899) *Reseña del Estado Social, Ecoomico e Industrial de la Isla de Puerto Rico al Tomar Posesión de Ella los Estados Unidos.* San Juan, PR: Academia Puertorriqueña de la Historia.

Coll Y Toste C (1892) Aspecto General De La Civilización De Puerto Rico en 1797, Desde El Punto De Vista Moral Y Material, Y Breve Estudio Comparativo Entre El Estado De Cultura De Aquella Época Y El Actual, Por Cayetano Coll Y Toste. *Boletín Histórico de Puerto Rico,* 1: 162–179.

Colton R (1911) *Report of the Governor of Porto Rico.* Washington, DC: Government Printing Office.

Commission for the Study and Treatment of Anemia (1904) *Report of the Commission for the Study and Treatment of "Anemia" in Porto Rico.* San Juan, PR: Bureau of Printing and Supplies.

Commission for the Suppression of Anemia in Puerto Rico (1905) *Anemia in Porto Rico: Preliminary Report.* San Juan, PR: Bureau of Printing and Supplies.

Davis GW (1900a) *Military Government of Porto Rico.* Washington, DC: Government Printing Office.

Davis GW (1900b) *Report on Civil Affairs of Puerto Rico.* Washington, DC: Government Printing Office.

Davison LP (1899b) Sanitary Report from San Juan. *Public Health Reports,* 14 (May 5): 636–642.

Davison LP (1899c) Sanitary Report from Ponce, PortoRico. *Public Health Service,* 14 (April 21): 549–550.

Davison LP (1899d) Letter to Adjunct General, Feb. 20. In Archivo General de Puerto Rico, *Documentos Municipales,* San Juan, Leg 126, Exp 164.

Dumont DE (1875) *Ensayo de una Historia Médico-Quirúrgica de la Isla de Puerto Rico.* Habana: La Antilla.

Editorials (1905) American Sanitary Achievements. *Journal of American Medical Association,* (Sept. 23): 924.

Fernós Isern A (1926a) The Development of the Public Health Organization of Porto Rico. *Porto Rico Health Review,* 2 (6): 3–10.

Fernós Isern A (1926b) The White-and the Tropics. *Porto Rico Health Review,* 2 (6): 3–10.

Franco Soto JA (1949) *Juan Recuerda su Pasado.* San Juan, PR: Imprenta Venezuela.

Froude JA (1888) *The English in the West Indies; Or, the Bow of Ulysses.* London: Longmans, Green, and Co.

García de Quevedo L (1915) La Anemia de Puerto Rico y Sus Causas. Paper presented at the Sesión Científica de la Sociedad Médica del Districto Norte, 17 June. University of Puerto Rico, Coleccíon Puertorriqueña Archives, 614.55 G216a.

Glennan AH (1899a) *Public Health Reports,* 14 (October 27): 1833.

Glennan AH (1899b) Sanitary Report For Mayaguez. *Public Health Service,* 14 (May 26): 763.

Glennan AH (1899c) Sanitary Report From Ponce, Puerto Rico. *Public Health Service,* 14 (April 21): 547–550.

Glennan AH (1899d) Sanitary Report From Porto Rico-Leprosy. *Public Health Reports,* 14 (February): 284–285.

Gompers S (1904) *Discurso Pronunciado en la Recepción Celebrada en su Honor por la Unión Central Obrera de Washington.* American Federation of Labor, University of Puerto Rico, Colección Puertorriqueña Archives.

González Font J (1903) *Escritos Sobre Puerto Rico: Noticias Históricas, Poesías, Articulos y Otros Datos.* Barcelona: Librería de José González Font.

Grant JB (1920) Letter to Dr. Heiser, 24 March. Rockefeller Foundation Archives, Record Group 1.1, 243, Box 2, Folder 33.

Grinnell AG (1914) The Physical Emancipation of Porto Rico. *The American Review of Reviews,* 15 (July-December): 719–724.

Greenleaf (1898) Letter to Dr. Groff, Aug. 27. National Archives, Record Group 112, Entry 26, #43656.

Gutiérrez Igaravídez P (1918) Significacíon, Importancia y Porvenir del Instituto de Medicina Tropical E Higiene de Puerto Rico. Paper presented at the Salones del Ateneo Puertorriqueno, 26 Feb., San Juan, PR.

Gutiérrez Igaravídez P (1912) *Un Caso de Pelagra.* San Juan, PR: Real Hermanos, Inc.

Hafner AW (1993) *Directory of Deceased American Physicians, 1804–1929: A Geneological Guide to over 149,000 Medical Practitioners Providing Brief Biographical Sketches Drawn From the American Medical Association's Deceased Physician Masterfile.* Chicago, IL: American Medical Association.

Henna JJ and Zeno Gandia M (1899) *The Case of Puerto Rico.* Washington, DC: Press of W. F. Roberts.

Henry GV (1898) Gen. Order #37, Passed Dec. 28. In Archivo General de Puerto Rico, *Documentos Municipales,* Leg. 125 1/2, Exp. 146.

Hernandez R and Fawcett Smith WM (1901) Letter to Governor Allen, March 22. National Archives, Record Group 59.

Herrmann KS (1907) *A Recent Campaign in Puerto Rico by the Independent Regular Brigade Under the Command of Brigadier General Schwan.* Boston, MA: E. H. Bacon.

Hill RB (1925) The Uncinariasis Problem. *Porto Rico Health Review,* 1 (1): 11–17.

Hoff JVR (1901) *Military Government of Porto Rico from October 18, 1898 to April 30, 1900: Appendices to the Report of the Military Governor, Epitome of Reports of the Superior Board of Health.* Washington, DC: Government Printing Office.

Hoff JVR (1900) The Share of 'the White Man's Burden' that has Fallen to the Medical Departments of the Public Services in Puerto Rico. *The Philadelphia Medical Journal,* (April 7): 796–799.

Hunt WH (1902) *Second Annual Report of the Governor of Porto Rico.* Washington, DC: Government Printing Office.

Hunt WH (1903) *Third Annual Report of the Governor of Porto Rico.* Washington, DC: Government Printing Office.

Hunt WH (1904) *Fourth Annual Report of the Governor of Porto Rico.* Washington, DC: Government Printing Office.

International Health Board (1922) *Bibliography of Hookworm Disease.* New York, NY: Rockefeller Foundation.

International Health Board (1920) *Rockefeller Foundation Annual Report.* New York, NY: Rockefeller Foundation.

International Health Board (1919) *Rockefeller Foundation Annual Report.* New York, NY: Rockefeller Foundation.

King GG (1929) *Letters of a Volunteer in the Spanish-American War.* Chicago, IL: Hawkins & Loomis.

King WW (2006) Porto Rico: Report on the High Mortality on the Island. *Public Health Reports,* 121 (Supplement 1): 38–43.

Kipling R (1899) The White Man's Burden. *McClure's Magazine,* 12 (4): 4–5.

Larned JN (1913) *History for Ready Reference,* volume 6. Springfield, MA: The C.A. Nichols Co., Publishers.

Lee B (1899) Letter to President of United States, January 9. National Archives, Record Group 112, Entry 26, #43656.

López Giménez E (1998) *Crónica Del '98: El Testimonio De Un Médico Puertorriqueño.* Madrid: Ediciones Libertarias Prodhufi, S.A.

Marcus J (1919) *Labor Conditions in Porto Rico.* Washington, DC: Government Printing Office.

Middeldyk RAV (1903) *The History of Puerto Rico: From the Spanish Discovery to the American Occupation.* New York, NY: D. Appleton and Company.

Morel Campos R (1896) *El Porvenir de Utuado: Estudio Historico Descriptivo y Estadistico.* Ponce, PR: Imprenta El Vapor.

Mountin JW, Pennell EH and Flook E (1937) Illness and Medical Care in Puerto Rico. *Public Health Bulletin,* (237): 1–63.

National Civil Service Reform League (1902) *The Situation in Porto Rico: Report of the Committee on the Civil Service in Dependencies of the National Civil Service Reform League.* New York, NY: National Civil Service Reform League.

Parke A (1901) Official Directory of the Civil Government of Porto Rico.

Pedreira AS (1937) *Un Hombre Del Pueblo, Volumen 1.* San Juan, PR: Imprenta Venezuela.

Permanent Commission for the Suppression of Uncinariasis in Porto Rico (1907) *Report for the Fiscal Year 1906–1907.* San Juan, PR: Bureau of Printing and Supplies.

Porto Rico Legislature (1902a) An Act Providing for the Appointment of a Director of Health, defining his duties as such, and establishing a Superior Board of Health, and for other purposes. Approved March 1.

Porto Rico Legislature (1902b) An Act Concerning Municipalities. Approved March 1.

Post RH (1907) *Annual Report of the Governor of Porto Rico.* Washington, DC: Government Printing Office.

Post RH (1904) Letter to Attorney General of Washington, DC, March 25. National Archives, Record Group 46, SEN58A-F19, Box 80.

Quevedo Báez M (1946) *Historia De La Medicina Y Cirugia en Puerto Rico, vol. 1.* Puerto Rico, PR: Asociación Médica de Puerto Rico.

Quevedo Báez M (1949) *Historia De La Medicina Y Cirugia de Puerto Rico, vol. 2.* Puerto Rico, PR: Asociación Médica de Puerto Rico.

Riera Palmer (1907) *Memorandum Presentado al Honorable Ayuntamiento de Mayaguez.* Mayaguez, PR: Tipografia La Voz de la Patria.

Roosevelt T (1906) *Message from the President of the United States Relative to his Recent Visit to the Island of Porto Rico.* Washington, DC: Government Printing Office.

Rowe LS (1904) *The United States and Porto Rico.* New York, NY: Longmans, Green, and Co.

Rowe LS (1901) The Insular Director of Sanitation and The Advisory Board of Health. *Report of the Commission to Revise and Compile the Laws of Porto Rico* 1 (1, 2, and 3): 236, 238.

San Juan Ayuntamiento (1888) *Informe Sobre el Estado Higiénico de la Poblacion que Presentan los Tenientes de Alcades al Excmo. Ayuntamiento de San Juan de Puerto Rico.* San Juan, PR: A. Lynn, Imprenta del Municipio.

Sanger JP, Gannett H and Willcox W (1900) *Report on the Census of Porto Rico, 1899.* Washington, DC: Government Printing Office.

McLeary J (1901) *Register of Porto Rico.* San Juan, PR: Press of the San Juan News.

Smith WMF (1901a) Letter to the Editor of *The Great Round World,* June 21. National Archives, Record Group 46, SEN56-F25, Box 102.

Smith WMF (1901b) Sanitation in Porto Rico. *Public Health Papers and Reports* 27: 166–174.

Smith WMF (1900) Letter to Governor Allen, October 31. National Archives, Record Group 46, SEN56-F25, Box 102.

Stiles CW (1913) Thymol Administration. *Public Health Reports,* 18 (29): 1497–1513.

Stiles CW (1903) Hookworm Disease (Uncinariasis)-A Newly Recognized Factor in American Anemias. *Brooklyn Medical Journal*, 17 (2): 51–56.

Sweet W (1904) Letter to Attorney General of Washington, DC, March 23. National Archives, Record Group 46, SEN58A-F19, Box 80.

Thayer WR (1916) *The Life and Letters of John Hay*, Volume 2. Boston, MA: Houghton Mifflin Company.

Todd RH (1925) *Informe Al Pueblo De San Juan Y Al Honorable Gobernador de Puerto Rico, Año Económico de 1924–25*. San Juan, PR: The Times Publishing Company.

U.S. Bureau of the Census (1935) *Schedules of the 1935 Special Censuses of Puerto Rico: Agriculture Schedules, 1935*. U.S. National Archives, Record Group 29.

U.S. Department of Commerce and Labor, Bureau of Statistics (1906) *Commercial Porto Rico*. Washington, DC: Government Printing Office.

U.S. Senate (1924) Committee on Territories and Insular Possessions. *The Civil Government of Porto Rico: Hearings Before the Committee on Territories and Insular Possessions*. 68th Congress, 1st Session, Feb. 18, 1924.

Vincent GE (1923) One War the World Needs: International Teamwork for World Health and Against Disease Makes for the Deeper Understanding between Nations which Destroys Suspicions and Antagonisms. *Our World: A Magazine of Understanding*, 2 (4): 48–54.

Weyl WE (1905) Labor Conditions in Porto Rico. *Bulletin of the Bureau of Labor*, 61 (November): 723–856.

Willoughby WF (1910) The Reorganization of Municipal Government in Porto Rico: Financial. *Political Science Quarterly*, 25 (1): 69–102.

Willoughby WF (1909) The Reorganization of Municipal Government in Porto Rico: Political. *Political Science Quarterly*, 24 (3): 409–443.

Yager A (1919) *Report of the Governor of Porto Rico*. Washington, DC: Government Printing Office.

Yager A (1915) *Report of the Governor of Porto Rico*. Washington, DC: Government Printing Office.

Yager A (1913) *Report of the Governor of Porto Rico*. Washington, DC: Government Printing Office.

Secondary

Abbot A(1988) *The System of Professions: An Essay on the Division of Expert Labor*. Chicago, IL: The University of Chicago Press.

Amador JG (2008) Redeeming the Tropics: Public Health and National Identity in Cuba, Puerto Rico, and Brazil, 1890–1940. Unpublished doctoral thesis, University of Michigan, Michigan.

Anderson W (2006) *Colonial Pathologies: American Tropical Medicine, Race, and Hygiene in the Philippines*. Durham, NC: Duke University Press.

Arana-Soto S (1978a) Unos Médicos Ilustres y una Época Terrible. *Revista del Instituto de Cultura Puertorriqueña*, 21 (81): 31–36.

Arana-Soto S (1978b) *La Sanidad en Puerto Rico Hasta el 1898*. San Juan, PR: Academia Puertorriqueña de la Historia.

Arana-Soto S (1978c) *El Dr. José Espaillat y la Enseñanza Médica en Puerto Rico*. Barcelona: Artes Gráficas Medinaceli.

Arana-Soto S (1974) *Historia De La Medicina Puertorriqueña*. Barcelona: Artes Gráficas Medinaceli.

Arana-Soto S (1968) *Catalogo de Poetas Puertorriqueños*. San Juan, PR: Sociedad de Autores Puertorriqueños.

Arana-Soto S (1966a) *Catalogo de Medicos de Puerto Rico de Siglos Pasados (Con Muchos de Éste)*. España: Imprenta de Aldecoa.

Arana-Soto S (1966b) *Catalogo de Farmaceuticos de Puerto Rico.* España: Imprenta de Aldecoa.

Arana-Soto S (1963) *Diccionario de Médicos Puertorriqueños (Que se han Distinguido Fuera de la Medicina).* España: Imprenta de Aldecoa.

Arana-Soto S (1962a) Los Médicos Abolicionistas. *Boletín de la Asociacíon Medica de Puerto Rico* 54: 238–240.

Arana-Soto S (1962b) Los Médicos Alcaldes. *Boletín de la Asociacíon Medica de Puerto Rico* 54: 22–23.

Arana-Soto S (1961) Luis Muñoz Rivera y Los Medicos. *Boletín de la Asociacíon Medica de Puerto Rico,* 53: 31–32.

Argüelles MP (1989) National Self-Determination and Puerto Rico, 1809–1948. Unpublished doctoral thesis, University of Virginia, Virginia.

Arnold D (2000) Science, Technology and Medicine in Colonial India. Port Chester, NY: Cambridge University Press.

Arnold D (1993) *Colonizing the Body: State Medicine and Epidemic Disease in Nineteenth-Century India.* Berkeley, CA: University of California Press.

Asenjo C (1933) *Quien es Quien en Puerto Rico.* San Juan, PR: Real Hermanos, Inc.

Ayala CJ and Bergad LW (2002) Rural Puerto Rico in the Early Twentieth Century Reconsidered: Land and Society, 1899–1915. *Latin American Research Review,* 37 (2): 65–97.

Azize Vargas Y and Aviles LA (1990) La Mujer en Las Profesiones de Salud. *Puerto Rico Health Sciences Journal,* 9 (1): 9–16.

Baber Z (2001) Colonizing Nature: Scientific Knowledge, Colonial Power and the Incorporation of India into the Modern World-System. *British Journal of Sociology,* 52 (1): 37–58.

Baralt GA (1999) *Buena Vista: Life and Work on a Puerto Rican Hacienda, 1833–1904.* Chapel Hill, NC: University of North Carolina Press.

Balasquide LA (1984) *Medicos Notables del Antaño Ponceño.* San Juan, PR: Instituto de Cultura Puertorriqueña.

Berbusse EJ (1966) *The United States in Puerto Rico, 1898–1900.* Chapel Hill, NC: University of North Carolina Press.

Bergad LW (1983a) Coffee and Rural Proletarianization in Puerto Rico, 1840–1898. *Journal of Latin American Studies,* 15 (1): 83–100.

Bergad LW (1983b) *Coffee and the Growth of Agrarian Capitalism in Nineteenth-Century Puerto Rico.* Princeton, NJ: Princeton University Press.

Bergad LW (1978) Agrarian History of Puerto Rico, 1870–1930. *Latin American Research Review,* 13 (3): 63–94.

Berger PL and Luckmann T (1966) *The Social Construction of Reality.* New York, NY: Anchor Books.

Bhabha H (1994) *The Location of Culture.* London: Routledge.

Birn AE (2009) The Stages of International (Global) Health: Histories of Success or Successes of History? *Global Public Health: An International Journal for Research, Policy and Practice,* 4 (1): 50–68.

Birn AE and Solórzano A (1999) Public Health Policy Paradoxes: Science and Politics In the Rockefeller Foundation's Hookworm Campaign In Mexico In the 1920s. *Social Science and Medicine,* 49 (9): 1197–1213.

Birn AE (1996) Public Health or Public Menace? The Rockefeller Foundation and Public Health in Mexico, 1920–1950. *Voluntas,* 7 (1): 35–56.

Blanes RA (1954) Isaac Gonzalez Martinez, 1871–1954. *Boletín de la Asociacíon Medica de Puerto Rico,* 46 (8): 387–390.

Brandt AM and Gardner M (1997) The Golden Age of Medicine? In: Cooter R and Pickstone JV (eds) *Companion to Medicine in the Twentieth Century.* New York, NY: Taylor & Francis, 21–37.

Briggs L (2002) *Reproducing Empire: Race, Sex, Science, and U.S. Imperialism in Puerto Rico.* Berkeley, CA: University of California Press.

Buckingham J (2002) *Leprosy in Colonial South India.* London: Palgrave.

Burnham JC (1997) American Medicine's Golden Age: What Happened to It? In: Leavitt JW and Numbers RL (eds) *Sickness and Health in America: Readings in the History of Medicine and Public Health.* Madison, WI: University of Wisconsin Press, 284–294.

Cabán PA (1999) *Constructing A Colonial People: Puerto Rico And The United States, 1898–1932.* Boulder, CO: Westview Press.

Cabranes JA (1979) *Citizenship and the American Empire: Notes on the Legislative History of the United States Citizenship of Puerto Ricans.* New Haven, CT: Yale University Press.

Caponi S (2002) Coordenadas Epistemológicas de la Medicina Tropical. *História, Ciências, Saúde-Manguinhos,* 10 (1): 113–149.

Carrasquillo RE (2006) *Our Landless Patria: Marginal Citizenship and Race in Caguas, Puerto Rico, 1880–1910.* Lincoln, NE: University of Nebraska Press.

Carreras CN (1974) *Hombres y Mujeres de Puerto Rico.* Mexico: Editorial Orion.

Carrion AM (1983) *Puerto Rico: A Political and Cultural History.* New York, NY: W.W. Norton & Company, Inc.

Cirillo VJ (2004) *Bullets and Bacilli: The Spanish-American War and Military Medicine.* New Brunswick, NJ: Rutgers University Press.

Cirillo VJ (2000) Fever and Reform: The Typhoid Epidemic in the Spanish-American War." *Journal of the History of Medicine and Allied Sciences,* 55 (4):363–397.

Coelho PRP and McGuire RA (2006) Racial Differences in Disease Susceptibilities: Intestinal Worm Infections in the Early Twentieth-Century American South. *Social History of Medicine,* 19 (3): 461–482.

Colgrove J (2002) The McKeown Thesis: A Historical Controversy and its Enduring Influence. *American Journal of Public Health,* 92 (5): 725–729.

Comaroff JL (1998) Reflections on the Colonial State, in South Africa and Elsewhere: Factions, Fragments, Facts and Fictions. *Social Identities,* 4 (3): 321–361.

Conrad P (1985) The Meaning of Medications: Another Look At Compliance. *Social Science and Medicine,* 20 (1): 29–37.

Córdova GF (1993) *Resident Commissioner Santiago Iglesias and His Times.* Río Piedras, PR: Editorial de la Universidad de Puerto Rico.

Cortés Zavala MT (2006) Ciencia y Salud: La Catedra de Medicina en Puerto Rico. In Opatrný J (ed) *Nación y Cultura Nacional en el Caribe Hispano.* Prague: Universidad Carolina de Praga, Editorial Karolinum, 169–176.

Crosby WH (1987) The Deadly Hookworm: Why Did the Puerto Ricans Die? *Archives of Internal Medicine,* 147 (March): 577–578.

Crosby WH (1986) Overtreating the Deficiency Anemias. *Archives of Internal Medicine,* 146 (April): 779.

Cubano Iguina A (2006) *Rituals of Violence in Nineteenth-Century Puerto Rico.* Gainesville, FL: University Press of Florida.

Cubano Iguina A (2005) Visions of Empire and Historical Imagination in Puerto Rico Under Spanish Rule, 1870–1898. In: Schmidt-Nowara C and Nieto-Phillips JM (eds) *Interpreting Spanish Colonialism: Empires, Nations and Legends.* Albuquerque, NM: University of New Mexico Press, 87–107.

Cubano Iguina A (1998) Political Culture and Male Mass-Party Formation in Late-Nineteenth-Century Puerto Rico. *The Hispanic American Historical Review,* 78 (4): 631–662.

Cubano Iguina A (1997) Criollos Ante el 98: la Cambiante Imagen del Dominio Español Durante su Crisis y Caida en Puerto Rico, 1889–1899. *Revista de Indias,* 57 (211): 637–655.

De Certeau M (1986) *Heterologies: Discourses on the Other.* Minneapolis, MN: University of Minnesota Press.

De Kruif P (1996) *Microbe Hunters.* Orlando, FL: Houghton Mifflin Harcourt.

Demert DJ, Bethony JM and Hotez PJ (2008) Hookworm Vaccines. *Clinical Infectious Diseases,* 46 (2): 282–288.

Dietz J (1986) *Economic History of Puerto Rico: Institutional Change and Capitalist Development.* Princeton, NJ: Princeton University Press.

Dubos R (1959) *Mirage of Health: Utopias, Progress, and Biological Change.* New York, NY: Harper & Brothers.

Engelhardt HT (1986) *The Foundations of Bioethics.* New York, NY: Oxford University Press.

Espinosa M (2009) *Epidemic Invasions: Yellow Fever and the Limits of Cuban Independence, 1878–1930.* Chicago, IL: University of Chicago Press.

Estades Font ME (1988) *La Presencia Militar De Estados Unidos En Puerto Rico 1898–1918.* Rio Piedras, PR: Ediciones Huracán, Inc.

Farley J (2003) *To Cast Out Disease: A History of the International Health Division of the Rockefeller Foundation (1913–1951).* New York, NY: Oxford University Press.

Farley J (1991) *Bilharzia: A History of Imperial Tropical Medicine.* Cambridge: Cambridge University Press.

Feliú F (2008) Science, Sight and the Ordering of Colonial Societies. In: Edwards E and Bhaumik K (eds) *Visual Sense: A Cultural Reader.* New York, NY: Berg Publishers.

Feliú F (2001) Rendering the Invisible Visible and the Visible Invisible: The Colonizing Function of Bailey K. Ashford's Antianemia Campaigns. In: Trigo B (ed) *Foucault and Latin America: Appropriations and Deployments of Discursive Analysis.* New York, NY: Routledge, 153–166.

Figueroa LA (2005) *Sugar, Slavery, and Freedom in Nineteenth-Century Puerto Rico.* Chapel Hill, NC: The University of North Carolina Press.

Fortuño Janeiro L (1934) *Album Histórico de Ponce (1692–1934).* Ponce, PR.

Foucault M (1980) *Power/Knowledge: Selected Interviews and Other Writings, 1972–1977.* New York, NY: Random House.

Freidson E (1970) *Profession of Medicine: A Study of the Sociology of Applied Knowledge.* New York, NY: Dodd, Mead & Co.

García GL (2000) I am the Other: Puerto Rico in the Eyes of the North Americans, 1898. *The Journal of American History,* 87 (1): 39–64.

García GL (1989) Economía y Trabajo en el Puerto Rico del Siglo XIX. *Historia Mexicana,* 38 (4): 855–878.

García CM and Quevedo E (1998) Uncinariasis y Café: Los Antecedentes de la Intervención de la Fundación Rockefeller en Colombia: 1900–1920. *Biomédica,* 18 (1): 5–21.

García Leduc JM (2003) *Apuntes Para una Historia Breve de Puerto Rico: Desde la Prehistoria Hasta 1898.* San Juan, PR: Editorial Isla Negra.

Gillett MC (1995) *The Army Medical Department, 1865–1917.* Washington, DC: Government Printing Office.

Go J (2008) *American Empire and the Politics of Meaning: Elite Political Cultures in the Philippines and Puerto Rico during U.S. Colonialism.* Durham, NC: Duke University Press.

Go J (2007) The Provinciality of American Empire: 'Liberal Exceptionalism' and U.S. Colonial Rule, 1898–1912. *Comparative Studies in Society and History,* 49 (1): 74–108.

Goffman E (1963) *Stigma:* Notes on the Management of Spoiled Identity. New York: Prentice-Hall.

Gonzalez JL (1980) *El Pais De Cuatro Pisos.* Rio Piedras, PR: Ediciones Huracán, Inc.

Goode J (2009) *Impurity of Blood: Defining Race in Spain, 1870–1930.* Baton Rouge, LA: Louisiana State University Press.

Guerra F (1975) *El Medico Politico: Su Influencia en la Historia de Hispano America y Filipinas.* Madrid: Afrodisio Aguado SA.

Guerra L (1998) *Popular Expression and National Identity in Puerto Rico: The Struggle for Self, Community, and Nation.* Gainesville, FL: University Press of Florida.

Gutiérrez del Arroyo I (1976) *El Dr. Agustin Stahl, Hombre de Ciencia: Perspectiva Humanistica.* Rio Piedras, PR: Universidad de Puerto Rico.

Hernandez Paralitici PH (1983) *Utuado: Notas Para su Historia.* San Juan, PR: Comité Historia de los Pueblos.

Hewa S (1995) *Colonialism, Tropical Disease, and Imperial Medicine: Rockefeller Philanthropy in Sri Lanka.* Lanham, MA: University Press of America.

Hoganson KL (1998) *Fighting for American Manhood: How Gender Politics Provoked the Spanish-American and Philippine-American Wars.* New Haven, CT: Yale University Press.

Ileto RC (1988) Cholera dn the Origins of the American Sanitary Order in the Philippines. In: Arnold D (ed) *Imperial Medicine and Indigenous Societies: Disease, Medicine and Empire in the Nineteenth and Twentieth Centuries.* New York, NY: St. Martin's Press, Inc., 125–148.

Jiménez Malaret R (1985) *Dr. Félix Tió y Malaret:* Ensayo Biográfico. San Juan, PR: Colección Hipatia.

Kalpagam U (2000) The Colonial State and Statistical Knowledge. *History of the Human Sciences,* 13 (2): 37–55.

Kauanui JK (2008) *Hawaiian Blood: Colonialism and the Politics of Sovereignty and Indigeneity.* Durham, NC: Duke University Press.

Kaufmann E (2001) Nativist Cosmopolitans: Institutional Reflexivity and the Decline of "Double-Consciousness" in American Nationalist Thought. *Journal of Historical Sociology,* 14 (1): 47–78.

Kraut AM (1994) *Silent Travelers: Germs, Genes, and the "Immigrant Menace."* Baltimore, MD: The Johns Hopkins University Press.

Kramer PA (2006) *The Blood of Government: Race, Empire, the United States and the Philippines.* Chapel Hill, NC: University of North Carolina Press.

Larson MS (1977) *The Rise of Professionalism: A Sociological Analysis.* Berkeley: University of California Press.

Levison JH (2003) Beyond Quarantine: A History of Leprosy in Puerto Rico, 1898–1930s. *História, Ciências, Saúde* 10 (Suppl 1): 225–245.

Lim ML (2001) A Perspective on Tropical Sprue. *Current Gastroenterology Reports,* 3 (4): 322–327.

Livingstone DN (1999) Tropical Climate and Moral Hygiene: The Anatomy of a Victorian Debate. *British Journal of Historical Sociology,* 32: 93–110.

Loveman M (2007) The U.S. Census and the Contested Rules of Racial Classification in Early Twentieth-Century Puerto Rico. *Caribbean Studies,* 35 (2): 3–36.

Lo MM (2002) *Doctors Within Borders: Profession, Ethnicity, and Modernity in Colonial Taiwan.* Berkeley: University of California Press.

Lopez I (2008) *Matters of Choice: Puerto Rican Women's Struggle for Reproductive Freedom.* Brunswick, NJ: Rutgers University Press.

Macdonald K (1995) *The Sociology of the Professions.* London: SAGE Publications.

Maldonado N (2010) The Changing Clinical Picture of Tropical Sprue. *Revista de Hematología,* 11 (2): 91–94.

Meléndez E (1993) *Movimiento Anexionista en Puerto Rico.* Rio Piedras, PR: Editorial de la Universidad de Puerto Rico.

Marín RJ (2006) *Tierra Adentro.* San Juan, PR: La Editorial Universidad de Puerto Rico.

Marks S (1997) Presidential Address: What is Colonial About Colonial Medicine? And What has Happened to Imperialism and Health? *The Society for the Social History of Medicine,* 10 (2): 205–219.

Márquez R (2007) *Puerto Rican Poetry: An Anthology from Aboriginal to Contemporary Times.* Amherst, MA: University of Massachusetts Press.

Martínez Vergne T (1999) *Shaping the Discourse on Space: Charity and its Wards in Nineteenth-Century San Juan, Puerto Rico.* Austin, TX: University of Texas Press.

McCoy AW, Scarano FA and Johnson C (2009) On the Tropic of Cancer: Transitions and Transformations in the U.S. Imperial State. In McCoy AW and Scarano FA (eds) *Colonial Crucible: Empire in the Making of the Modern American State.* Madison, WI: University of Wisconsin Press, 3–33.

Méndez JL (1983) *Para Una Sociologia De La Literatura Puertorriqueña.* Rio Piedras, PR: Editorial Edil, Inc.

Mignolo WD (2002) The Geopolitics of Knowledge and the Colonial Difference. *The South Atlantic Quarterly,* 101 (1): 57–96.

Ming-Cheng Lo M (2002) *Doctors Within Borders: Profession, Ethnicity, and Modernity in Colonial Taiwan.* Berkeley, CA: University of California Press.

Negron De Montilla A (1975) *Americanization in Puerto Rico and The Public-School System, 1900–1930.* Barcelona: Editorial Universitaria.

Negrón-Portillo M (1990) *Las Turbas Republicanas, 1900–1904.* Rio Piedras, PR: Ediciones Huracán, Inc.

Nouzeilles G (1997) La Espinge De Monstruo: Modernidad e Higiene Racial en La Charca de Zeno Gandia. *Latin American Literary Review,* 25 (50): 89–107.

Pacheco Padró A (1954) *Isaac González Martínez: Su Vida y Su Obra.* Ciudad Trujillo: Editora Montalvo.

Pagan B (1959) *Historia de los Partidos Politicos Puertorriqueños (1898–1956).* San Juan, PR: Librería Campos.

Palmer S (2010) *Launching Global Health: The Caribbean Odyssey of the Rockefeller Foundation.* Ann Arbor, MI: University of Michigan Press.

Palmer S (2009) Migrant Clinics and Hookworm Science: Peripheral Origins of International Health, 1840–1920. *Bulletin of the History of Medicine,* 83 (4): 676–709.

Parsons T (1950) *The Social System.* London: The Free Press.

Patterson KD (1989) Colonial Medicine. *Journal of African History,* 30 (3): 511–512.

Peard JG (1999) *Race, Place, and Medicine: The Idea of the Tropics in Nineteenth-Century Brazil.* Durham, NC: Duke University Press.

Picó F (2006) *History of Puerto Rico: A Panorama of its People.* Princeton, NJ: Markus Wiener Publishers.

Picó F (2004) *Puerto Rico, 1898: The War After the War.* Princeton, NJ: Markus Weiner.

Picó F (1993) *Al Filo Del Poder.* Rio Piedras, PR: Editorial de la Universidad de Puerto Rico.

Picó F (1986) *Historia General De Puerto Rico.* Río Piedras, PR: Ediciones Huracán, Inc.

Picó F (1981) *Amargo Café: Los Pequeños y Medianos Caficultores de Utuado en la Segunda Mitad del Siglo XIX.* Río Piedras, PR: Ediciones Huracán, Inc.

Pilar Argüelles MD (1989) National Self-Determination and Puerto Rico, 1809–1948. Unpublished doctoral thesis, University of Virginia, Virginia.

Preston AM (2001) Treatment of Tropical Sprue: the World of Dr. Bailey K. Ashford Examined in Retrospect. *Puerto Rico Health Sciences Journal,* 20 (3): 225–228.

Quintero Rivera AG (1981) Clases Sociales E Identidad Nacional: Notas Sobre El Desarrollo Nacional Puertorriqueño. In: Quintero Rivera AG, González JL, Campos R and Flores J (eds) *Puerto Rico: Identidad Nacional Y Clases Sociales.* Río Piedras, PR: Ediciones Huracán, Inc., 13–44.

Quiroga J (1997) Narrating the Tropical Pharmacy. In: Negron-Muntaner F And Grosfoguel R (eds) *Puerto Rican Jam: Rethinking Colonialism and Nationalism.* Minneapolis, MN: University of Minnesota Press, 116–126.

Ramírez de Arellano AB (1990) The Politics on Medical Education in Puerto Rico: 1946–1950. *Puerto Rico Health Sciences Journal,* 9 (2): 185–192.

Ramírez de Arellano AB (1989) A "Class A" Institution: The Struggle for the University of Puerto Rico School of Medicine. *Puerto Rico Health Sciences Journal,* 8 (2): 265–270.

Ramírez de Arellano AB and Seipp C (1983) *Colonialism, Catholicism, and Contraception.* Chapel Hill, NC: The University of North Carolina Press.

Rigau-Pérez JG (2010) El Servicio de Salud Publica de los Estados Unidos en Puerto Rico, 1898–1918. Op. Cit.: *Boletin del Centro de Investigaciones Historicas,* (19): 143–178.

Rigau-Pérez JG (2000a) Bailey K. Ashford, Más Allá de Sus Memorias. *Puerto Rico Health Sciences Journal,* 19 (1): 51–55.

Rigau-Pérez J (2000b) La Salud en Puerto Rico en el Siglo XX. *Puerto Rico Health Sciences Journal,* 19 (4): 357–368.

Rigau-Pérez J (1989) The Introduction of Smallpox Vaccine in 1803 and the Adoption of Immunization as a Government Function in Puerto Rico. *Hispanic American Historical Review,* 69 (3): 393–423.

Rigau-Pérez J (1985) Strategies that Led to the Eradication of Smallpox in Puerto Rico. *Bulletin of the History of Medicine,* 59 (1): 75–88.

Ring NJ (2009) Mapping Regional and Imperial Geographies. In McCoy AW and Scarano FA (eds) *Colonial Crucible: Empire in the Making of the Modern American State*. Madison, WI: University of Wisconsin Press, 297–308.

Ríos-Font W (2005) El Crimen de la Calle de San Vicente: Crime Writing and Bourgeois Liberalism in Restoration Spain. *MLN*, 120 (2): 335–354.

Rivera Rivera M (1980) *Concepto y Expresión del Costumbrismo en Manuel A. Alonso Pacheco (El Gíbaro)*. San Juan, PR: Instituto de Cultura Puertorriqueña.

Rodríguez-Santana IM (2005) Conquests of Death: Disease, Health and Hygiene in the Formation of a Social Body. Unpublished doctoral thesis, Yale University, Connecticut.

Rodríguez-Silva IM (2012) *Silencing Race: Disentangling Blackness, Colonialism, and National Identities in Puerto Rico*. New York, NY: Palgrave Macmillan.

Rodríguez-Silva IM (2004) A Conspiracy of Silence: Blackness, Class, and National Identities in Post-Emancipation Puerto Rico (1850–1920). Unpublished doctoral thesis, University of Wisconsin-Madison, Wisconsin.

Rodríguez Otero E (2008) Obras Completas, Vol. IV: Ateneo. San Juan, PR: Sucesores de Eladio Rodríguez Otero.

Rodriguez-Trias H (1984) The Women's Health Movement: Women Take Power. In Sidel VW and Sidel R (eds) *Reforming Medicine: Lessons of the Last Quarter Century*. New York, NY: Pantheon Books, 107–126.

Rosa-Nieves C and Melón EM (1970) *Biografías Puertorriqueñas: Perfil Histórico de un Pueblo*. Sharon, CT: Troutman Press.

Rosenbloom D (2008) The Politics-Administration Dichotomy in U.S. Historical Context. *Public Administration Review*, 68 (1): 57–60.

Scarano FA (2012) Doctors and Peasants at the Intersection of Empires: The Early Hookworm Campaigns in Puerto Rico. Paper presented at the Annual Meeting of the American Studies Association, 15–18 November, San Juan, PR.

Scarano F (1999) Desear el Jíbaro: Metáforas de la Identidad Puertorriqueña en la Transición Imperial. *Illes i Imperis: Estudios de la Historia de las Sociedades en el Mundo Colonial y Post-Colonial*, 2 (Spring): 65–76.

Scarano F (1998) Liberal Pacts and Hierarchies of Rule: Approaching the Imperial Transition in Cuba and Puerto Rico. *The Hispanic American Historical Review*, 78 (4): 583–601.

Scarano F (1996) The Jíbaro Masquerade and the Subaltern Politics of Creole Identity Formation in Puerto Rico, 1745–1823. *American Historical Review*, 101 (5): 1398–1431.

Scarano FA (1993) *Puerto Rico: Cinco Siglos De Historia*. San Juan, PR: McGraw-Hill.

Schwartz SB (1992) The Hurricane of San Ciriaco: Disaster, Politics, and Society in Puerto Rico, 1899–1901. *The Hispanic American Historical Review*, 72 (3): 303–334.

Silvestrini BG and Luque De Sanchez MD (1992) *Historia De Puerto Rico: Trayectoria De Un Pueblo*. San Juan, PR: Cultural Panamericana.

Silvestrini BG (1982) El Impacto de la Politica de Salud Publica de los Estados Unidos en Puerto Rico, 1898–1913. In Silvestrini BG (ed) *Politics, Society and Culture in the Caribbean: Selected Papers of the XIV Conference of Caribbean Historians*. San Juan, PR: Editorial de la Universidad de Puerto Rico, 63–81.

Sontag S (1989) *Illness as Metaphor and AIDS and its Metaphors*. New York, NY: Anchor Books.

Starr P (1984) *The Social Transformation of American Medicine*. New York, NY: Basic Books.

Stern AM (1999) Buildings, Boundaries, and Blood: Medicalization and Nation-Building on the U.S.-Mexico Border, 1910–1930. *Hispanic American Historical Review*, 79 (1): 41–81.

Stolzfus RJ, Dreyfuss ML, Chwaya HM, and Albonico M (1997) Hookworm Control as a Strategy to Prevent Iron Deficiency. *Nutrition Reviews*, 55 (6): 223–232.

Szreter S (1988) The Importance of Social Intervention in Britain's Mortality Decline c. 1850–1914: a Reinterpretation of the Role of Public Health. *Social History of Medicine*, 1 (1): 1–38.

Tesh SN (1988) *Hidden Arguments: Political Ideology and Disease Prevention Policy*. New Brunswick, NJ: Rutgers University Press.

Thompson L (2007) *Nuestra Isla y Su Gente: La Construcción del "Otro" Puertorriqueño en Our Islands and Their People.* Río Piedras, PR: Universidad de Puerto Rico.

Tio A (1987) La Farmacia de Don Fidel Guillermety Quintero. *Boletín de la Asociacíon Medica de Puerto Rico,* (37–38): 247–252.

Tomes N (2009) Introduction. In McCoy AW and Scarano FA (eds) *Colonial Crucible: Empire in the Making of the Modern American State.* Madison, WI: University of Wisconsin Press, 273–276.

Tomes N (2001) Merchants of Health: Medicine and Consumer Culture in the United States, 1900–1940. *The Journal of American History,* 88 (2): 519–547.

Tomes N (1999) *The Gospel of Germs: Men, Women and the Microbe in American Life.* Cambridge, MA: Harvard University Press.

Topik SC (2000) Coffee Anyone? Recent Research on Latin American Coffee Societies. *Hispanic American Historical Review,* 80 (2): 225–266.

Torres-Gómez JM (1999) Un Hiato en la Vida de la Asociación Médica de Puerto Rico. *Puerto Rico Health Sciences Journal,* 18 (1): 65–70.

Torres-Robles CL (1999) La Mitificación y Desmitificación del Jíbaro como Símbolo de la Identidad Nacional Puertorriqueña. *The Bilingual Review/La Revista Bilingüe,* 24 (3): 241–253.

Trías Monge J (1997) *Puerto Rico: The Trials of the Oldest Colony in the World.* New Haven, CT: Yale University Press.

Trigo B (2000) *Subjects of Crisis: Race and Gender as Disease in Latin America.* Hanover, MA: Wesleyan University Press.

Trujillo-Pagán NE (2009) The Politics of Professionalization: Puerto Rican Physicians Between Spanish and U.S. Colonialism. In: De Barros J, Palmer S and Wright D (eds) *Health and Medicine in the circum-Caribbean, 1800–1968.* New York, NY: Routledge, 142–164.

Trujillo-Pagán NE (2003) Health Beyond Prescription: A Post-Colonial History of Puerto Rican Medicine at the Turn of the Twentieth Century. Unpublished doctoral thesis, University of Michigan, Michigan.

Tyrrell I (2010) *Reforming the World: The Creation of America's Moral Empire.* Princeton, NJ: Princeton University Press.

Urrego MA (2002) Cambio de Soberanía y Confrontación Moral en Puerto Rico, 1898–1920. *Revista Mexicana del Caribe,* 7 (13): 125–152.

Valdés DN (2011) *Organized Agriculture and the Labor Movement Before the UFW: Puerto Rico, Hawaii, California.* Austin, TX: University of Texas Press.

Wailoo K (1999) *Drawing Blood: Technology and Disease Identity in Twentieth-Century America.* Baltimore, MD: Johns Hopkins University Press.

Waitzkin H (1991) *The Politics of Medical Encounters.* New Haven, CT: Yale University Press.

Wamester Bares S (2008) The Puerto Rican Novel 1849–1910, Somatic Fictions of Identity: Writing Nationality on the Limits. Unpublished doctoral thesis, New York University, New York.

Wells H (1969) *The Modernization of Puerto Rico: A Political Study of Changing Values and Institutions.* Cambridge, MA: Harvard University Press.

Willrich M (2011) *Pox: An American History.* New York, NY: Penguin Press.

Wintermute BA (2011) *Public Health and the U.S. Military: A History of the Army Medical Department, 1817–1917.* New York, NY: Routledge.

Wolf ER (1956) San José: Subcultures of a "Traditional" Coffee Municipality. In Steward JH, Manners RA, Wolf ER, Seda EP, Mintz SW and Scheele RL (eds) *The People of Puerto Rico: A Study in Social Anthropology.* Urbana, IL: University of Illinois Press, 171–264.

Worboys M (2000) Colonial Medicine. In Cooter R (ed.) *Medicine in the Twentieth Century.* Australia: Harwood Academic Publishers, 67–80.

INDEX